China's Intrepid Muse

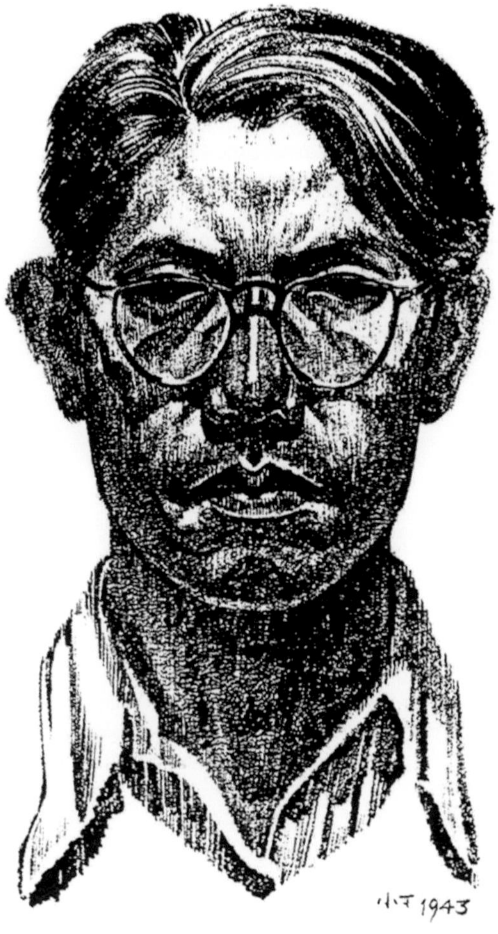

Ding Cong, self-portrait (1943)

China's Intrepid Muse

The Cartoons and Art of Ding Cong

Marcia R. Ristaino

FLOATING WORLD
EDITIONS

In memory of Dick Ristaino

First edition, 2009

Published by Floating World Editions, Inc., 26 Jack Corner Road, Warren, CT 06777. Printed in China.

ISBN: 978-1-891640-57-5

Library of Congress Cataloging-in-Publication data available

Contents

Preface *vi*

Introduction 1

The Artist and His Context 6

Wartime and Wanderings 30

Xiao Ding's Art at its Peak 60

Mao Attacks the Arts 73

Rehabilitation and Return 101

Afterword *121*

Notes *123*

Selected Bibliography *125*

Index *128*

Preface

Ding Cong (1916–2009) is China's most famous cartoonist and caricaturist, whose work and life provide a rich narrative of nearly a century of China's modern history. Although best known for his cartooning, he is also one of China's great artists of the twentieth century. Ding Cong was born in Shanghai into a family famous in the arts. He was especially active there during the 1930s, contributing cartoons and artwork to the burgeoning press and publication outlets. A politically daring artist, he suffered terribly during the Anti-Rightist Movement (1957–68) and the Cultural Revolution (1966–76), losing more than twenty years of his creative life.

I had the privilege and pleasure of meeting with Ding Cong and his wife, Shen Jun, at their apartment in northwest Beijing during 2007 and 2008. I was warmly greeted by the couple on three occasions, and Ding Cong was gracious in answering questions about his life and work and very generous in showing me his cartoons and art. I was also permitted to make a 45-minute video of the couple, with support from the Beijing Technical College. The video provides additional background to Ding Cong's life story and provides a sense of personal connection with this artist. This book is based primarily on these interviews, the video, and the cartoons and artwork he shared with me.

Urban artists like Ding Cong were acquainted with Western artistic trends. His active participation in his family's artistic circle afforded him opportunities to learn about major Western schools of artistic expression. Living in cosmopolitan Shanghai in the 1920s and 1930s, he was able to peruse *The New Yorker* and *Vanity Fair*, his two favorite magazines. He made friends with one of the great Mexican muralists, Miguel Covarrubias, who came to China and inspired Ding Cong with his realism and the public orientation of his art.

With these Western influences, Ding Cong and others created a new art form in China, one that illuminated, but also conformed to, the realities that China faced. The cartoon was a Western import to China, but soon became a means for these artists to express the needs and hopes of a transitional generation committed to ensuring China's national salvation. The conscious motivations of the participants are perhaps most clearly mirrored through cartoon art, using humor, black humor, and an overall vision that intended to capture and then to shape the public mood. Ding Cong continued to practice his art into his nineties, painting his last cartoon in 2005. Until his recent death he lived in retirement with his artist wife in Beijing.

This work was prepared to accompany a conference and exhibition entitled "Public Art and Illustration: The Example of Chinese Cartoonist Ding Cong," co-sponsored by the Library of Congress and George Mason University in October 2009. I am humbly grateful to both institutions for supporting and encouraging these efforts. My special thanks are to the John W. Kluge Center for Scholars at the Library of Congress for providing me office and staff support and the lovely venue for the conference events, and the College of Visual and Performing Arts of George Mason University for preparing and managing the exhibition of Ding Cong's cartoons and artwork. I was ably assisted along the way by Wan-chun Wu, who worked tirelessly and cheerfully as my research assistant.

Many colleagues provided the essential support in bringing to completion this substantial work. My gratitude is to Dr. Carolyn Brown, Director of the Kluge Center, and to John Reeder, Dean of the College of Visual and Performing Arts for their sustaining endorsement of the project. Nick Liu, a Ph.D student at Beijing Technical College, served as director and the interviewer for the video in Beijing. Professor Carla Hinton generously advised and made some additions to the project video. Professor Edward McCord read the project manuscript and recommended its publication. My dedicated editor and publisher, Ray Furse, had to compress our schedules and concentrate various efforts to make the short deadlines for publishing this work in time for the Conference and Exhibition events. Dr. Zhu Hongzhen, a friend of the Dings, offered advice and valuable information. Special thanks to Professor Michael Sullivan for lending high-quality images of several of Ding Cong's works from his own collection.

Others who helped in various ways include Betty McIntosh, who worked with Ding Cong in Kunming, China, during World War II. Murray Minster helped make the project's connection with George Mason University. Friends and colleagues who gave moral support and encouragement that were so welcomed included Yu Maochun, Frank Joseph Shulman, Fang Gann, Mary Lou Reker, Marilyn Clemens, Wu Ma, and Dr. Shu Mengde.

Finally, this brief survey of Ding Cong's career is predominantly based on the artist's recollections, notes, and artwork. Although it touches on many momentous events of China's past century, it is not meant to provide a complete picture of that tumultuous period. For additional background information, interested readers are encouraged to consult a history of modern China. Except for photographs, all images are by Ding Cong.

Introduction

> *With public sentiment, nothing can fail; without it nothing can succeed. Consequently he who moulds public sentiment, goes deeper than he who enacts statutes or pronounces decisions.*
>
> —Abraham Lincoln

George Orwell once said "Every joke is a little revolution." The same might be said of a well crafted cartoon. Cartoonists thrive on change and because China has experienced so many radical changes during the twentieth century, it is an ideal country in which to observe the nuance and commentary of the cartoon. Changes have come with the lengthy period of transition during which China has moved away from its imperial past into experimenting with various modern institutions, finally establishing a Communist state in 1949, and then more recently adding to it many aspects of a capitalist society. These momentous changes have caused personal identity crises for many, posing questions as to who they were in the new and often alien environment. In the interim, the rupture and chaos in the political and cultural spheres have inspired unusual innovation and poignant commentary by the cartoonists. With that in view, this study will examine the life and work of China's most influential modern caricaturist and cartoonist, Ding Cong (丁聪, 1916–2009). His artwork reveals much about the society in which he has lived and worked.[1] His artistic vision allowed him to play a leading role in expressing and even defining

China's cultural responses to the cataclysmic events that took place in the twentieth century.

The cartoon is a potentially powerful tool, especially in a relatively closed society like that of China. It allows its creator to convey thoughts and ideas which otherwise cannot be stated directly. Of course, it also assumes that the creator is sensitive and savvy about what might get past the censors and what probably will not. The obvious value of the cartoon is that it allows unique insight into what really counts within the society, and provides a different perspective on how a large portion of the society privately views important events and policies. When coupled with the development in China of a modern and vibrant vernacular press to serve as the medium, the cartoonist acquired the potential to reach and influence a mass audience

The cartoon in China is an import from the West, beginning in the nineteenth century when missionaries and the force of foreign aggression or gunboat diplomacy threatened China's sovereignty. The Opium Wars of the mid-nineteenth century and the Boxer Rebellion of 1900 unleashed violent Chinese emotions and long pent up resentments. Japan's invasion and occupation of most of the Chinese mainland during World War II greatly added to the pervasive sense of humiliation at the hands of foreigners. These powerful subjects, sovereignty and national survival, found ready expression in the cartoon art form new to China, and contributed to the popular cry of "100 years of national humiliation" that needed to be avenged.

The Chinese term for cartoon, *manhua*, relates to the Japanese term with the same meaning, *manga*, although reference to the term can be found in China as early as the Song Dynasty (960–1279). Chinese artists trained in Japan during the early twentieth century brought the concept back to China and then perfected their own styles, mostly based on

Western models, and influenced others who became enamored of the medium. The cartoonist Feng Zikai (1898–1975), was the first to use the term *manhua* for the new art form and created the original shape and style of the Chinese cartoon.

In this study Ding Cong will serve as our interpreter, providing a glimpse into the private world of Chinese living during the century. Ding was born in Shanghai in 1916, at a time when that coastal city was a vibrant commercial center, and beginning to eclipse Beijing as the hub of literary, artistic, and political activity. The great Taiping Rebellion of the mid-nineteenth century had ravaged south China, causing many with the means to collect art and those with artistic talent to flock into Shanghai, the foreign protected treaty port. Ding's family (figs. 1, 2) fit this mold in that his father, Ding Song (1879–1969), was a renowned artist and cartoonist who founded the prestigious Fine Arts Institute of Shanghai and

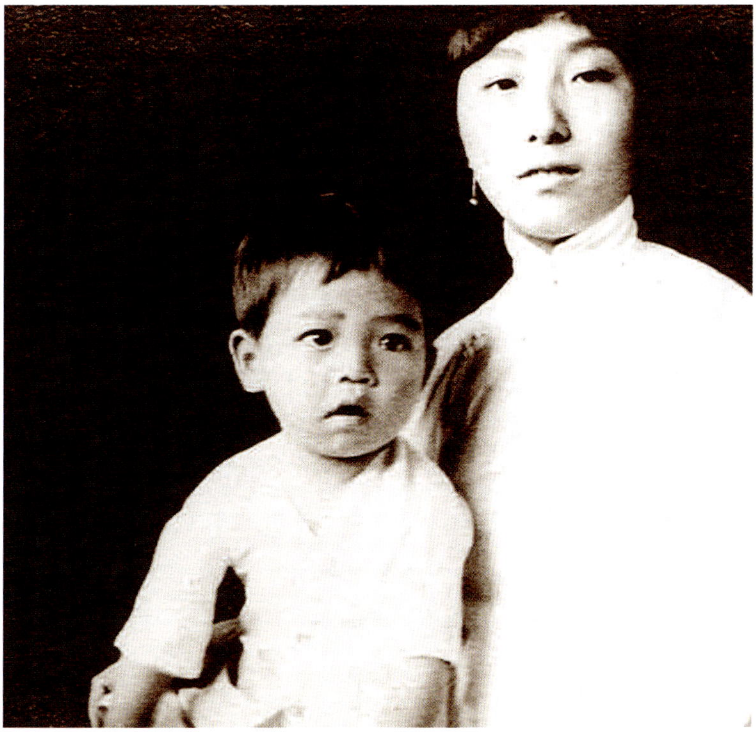

1. Mother and son

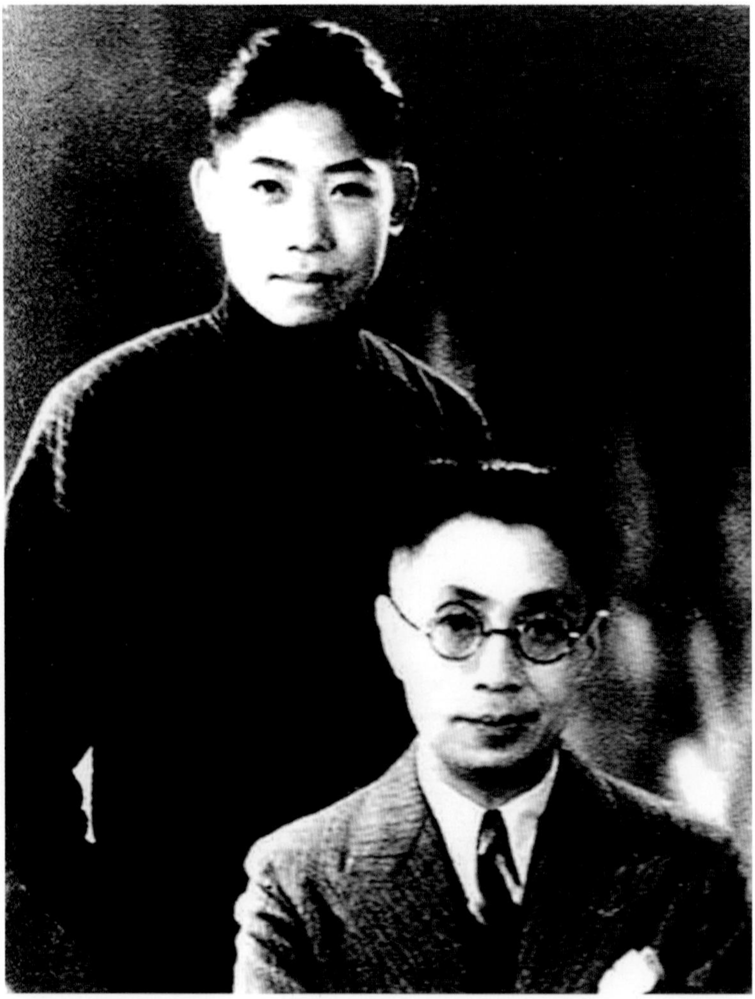

2. Ding Cong with his cartoonist and artist father, Ding Song (1946)

served as a pioneer of Western art in China. He also established the first cartoon association in China. Ding's childhood home was always filled with visiting painters, talented writers, theater people, and opera stars. They were only too willing to share their experiences and insights so that Ding Cong could benefit from their talent and examples of their art. His home became a noted salon with weekly Saturday gatherings where those involved could discuss the arts, China's future, and the course of their own works and contributions.

Unlike China, the West has had a long tradition of political cartoons. One thinks of Honoré Daumier (1808–79) who regularly furnished satirical political cartoons to Paris weeklies, and was sentenced to jail for his negative depictions of the French king. The British cartoonist Sir David Low's stinging depictions of Adolph Hitler caused his work to be banned in Italy and Germany. Propaganda Minister Goebbels claimed that his work damaged Anglo-German relations. In Germany, the political cartoonist George Grosz was greatly admired for his remorseless satirical cartoons of German politicians. In America, Herbert Block, known as Herblock, was always ready with his stinging wit to accent the political scandals and foibles of politicians of the day. In earlier times, Thomas Nast made his mark as a political cartoonist.

As noted, the cartoon was appropriate in China because of the plethora of upheavals and radical political events that took place during the twentieth century. To provide just a bare-bones listing in the order of appearance, there was first a Chinese intellectual revolution, succeeded by a political revolution, followed by an international war, a civil war, comprehensive social-economic revolution, and finally, by the technological and global revolution, if it might be called that, which is currently encompassing and challenging the world. So in addition to bringing to light the thoughts and responses of those affected by these transitional and often chaotic times, this Chinese cartoonist's work can provide a good visual narrative of modern Chinese history and the national struggle for world acceptance and respect. Ding Cong's vision is further enhanced by his additional and sometimes surpassing talents as a painter, woodblock artist, and caricaturist. He is best known for his cartooning, but he is also one of China's great artists of modern times.

The Artist and His Context

Do not misread the laughter in these drawings,
Embedded in them is a bitter sense of sorrow.

—Xiao Ding

The nature of the times in which Ding Cong was born requires further elaboration in order to understand his intellectual formation and the wellsprings of his bold imagination. The failure of the Chinese Republic founded in 1912 to address the nation's problems inspired the New Culture Movement, an intellectual awakening accompanied by a significant literary movement. Chinese artists, cartoonists, and intellectuals, doubting their ancient culture and looking to the West for ideas and inspiration, organized literary societies and debated the relative merits of Eastern and Western cultures. New publications proliferated to express the many ideas that emerged in the more diverse urban culture. Students and professors mobilized around the frightening realization that China was disintegrating. To forestall that outcome, the cry was that the old imperial system and its institutions had to be replaced. Even the family system, at the heart of the Confucian society, was seen as oppressive and became an object for derision. The difficult and arcane Chinese language of the classics needed complete overhaul to bring it closer to the language of speech and everyday use. Literature needed to deal with the issues of real life, and, most important for this study, the pictorial arts, rather than remain fascinated with landscapes, birds, and flowers, was called upon to depict the reality of Chinese life.

These new requirements can easily be seen as revolutionary in scope and effect. A new politics, a new literature, new art and art forms, and even a new language suggested the need for a completely new identity for the Chinese. Writers began composing their works in the vernacular, based on colloquial speech; artists copied Western techniques, and new political forms became the objects of movements. Sun Yat-sen initiated a political revolution that ushered in the Chinese Republic in 1912, marking the end of the imperial Qing Dynasty (1644–1911). Yuan Shi-kai's attempt to reverse this modernizing course inspired a decisive reaction, complete with negative cartooning. The prospects for still more revolution were pushed ahead by the social and political impact of the May Fourth Movement of 1919, precipitated by the signing over to Japan at Versailles former German "concessions" in Shandong Province, including Qingdao city. This humiliating event provoked massive and angry demonstrations against the new but corrupt and impotent government in Peking. It intensified the growing disappointment with the Republican Revolution of 1911–12, which had failed to unite the country and avert the recent foreign aggression.

The Chinese Communist Party established its presence and organized its First Congress in Shanghai in 1921. Change was happening at whirlwind speed in Shanghai, with massive strikes by factory workers followed by blowback from foreign powers trying to preserve their privileged and lucrative lifestyles, guaranteed by the power of extraterritoriality and gunboat diplomacy. According to the so-called "unequal treaties" marking the end of the Opium Wars, China's sovereignty over its territory and its laws did not apply to the foreign powers residing in the treaty ports. Numerous newspapers and newsletters appeared, written in the vernacular and using modern print technology, to report, illustrate, and debate the many changes and tumultuous events as they occurred. The awakening and continued shake-up of Chinese society could hardly be avoided under these severe challenges and conditions. The emotions it stirred required new and different channels of expression.

Early Life in Shanghai

Shanghai was the cosmopolitan center of China, where the new ideas coming from the West affected everyone. It offered many channels for creative adaptations of Western ideas while still maintaining roots in Chinese soil. The city was divided into three parts, based on the stipulations of nineteenth century treaty agreements. The French had the French Concession, a largely residential area intended mainly for Westerners; the British ran the International Settlement, the center of business, and included participation from Americans, Dutch, Japanese, and other foreigners; and the Chinese managed the surrounding areas largely inhabited by Chinese.

By the end of the Qing dynasty, Western art in China had been taught by the Jesuit fathers at their compound in Siccawei, a western section of Shanghai now known as Xujiahui. Young Chinese learned to paint and draw ecclesiastical subject for the needs of the Catholic Church. The school eventually became part of Aurora University, located in the French Concession. Another, independent school, known as the Sino-Western Drawing and Painting School, at which Ding Cong's father was a student, became a new arts teaching center. One of its students, Liu Haisu, in 1912 went on to establish his own school, with twelve students working in a rented house. This school, the Shanghai Painting and Art Institute, became a major center for the development of Western art in China before World War II. By 1915, it was known as the Shanghai Art Institute (Shanghai Meizhuan).[2]

The young Ding Cong attended a Christian middle school in the French Concession where he could gain access to the latest issues of the *London Daily News*, *The New Yorker*, and *Vanity Fair*, or he might purchase copies at the many local newsstands. Sometimes, he was able to buy older or unsold issues at a cheaper rate. These publications had a very strong influence on him, especially their lively cartoons and graphic art work. He quickly recognized their intrinsic power to set new trends and establish new tastes.

Ding's father, Ding Song, an accomplished artist himself, did not want his son to become a cartoonist. This son was the first of twelve children, six of whom did not survive. Being the eldest, he was expected to set a good example and help with the family's finances by earning money. His father wanted him to follow a profession that would provide a good livelihood. He worried about the salon's and his family's strong influences on his son, who already showed a talent for drawing and artistic interest (fig. 3). Hoping to curb this trend, Ding Song insisted that no paper or brushes be given to his son who must focus his full attention on practical pursuits. These parental demands meant that his son was mainly self taught, and in the end, failed in the face of Ding Cong's ardent love for drawing and his insistence that he be allowed to follow his own artistic interests.

3. Sketch by Xiao Ding at age four

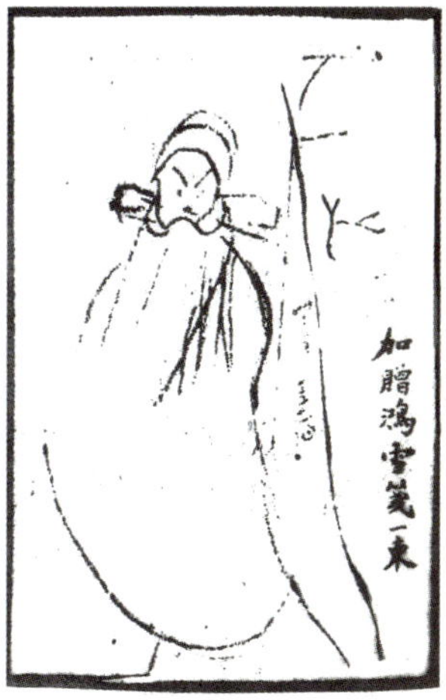

Ding Cong worked under the pen name Xiao Ding (小丁), which in English means "Little Ding." It is the name given to him by the influential painter Zhang Guangyu (1900–64), an important participant in the family salon's gatherings, and founder of the influential magazine *China Cartoons* (*Zhongguo manhua*). Xiao Ding is the name Ding Cong used to sign all of his cartoons and artwork and will be used subsequently in this work. Denied access to suitable paper and supplies by his father, Xiao Ding made do with simple scraps of paper and pencils and, based on practice and his observations of other artists' work, became his own teacher. His favorite subjects for sketching were the famous opera stars that frequented his childhood home (figs. 4, 5). Despite his bare resources, Ding's talents were not missed by those who saw his work. He, along with Zhang Guangyu, became part time students at Liu Haisu's art school where, for three dollars a month, he could visit artists' studios and discuss his work. In his limited spare time, he also became an accomplished amateur musician on both the flute and *erhu*, a two-

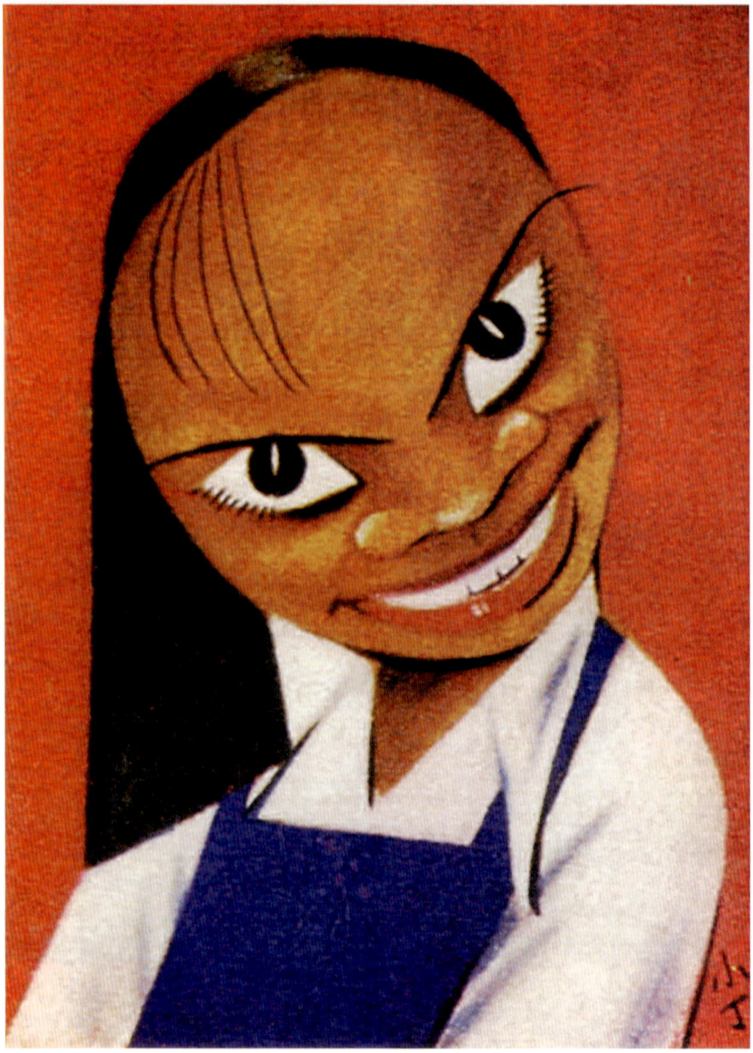

4. Caricature of the Shanghai songstress, opera, and film star, Wang Renmei (1936)

stringed, fiddle-like instrument, often entertaining friends with his music. His interests and talents left little doubt that he was destined for a life in the arts.

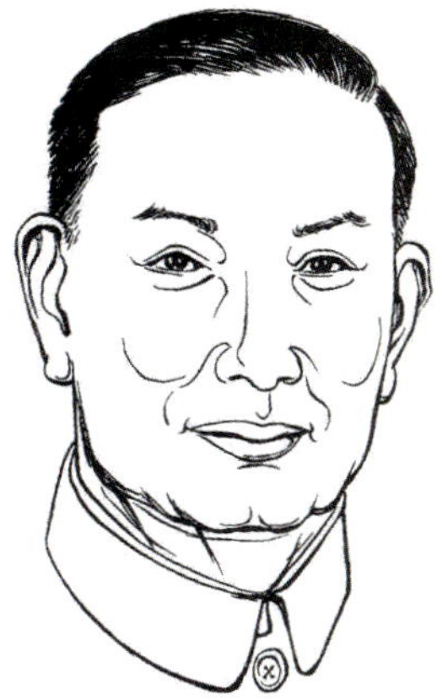

5. Portrait of the opera star Mei Lanfan

During his high school years, Ding's home life offered another important influence. Attending Hollywood movies became a favorite pastime of Shanghai Chinese. These films offered a prized window to a new visual world, one continuously reinforced by their showings at movie houses in the foreign concessions.[3] Ding's father had a friend in the burgeoning movie industry in Shanghai. Through the support and admiration of this friend, Ding got a job as a part-time editor of a movie magazine. The job allowed him to draw movie cartoons and, best of all, portraits of celebrated movie stars. The personal style he developed preserved his Chinese roots by being close to the brush and ink style of calligraphy. But his use of the pen rather than the Chinese brush was Western, as were his subjects. He neglected the traditional bird and flower subjects of traditional painting in order to perfect his renderings of people and real life situations. Xiao Ding had a special talent for highlighting the facial expressions of his subjects, a feature absent from traditional Chinese paintings, in which facial expressions appear frozen or formal. Although still quite young, he entered some of his best work in the first national exhibit of cartoon art held in Shanghai in November 1936 (fig. 6). Several attending guests commented on how well he captured the individual character of his movie star subjects by including their seductive poses, sidelong glances, and knowing looks. His earlier "secret" work, painting popular opera stars, afforded him the necessary confidence to capture the new look and glamour of the Shanghai movie stars.

Ding's father tried his hand at getting his son gainfully employed. Unaware of his son's reticence around young women, he made arrangements for his son to teach painting at a local school for girls. The work made Xiao Ding extremely

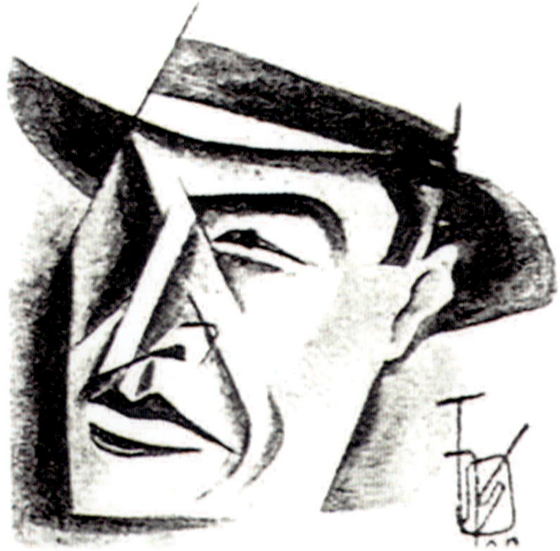

6. Drawing of the Shanghai movie star, Jin Yan

nervous during the class periods as the female students gathered around him for their lessons. This was not the case with his good friend Zhang Leping, creator of the delightful cartoon character, San Mao (Three Hairs), who was very envious of Xiao Ding's access to so many girls in his classroom. He begged Xiao Ding to arrange for him a similar position at the school, but to no avail.

Xiao Ding was described by those who knew him in his prime as a jolly fellow with an ebullient personality and surprising, boisterous laugh. Somewhat round in shape, partly owing to his short stature, he was well known for his wit and infectious sense of humor. Humor appears throughout his work, although more often in his later works when conditions in China had improved. His earlier works reflected the desperate and trying times, usually with an added touch of sarcasm or biting social commentary. His works exude an internal, often fierce energy that deals directly and unambiguously with his subjects. He strikes out at a theme and spares little subtlety, unless the degree of censorship of the time requires some masking. His strength is that his work often is able to communicate ideas too complicated for verbal expression. His bold pictures can work magic by taking a popular or familiar subject and overlaying it with rich, emotive symbols, an emotional vocabulary that is well known to his audience. On occasion, he might use allusions from historical events, or work with a selection from folklore to make his point. This technique came in handy during periods of heavy censorship. The stricter the censorship, the more layers or cultural veils needed to shroud or seclude the edgy and even subversive message. As we will see, he was also a fine graphic artist who created designs and illustrations for publishers of books, magazines, and journals.

Xiao Ding lived in an important era that favored his special talents. The succession of major events in Shanghai during the 1920s gave the blooming publishing scene plenty to write about. Xiao Ding's father and friends made these the subject of many of their discussions and gatherings. One of the most momentous incidents happened in May 1925, when a fatal shooting of a Chinese worker in a Japanese cotton mill was followed by the British attack on young demonstrators who had protested the earlier Japanese action, and also the deplorable conditions for workers in the mills. This seminal event galvanized the Chinese and, in many ways, marked the beginning of a full-blown social revolution. People who until then had thought change was centered in the cultural and intellectual areas now understood the national crisis.

The awakening to the need for change now reached down to include many more ordinary Chinese. The Communists, especially, came to recognize and employ the power of mass movements. In the cities, they goaded the workers into strikes, and in the countryside, they began to make headway at spreading new ideas about class relationships and organized violent peasant revolts around them. Their work there benefited from organized peasant associations which were already very familiar with poverty and the struggle to survive in the countryside.

Tensions grew between progressives who belonged to organized study groups and struggled with eclectic ideas from the West, such as "democracy and science" and revolutionary nationalism, and those who embraced the principles of Marxism-Leninism and a thorough-going social revolution. Especially in the 1920s, the latter group accepted direction and guidance from the Communist International (Comintern) and its advisors in China. There were many other philosophies or allegiances in the mix of the times, but these two trends or groupings, the progressives and the revolutionaries, best fit the general contours of this period. In 1922, the Guomindang (Nationalist Party) and the Chinese Communists began to pool their talents and resources in a united front, hoping that their unity would help bring the same to the country and provide strength against warlords and foreign imperialism. A military academy, directed by Chiang Kai-shek (in *pinyin* Jiang Jieshi), produced a new, more modern officer corps from members of both political camps and trained them in modern military skills. These officers provided the core leadership of the Northern Expedition, starting in early July 1926 from Canton in the south. Its primary mission was to get rid of the many warlords, who were acting as independent kingdoms and undermining China's capacity to think and act as a nation.

When the forces reached Shanghai in April of 1927, however, instead of continuing the drive for unity and the elimination of warlords, Chiang Kai-shek formed alliances with powerful secret societies and conservatives, and without any forewarning, he turned their combined power against the leftists and Communists. The Chinese Communist Party and its leftist followers were badly damaged by this split in the united front, and its members never again trusted Chiang and the Nationalists.[4] Many talented writers, artists, and cultural leaders, some friends or acquaintances of the Ding family, had become more closely associated with the left in the 1920s, and suffered severe repression during this watershed crackdown.

The strikes, boycotts, and even the activities of literary societies of the 1920s received crucial support from those able to write persuasive posters, leaflets, and placards for use at public events. Writers published stories in the newspapers about the evils of the old society, especially the suffocating

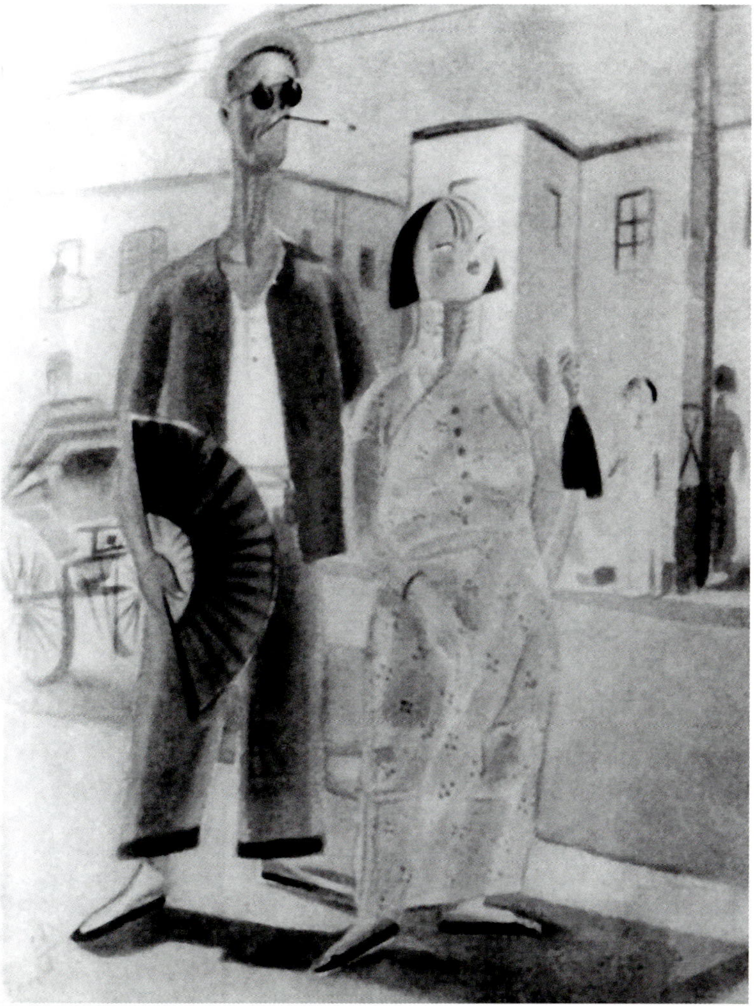

7. A Shanghai gangster and prostitute (1936)

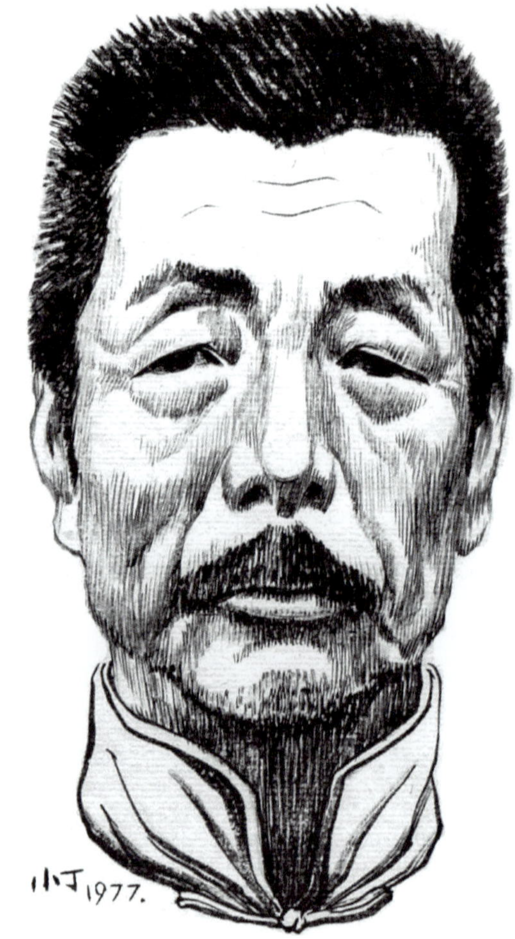

8. Portrait of Lu Xun (1977). Courtesy of Michael Sullivan

family system, the plight of women, the vast divide between the rich and poor, the deplorable conditions in the country-side, urban violence, and so on (fig. 7). Venues for the display of this kind of work were often quite basic. Cartoonists like Xiao Ding might publish their work in books and newspapers, or on posters, leaflets, and pamphlets. The methods of dissemination were varied and might include distributing at street corners, pasting on poles or walls, or carrying on sign-boards or banners. The efforts of Xiao Ding and others to map out in their art solutions to China's many ills in this period and the 1930s certified the cartoon as an important tool for introducing new ideas and promoting change. They enjoyed several publishing outlets, as there were nineteen cartoon magazines published in Shanghai.[5] Two prominent newspapers for cartooning were *Shen Bao* and *Da Gongbao*. The period also produced a golden age, perhaps the richest period in modern Chinese literature.[6] Those who participated were pioneers in setting a new course for the arts and literature. It is worthwhile to consider a few authors who greatly influenced Xiao Ding, and he them.

Leading Literary Figures

Lu Xun (1881–1936) is usually identified as China's greatest modern writer, especially of social satire (fig. 8) One can imagine his impact by the broad scope of his activities. In addition

9. Illustration for Lu Xun's short story Diary of a Madman

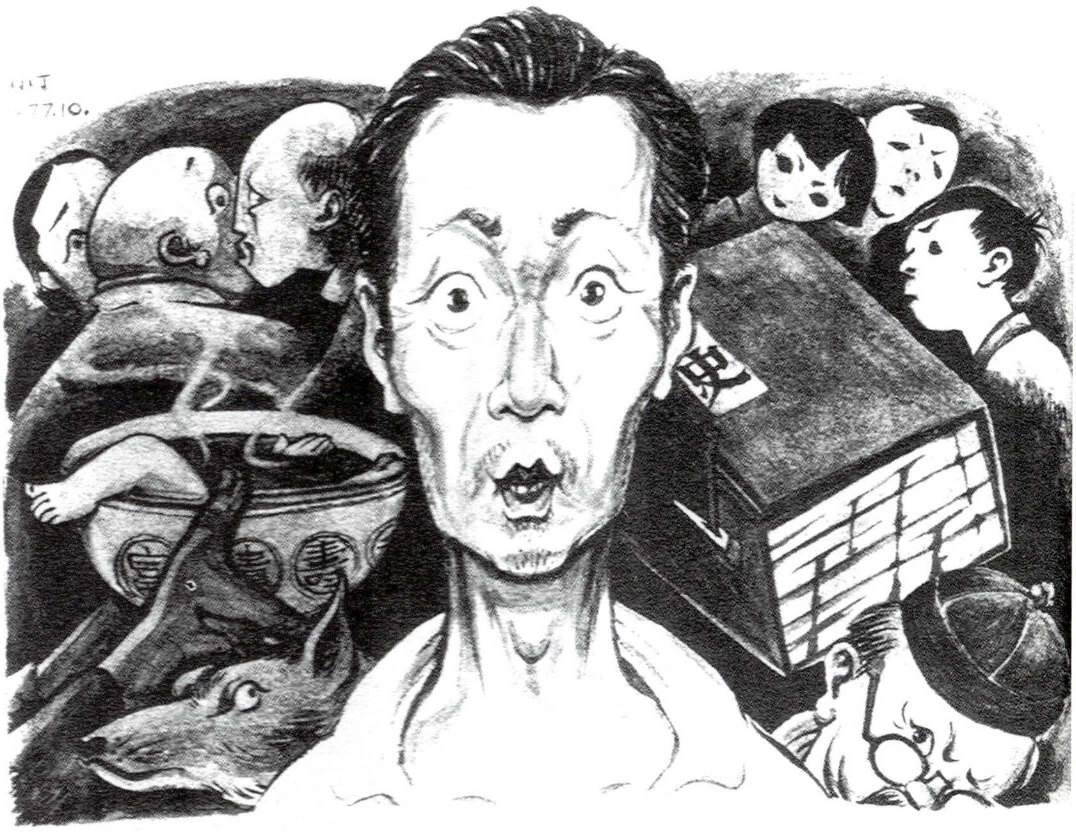

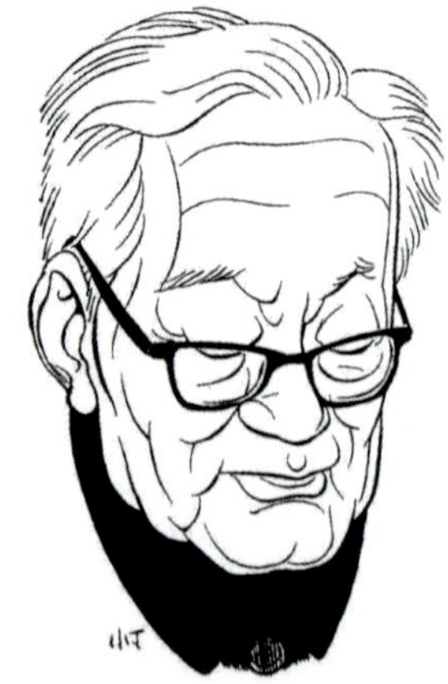

10. Portrait of Ba Jin.

to writing short stories, he produced essays, criticism, and works on literary theory. His fame came mainly from his short stories. One of his most celebrated was *Diary of a Madman*, published in 1918 (fig. 9) in the popular journal *New Youth (Xin qingnian)*. This journal became the voice of the May Fourth Movement, advocating intellectual and artistic freedom. Lu Xun's story is a condemnation of traditional Chinese society and culture, which the protagonist describes as destructive, even "man-eating." In fact, he believes he is being held captive by cannibals. The story is purposefully shocking and intends to awaken society to the national crisis and dire need for change. Lu Xun was a key participant in the literary debates of the 1920s and 1930s, and a founding member of the influential League of Left-Wing Writers (1932–36) based in Shanghai. Xiao Ding admired his stirring imagination and clear writing style, saying that these qualities made the work easy for him to illustrate. Xiao Ding illustrated all of Lu Xun's short stories.

Another influential figure was Mao Dun (1896–1981), a pen name for Shen Yanbing. Upon meeting Xiao Ding for the first time, Mao Dun commented that he looked just like an artist, with long and tousled hair and a pallid complexion set off by his large bowtie. He described Xiao Ding's cartoon art as arresting, concise, and forceful (fig. 12), the work of a happy and energetic artist.[7] In his celebrated work *Midnight (Ziye)*, Mao Dun presents a sweeping survey and dissection of Shanghai society, populating his story with reactionary capitalists, some revolutionaries, and a few Communists. He portrays with empathy each segment of the working poor and their desperate struggle to deal with failure and defeat in life. The narrative operates against a backdrop of horrific military battles that deeply scarred particularly the Chinese sectors of Shanghai in the 1930s.

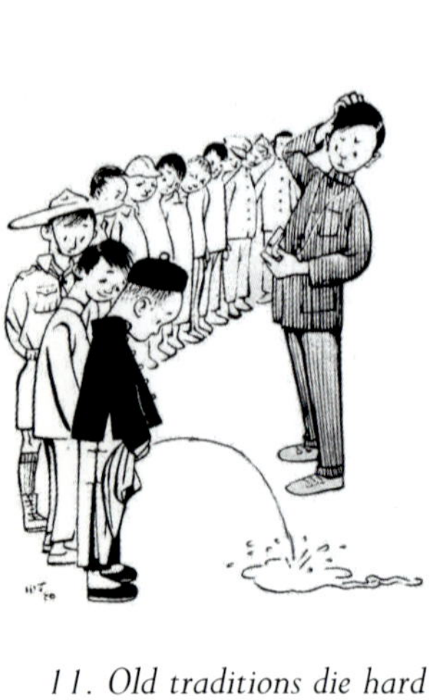

11. Old traditions die hard

The renowned author Ba Jin (1904–2005; fig. 10) in his novel *The Family (Jia)*, explains the pressures and strains that

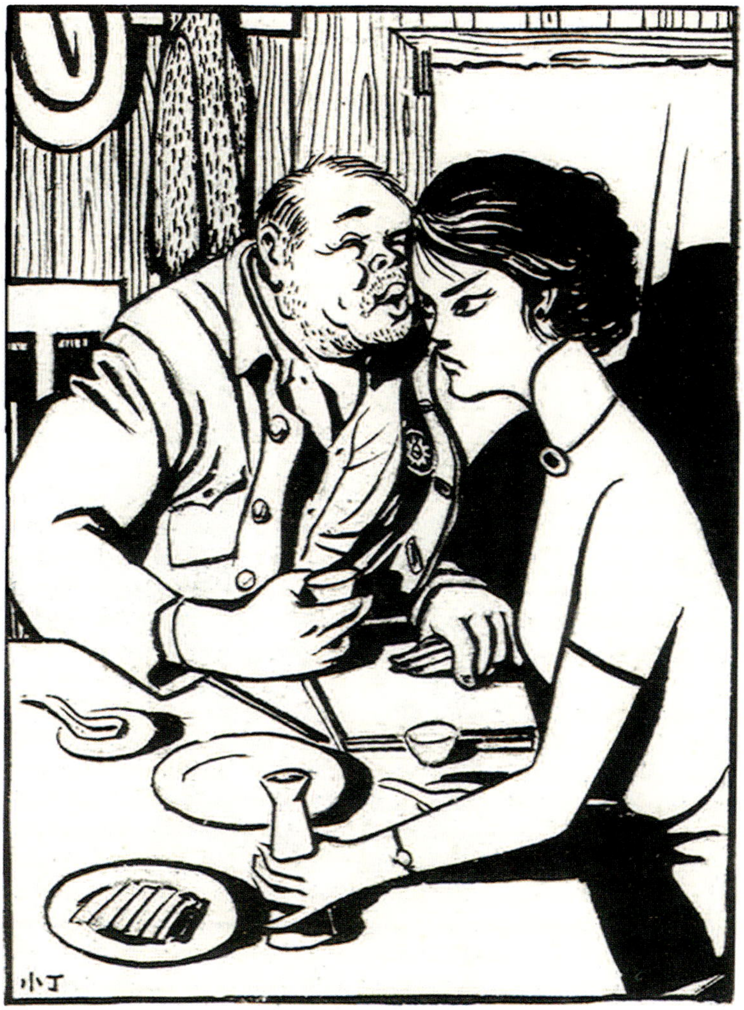

12. Illustration for Mao Dun's novel Midnight

the feudal household structure exerts on its members, and shows the family as a destroyer, rather than a source of nurturing, in the lives of his characters. His central themes were also common in Xiao Ding's work.

Most of these writers and artists were part of the movement dedicated to examining the old society and Confucian system and exposing its poisonous effects. Their social satire points out the human needs and desires of people lost in a state of dislocation and hopelessness. The literary sources they translated and consulted for vision and inspiration included

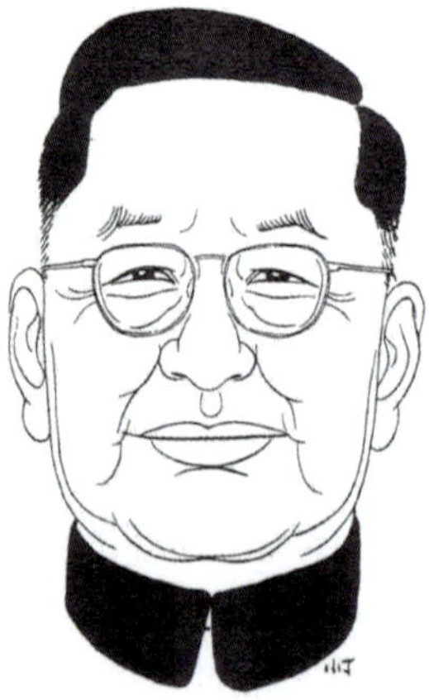

13. Portrait of Lao She

Western writers such as Charles Dickens, John Dewey, Marx, Tolstoy, Darwin, Turgenev, Ibsen, Gogol, and others. The writings of these Chinese authors gave Xiao Ding plenty of material to mine for his cartoons, and inspired him to find a way out for China, safe from the predatory warlords, enervating political turmoil, and continuing outside aggression.

Xiao Ding's favorite author was Lao She (1899–1966; fig. 13), although he had to struggle to make that choice among those noted authors just discussed. The appeal was Lao She's insistence on a sincere and realistic depiction of all categories and members of Chinese society, and one that was completely intelligible to the reader. Lao She described the principles of the May Fourth Movement as having created the conditions for his becoming a writer, saying it gave him a new soul as well as a new literary language. His humanitarian impulses and proclaimed search for love, beauty, and truth might seem naïve and even pedestrian to today's reader, but at the time, they were quite novel. Lao She, the writer, worked towards revealing explicitly the injustices so prevalent in traditional society. Using crisp and often racy language, he was able to capture the flavor and intensely human qualities of his characters. This success was especially true in his famous novel *Luotuo xiangzi*, known in English as *Rickshaw Boy*, in which he employs humor along with acute observation to reveal the raw human experiences and basic needs of his characters (figs. 14–16) Like Lao She, Xiao Ding favored using justice and injustice as subjects for his art. It is easy to imagine how strongly the following passage from *Rickshaw Boy* must have affected Xiao Ding:

> ...for the poor, when the storm is over and the worker is ill, the whole family starves. Each storm adds to the number of girls turned prostitutes and boys turned thieves, and there are more men to fill the jails. The rain falls on the rich and poor alike, and

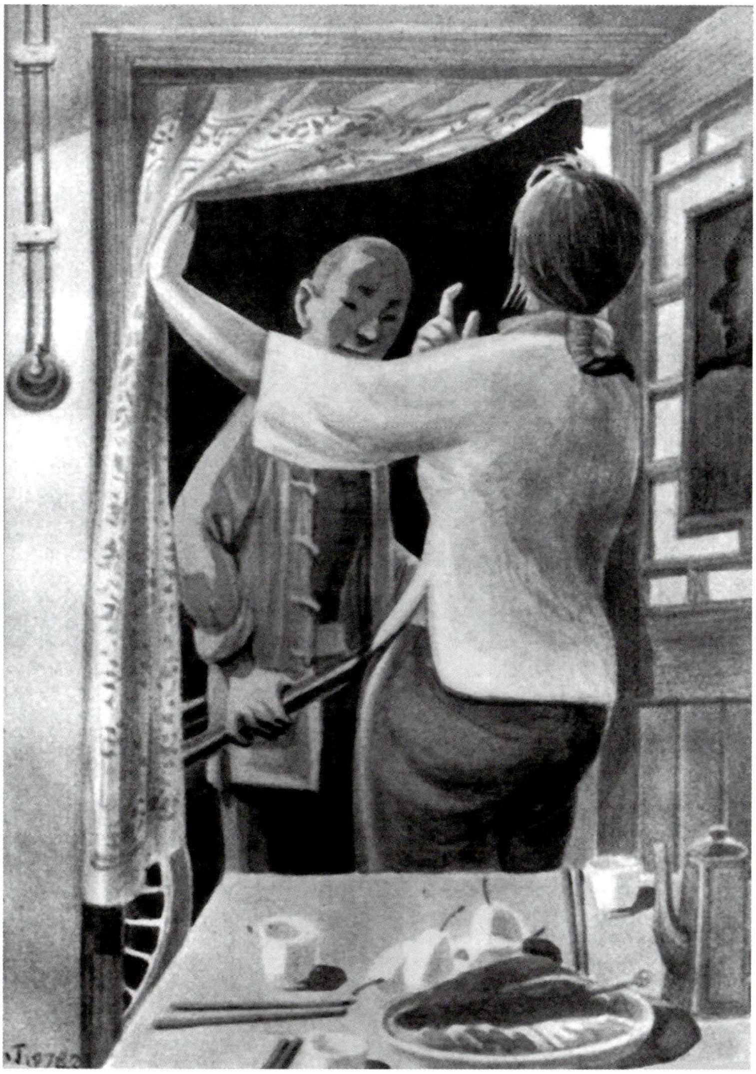

14. Illustration for Lao She's novel Rickshaw Boy (1978)

> on the just and the unjust. But the bitter truth is that there is no equity even in the fall of rain, because the world on which it falls is so unjustly ruled.[8]

Lao She captured the tragic life of a rickshaw puller and his impoverished family in 1920s Beijing. Xiao Ding provided illustrations for a later edition of the book, which was first published in 1936. His delicate shading and visual sophistication convey the sad and somber essence of the novel's characters.

Influence of Mexican Artists

Xiao Ding shared ideas with one of the great muralists of Mexico, Miguel Covarrubias (1904–57). Covarrubias had dedicated his art to revealing the underlying political and social conditions that led to the Mexican Revolution (1910–20), and the two became friends in Shanghai in the early 1930s. The Mexican artist's work had appeared in the *New Yorker* and *Vanity Fair* which, as previously noted, were favorite publications of Xiao Ding. Both artists were committed to art as an outlet for protest, even confrontation. Both also saw a role for humor in serving that end. Unfortunately, their willingness to inject levity into their work caused some in academic circles to dismiss them as "popular" artists. Because it sometimes appeared on postcards or street posters, the cartoon suffered diminished status for many, who deemed it a lesser, vulgar form of art. Lu Xun, on the other hand, claimed that "comic strip art may not produce a Tolstoy or Flaubert, but it contains the possibilities of a Michelangelo or da Vinci."[9] Showing his skill and versatility with both traditional and modern Chinese themes, Covarrubias illustrated the 1949 edition of *All Men are Brothers*, Pearl Buck's noted translation of the Chinese novel *Shui hu chuan*.

Another major Mexican painter who influenced Xiao Ding and his colleagues was Diego Rivera (1886–1957). Rivera had helped establish the Mexican Mural Renaissance in the 1920s to 30s with his large wall works in fresco. Reproductions of his works were in high demand for study and teaching in Shanghai art circles. Two other Mexican revolutionary artists whose influences were felt in painting and caricature included José Orozco (1882–1949), a social realist muralist, and David Alfaro Siquieros (1896–1974), a painter and political activist who had attempted to assassinate Leo Trotsy. Finally, the painting style and artistry of the Spaniard Francisco

Goya (1746–1828) intrigued Xiao Ding, especially his scenes of everyday life portrayed in his so-called tapestry cartoons. Like these Mexican artists, Xiao Ding saw the cartoon and his illustrations as public art.

Shanghai in Torment

Xiao Ding published his first cartoon in 1932 at the age of sixteen. This original piece of work would have been an important addition to his overall collection. Probably because he was unsure of its worth at this early stage in his career, or unaware of the proper procedures, he sent his original art to the publisher for consideration, without making a copy for himself. Later in his career, he learned the importance of making copies of his work to send to the publishers. As noted, he worked in a vibrant artistic community in cosmopolitan Shanghai. Urban amenities included a Western orchestra with White Russian and Jewish refugee musicians, frequent Western theater productions, and many Western film showings.

Xiao Ding's family had moved to the French Concession, which provided better protection from Chinese government censorship and police. Still, foreign police raids on suspected hotbeds of political resistance happened often and resulted in the seizure of large quantities of artwork and literature. After careful perusal by the foreign concession police, the captured materials, as well as the authors, were turned over to the Chinese police. After interrogation and often torture, the authors were either jailed or executed. Xiao Ding said he learned to operate under these dangerous conditions by stopping work in periods of heavy censorship, waiting patiently until things cooled down, and then beginning again, cautiously.

The Shanghai artistic and literary scene was a boiling cauldron of factions including: those who still wanted to revere the old; reformists who would go only so far with the new thinking; those disillusioned because the Republican Revolution of 1912 had not improved the lot of the poor; admirers of the Soviet Union; leftists; committed Marxists; anarchists; and Communists. The Nationalist Government, in power since 1928, had not developed a program that could satisfy and inspire the intellectuals and leftists who were looking for ways to strengthen China and to address crucial social needs.

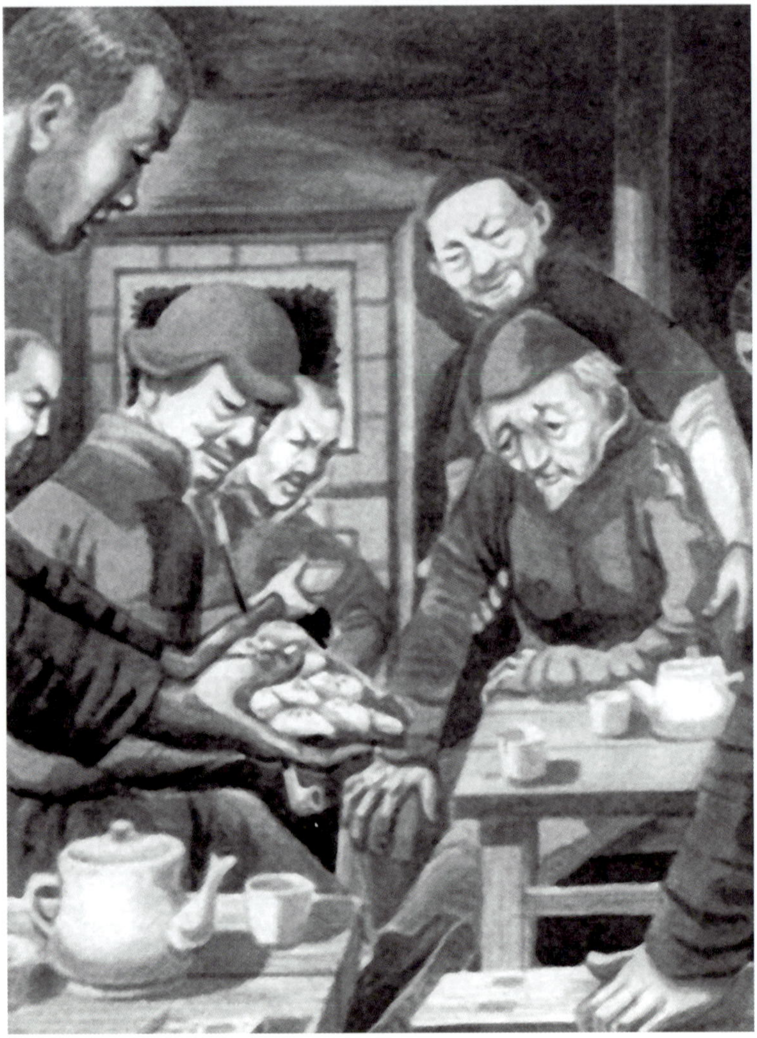

15. Gathering at the tea house, from Rickshaw Boy *(1978)*

Internal factionalism, fueled by different political voices, plagued the Nationalist Party and made setting a course and projecting a coherent message very difficult. The Communist Party, too, suffered from serious dissension within its ranks.

In early 1932, the fierce Japanese attack on the densely populated Chinese portions of Shanghai, complete with devastating aerial bombing of dense urban areas, was horrifying and greatly enhanced public demand for effective official response and action. Patriotism arose as a powerful motivating force. The thrilling courage of Chinese fighters pitted against better armed Japanese forces galvanized a population ready to make a commitment to whatever was necessary for national salvation. The urgent call to the public declared that none could remain innocent bystanders to this ongoing tragedy; instead, all must actively participate in the cause of national salvation. Backed up by the development of a modern vernacular press, the social and political turbulence fed by the war, strikes, demonstrations, and clandestine meetings, became matters known to the public as never before.

The cartoons appearing in the press became a simple and powerful means for expressing the immediate public emotions. They played a key role in the militant cultural movement committed to saving the nation from extinction. Xiao Ding's solid and aggressive lines captured the new ideas in ways that were direct and potent. He evoked his themes with highly charged colors and simple subjects to essentially jar the reader into recognizing his point. As an art form, the cartoon became far more accessible to the masses than traditional paintings, which were often accompanied by obscure literary references. Xiao Ding made the cartoon image closely reflect the experiences of the common people, and communicated their fears through its visual power. His work was a creative blending of art and politics and it succeeded because Xiao Ding understood how to transform human experience into public art.

Woodcuts (*muke*) were another favorite artistic and public media of the period, and greatly favored and supported by Lu Xun from his home in the Japanese Concession in the Shanghai International Settlement. Woodcuts in China can be traced as far back as the Tang Dynasty (618–907). Their utility for cartoonists was particularly appropriate to the upheavals of the 1930s. Printing resources were in short supply; with woodcuts, it was easy to produce many printings of a picture or cartoon for distribution. Xiao Ding was an active participant in the "woodcut movement" of this period, which enjoyed considerable influence and success in Shanghai and Hangzhou, only to be driven underground by the authorities. Several new magazines associated with the movement published woodcuts and cartoons. Their titles are suggestive of their intended purpose and radical flavor: *Torrent*, *Big Dipper*, *Art*, *Siren*, *Beacon*, *Dawn*, *Outcry*, and *Struggle*.

The Guomindang censors carefully monitored the full range of publications and crushed those they considered subversive. At their direction, many artists and writers were executed or jailed. But as some were crushed, another group would pop up and continue the work of relating their art to the struggle. The new patriotic National Salvation Movement included members with many shades of opinion. The salvation movement's organizations provided useful outlets for the different voices trying to be heard amidst the legions of discontented. New organizations formed overnight and added pressure on the government, as it tried to maintain control and order. By July 1937, the most prominent organization for the cartoon artists was National Salvation Cartoon Association.

Moving Inland and to the Countryside

Following the momentous crackdown of April 1927 and the continued hunting down of leftists and Communists by the

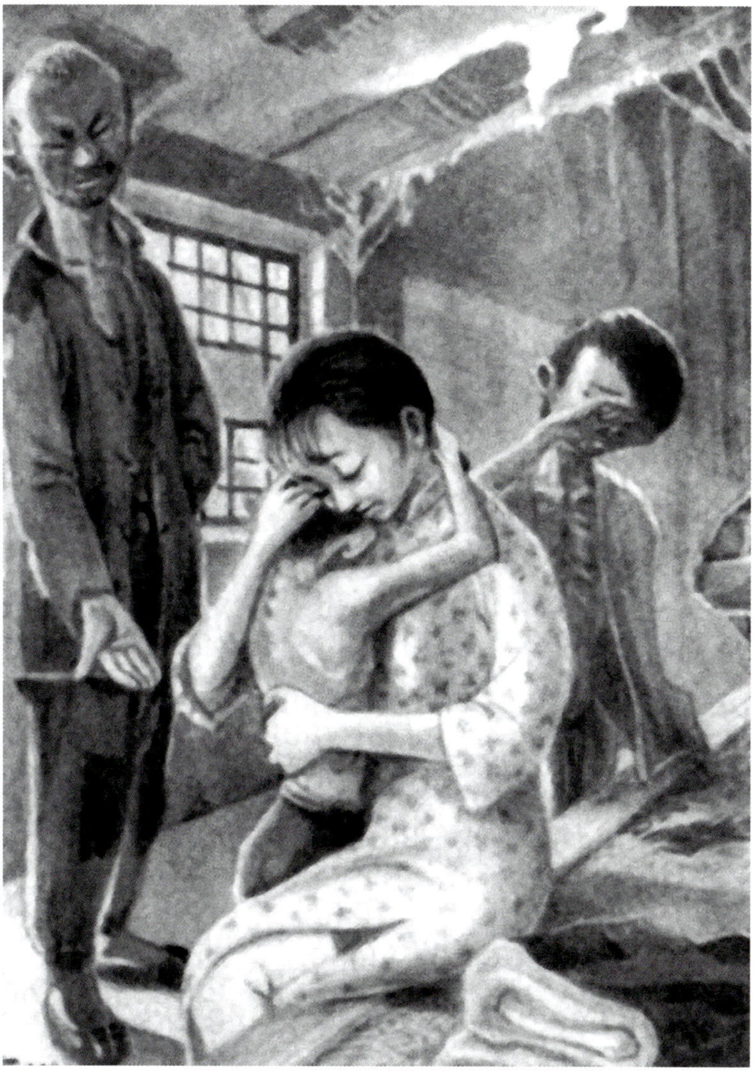

16. The poverty and sadness of the rickshaw driver's life (1978)

Nationalist forces, these sometimes allied forces focused their efforts on finding refuge inland. The Communist Party established several bases in rural areas. At this time, Comintern guidance to the Party wavered in many directions, owing to bitter factionalism and the unique conditions in China. But having lost its strength in the cities, the Party reacted by establishing its most important rural base area in remote Jinggangshan, a region straddling two south China provinces, with its capital at Ruijin. In addition, the period from 1929 to 1932 marked the rise of the Red Armies, which in turn increased the number of peasant partisans and rural mass organizations. These new developments involving the struggle to survive and grow in the interior provided ready new subjects for local artists and cartoonists.

The Red Armies provided the essential muscle to provide security for Party members and back up for Party policies. Under Mao Zedong's and Zhu De's leadership, this new Communist base area served as a center for organizing peasant armed uprisings, with cadres working in the spirit of Mao's famous metaphor of "sending fish [Communists] to water [the masses]." This attention to base area building and agrarian revolution, however, was interrupted by military necessity, as the base became a central target of Chiang Kai-shek's Nationalist troops. Using a strategy of tightening encirclement, Chiang, heeding the advice of his German military advisor, launched a decisive fifth campaign against the Jinggangshan base. The campaign produced an effective blockade of the base, where crucial supplies were already very scarce. Faced with looming annihilation, the beleaguered Communists began the great trek westward, which became known as the Long March (1934–35). Only one tenth of those who participated in the epic military maneuver survived. During its legendary course, Mao began his ascendancy to central party leadership. The Long March terminated in northern Shaanxi Province, where the Communists consolidated their power with a base centered on the town of Yan'an. This new base became a magnet for artists who thought they had escaped the urban dangers and restrictions encountered under the Nationalists. Seeking creative independence, in October 1938 they opened the Lu Xun Academy of Arts and Literature in a former Catholic church, under the direction of the Party's literary critic, Zhou Yang.

Still far from safe from enemy attacks, the leftist writers and artists began to benefit indirectly from the unrelenting pressure of Japan on China. It served as a useful distraction as Chiang Kai-shek directed his armies in the northeast and northwest to blockade and campaign against the new Communist base. To further emphasize and press his decision of "bandit suppression," Chiang flew to Xi'an in December 1936. He intended to admonish his generals about their lax efforts, but soon found firm resistance to his policy of "pacification [of the Communists] first, then resistance [to Japan]," a view shared by many in the arts who chaffed under the Nationalist regime. Unable to convince him of the wrongness of his policy, the generals boldly arrested and kidnapped Chiang, who, it is said, attempted to flee in his nightclothes by scrambling up a hillside, losing his false teeth in the effort. They held him captive for fourteen days and, in essence, demanded that the national priority be changed to fight Japan rather than suppress the Communists. The outcome was the formation in 1937 of the second united front between the Communist and the Nationalist forces in a new alliance against Japan.

Wartime and Wanderings

Cartoons are weapons for artists to fight against darkness;
I have mine handy when times are long and gloomy.

—Xiao Ding

War of Resistance Against Japan

Shanghai was bursting with patriotic organizations making urgent calls for anti-Japanese action. The memory of the 1932 attack was still fresh, and Japanese aggression in north China seemed to question the country's very survival. Then in August 1937, the nation's worst fears materialized when the Japanese launched a brazen and devastating attack on the Chinese sectors of Shanghai. For Chinese in Asia, this momentous event marked the beginning of World War II.

The cartoon quickly became another instrument of war against the Japanese. As John Lent has argued, innovations of cartoonists operating under wartime conditions emphasized a realistic approach, appealed to a mass audience, and were socially oriented.[10] They produced a New Art Movement (*Xin meishu yundong*), clearly linked to the national struggle for survival. The cartoonists' desire to disseminate their contributions widely led to the creation in Shanghai in 1937 of the National Salvation Cartoon Propaganda Corps (*Jiuwang manhua xuanchuandui*), which planned to move ahead of advancing Japanese troops. Corp teams traveled to Nanjing, Wuhan, Changsha, Guilin, Chongqing, and elsewhere, spreading propaganda, mounting street exhibits, and staging favorite dramas.

Xiao Ding and others in his circle found life in Shanghai, with the constant pressures from the Guomindang censors and police, intolerable and certainly unsafe. Ding moved to Hong Kong in late summer of 1937, where he expected to find a more tolerant, if less active and stimulating, atmosphere. Other artists and writers migrated elsewhere, some to the northwest Communist base area and others to provinces across the country. In Hong Kong, Ding was able to continue to produce powerful and deadly serious anti-Japanese cartoons and sketches. His robust and compelling drawings drew upon all of the themes and issues of the 1930s. His clean and simple drawings, depicting the emotionally charged times, reflected his intention to turn his images and their suggestiveness into lessons for the people, to help them understand what was happening to their country. When the spirit of his images was one of mocking and jovial vitality, he carefully avoided any decorative traces in his work, preferring instead a simple, clean message, bold lines, and a dynamic rhythm. At other times, he might employ an overlay of exciting and even playful detail to capture his audience. All of this work benefitted greatly from the good printing facilities available in Hong Kong.

Flight to Hong Kong

Xiao Ding fled Shanghai aboard a French ship. Settling temporarily in the relatively safe crown colony of Hong Kong, he continued to produce numerous, passionate cartoons using the anti-Japanese theme. His life was full of various projects, including the editorship and serving as illustrator of the popular Hong Kong edition of the magazines *Young Companion Pictorial* (*Liangyou huabao*), and *China Today* (*Jinri Zhongguo*), which had worldwide distribution, with editions in Chinese, French, Russian, and English. In 1937, after the National Salvation Propaganda Corps formed propaganda teams that fanned out across the country, some came to work in Hong Kong. Officially, this body was supervised by the Guomindang, but in practice, it worked under Guo Morou, who was a progressive leader in its political department. Guo maintained close relations with the Chinese Communist Party through his contact Zhou Enlai.[11]

Because of the local availability of newspapers, magazines, mimeographs, murals, posters, and other public media, corps members believed that the cartoon was the most promising agent for promoting political and social change. Corps participation was welcomed by local drama groups, as they put on popular cartoon shows meant to inspire anti-Japanese resistance and to raise local morale, especially among the troops (fig. 17). Their cartoons and shows became persuasive rallying tools for the anti-Japanese campaign. A corps mem-

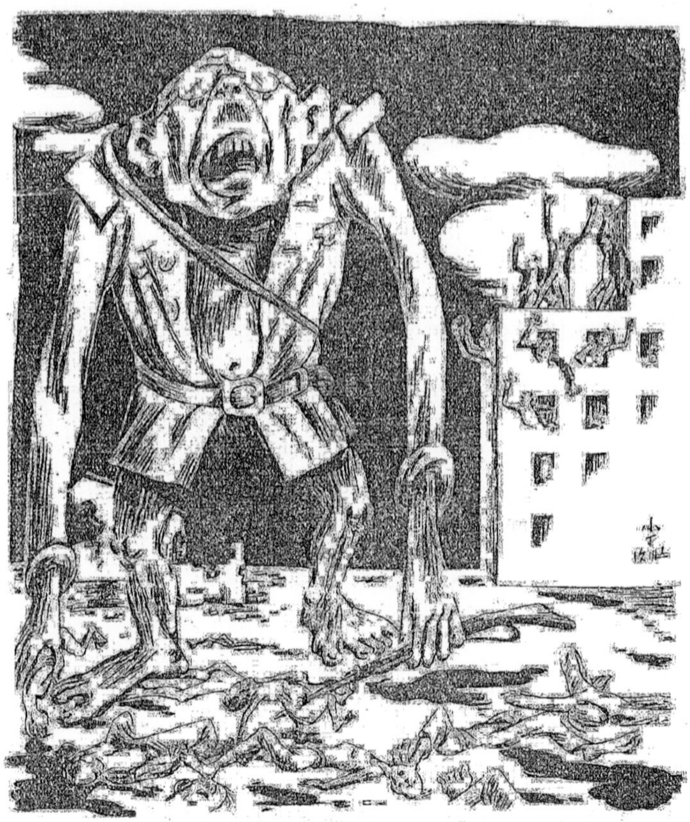

17. "A 'Civilized' King Kong" portrays the Japanese army as the marauding movie monster (1937)

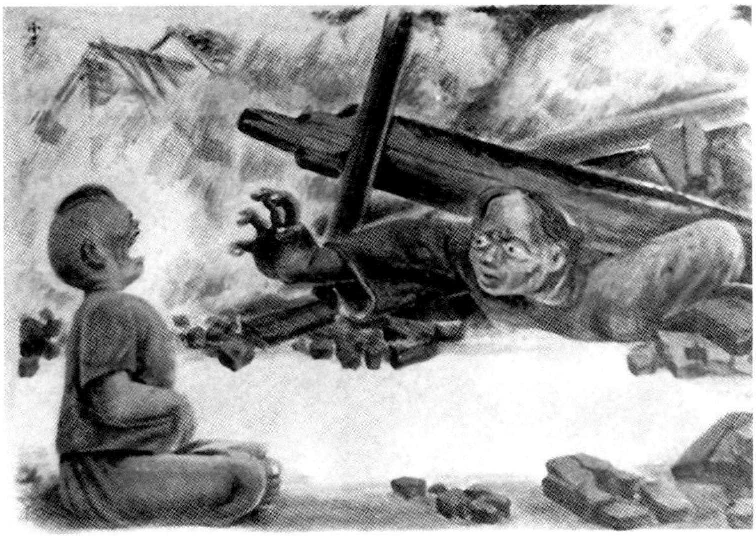

18. A young child calls to its trapped mother (1938 or 1939)

ber with first-hand experience described the source of his artistic inspiration as follows: "From Shanghai to Nanjing, the enemy planes tailed us and bombed trains and people, leaving a trail of fire and a land of moaning."[12] Xiao Ding's painting of a miserable, wailing child calling for its trapped mother (fig. 18) gives a graphic look at the pain and personal horrors of war. It is reminiscent of the well known Western war photograph taken in Shanghai of a crying baby, injured, alone, and abandoned on a railroad track. Terrifying and tragic experiences, documented in images such as this Japanese attack on a Chinese neighborhood (fig. 19), inspired cartoonists everywhere to put on cartoon shows built around particular themes or memorable events. The result was the proliferation of interesting and moving forms of picture storytelling. Spoken storytelling in the teahouse theaters had traditionally been a favored Chinese medium for entertainment and even instruction, and cartoon shows became a new variant of this traditional art form.

The storytelling artist might use symbols to convey his point. Snakes, dogs, or pigs usually depicted the public enemy, while lions and tigers suggested courage and steadfastness.

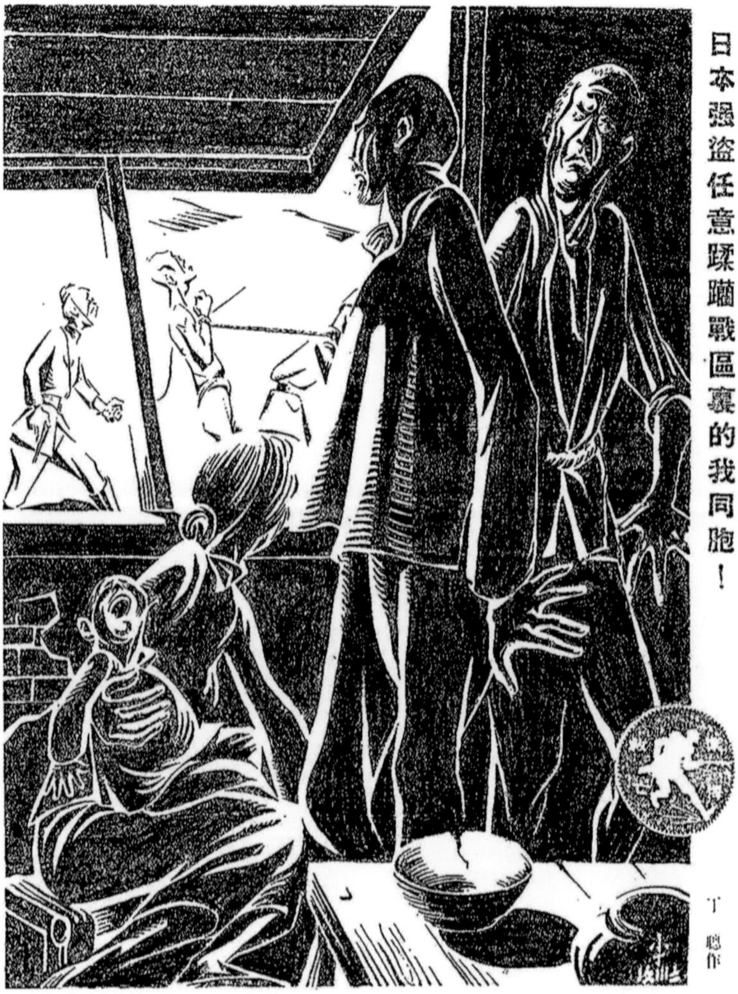

19. Japanese forces attack the neighborhood (1937)

Collaborators with the Japanese might appear as small and cringing or obsequious creatures. The artists' common intention was to ward off any feelings of powerlessness on the part of the people, which might produce weakness in the public willingness to resist Japanese aggression. The calculated battle cry aimed at the unity of the country against the enemy and universal participation in the national struggle.

Xiao Ding was an active participant in these artistic projects, designing stage sets, advertisements, and posters for the local theater groups. He continued to contribute work to the Corps's official publication, *Resistance Cartoons* (*Kangzhan man-*

hua). In 1939, Xiao Ding's friend Ye Qianyu, who was also director of the National Salvation Cartoon Propaganda Corps, came to Hong Kong from Wuhan. Ye had created the first cartoon series in China during the 1930s and was very influential in fine arts education. He wrote a book, *The True Records of the Japanese Aggressor's Atrocities*, on the brutal Japanese actions in China, which Xiao Ding helped with and edited.

Following this project, the two put together a major exhibit in the lobby of the Hong Kong Central Theater dealing with the war of resistance against Japan. The American journalist Edgar Snow attended a preview of this exhibit (fig. 20). Xiao Ding offered several of his cartoons and helped select other entries. Most important, he received special recognition among the growing anti-Japanese movement in Hong Kong when Madame Sun Yat-sen (Song Qingling), who

20. Visitors at an anti-Japanese war art exhibit in Hong Kong (April 1939). Guests and participants included (from left to right) Ye Qianyu, Edgar Snow, Israel Epstein, Jin Zhonghua, Zhang Guangyu, Ding Cong, and Chen Xianqi

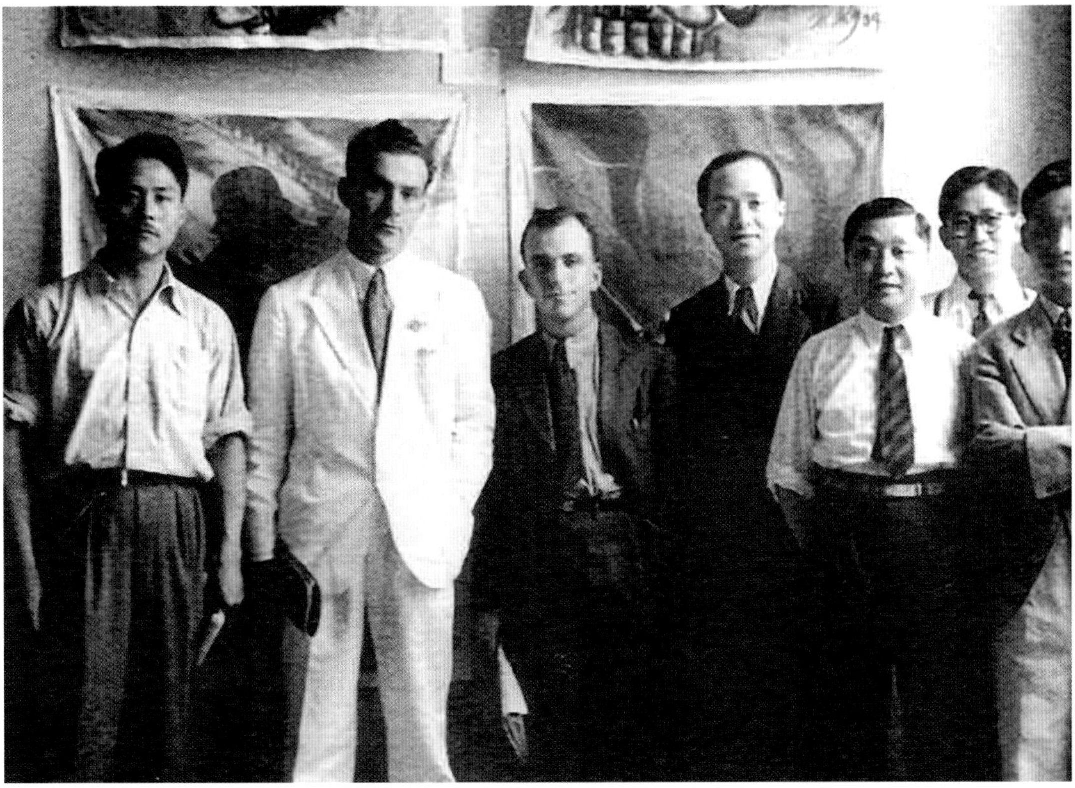

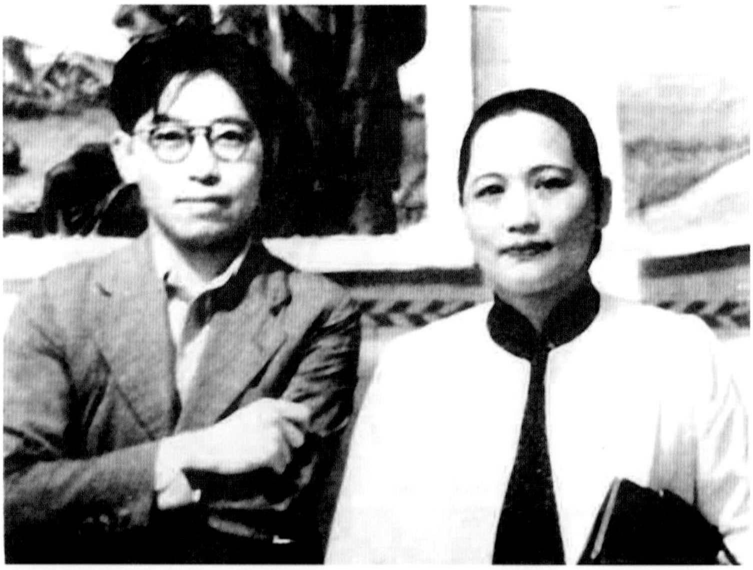

21. Madame Song Qingling and Ding Cong stand together at this 1939 anti-Japanese art exhibit in Hong Kong

visited the exhibit (fig. 21), selected his painting *Fugitives* (*Taowang*) as the best of all the propaganda illustrations. True to his principles, Ding had based this painting (fig. 22) on a photograph of a real life refugee event. After the exhibition Xiao Ding sold the painting for ten silver coins, which he then donated to the League for the Resistance Against Japanese Aggression. Madame Sun planned to use his painting as the logo for her organization Defend China Alliance (*Baowei*

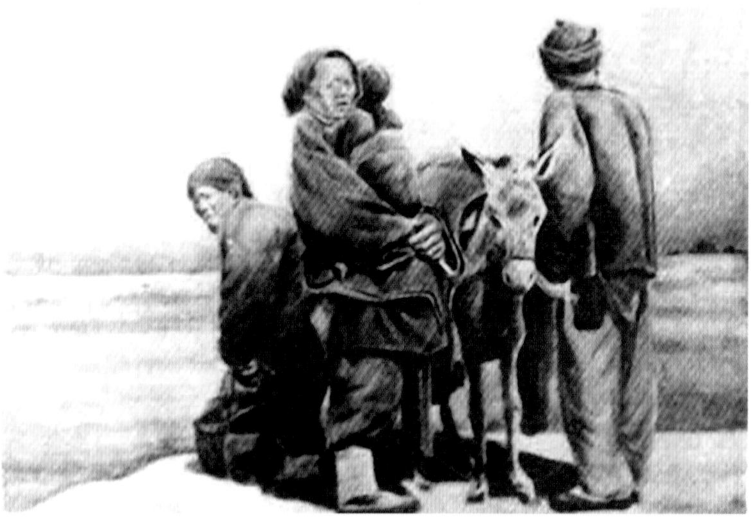

22. Madame Song selected Xiao Ding's painting Fugitives *for her organization's logo*

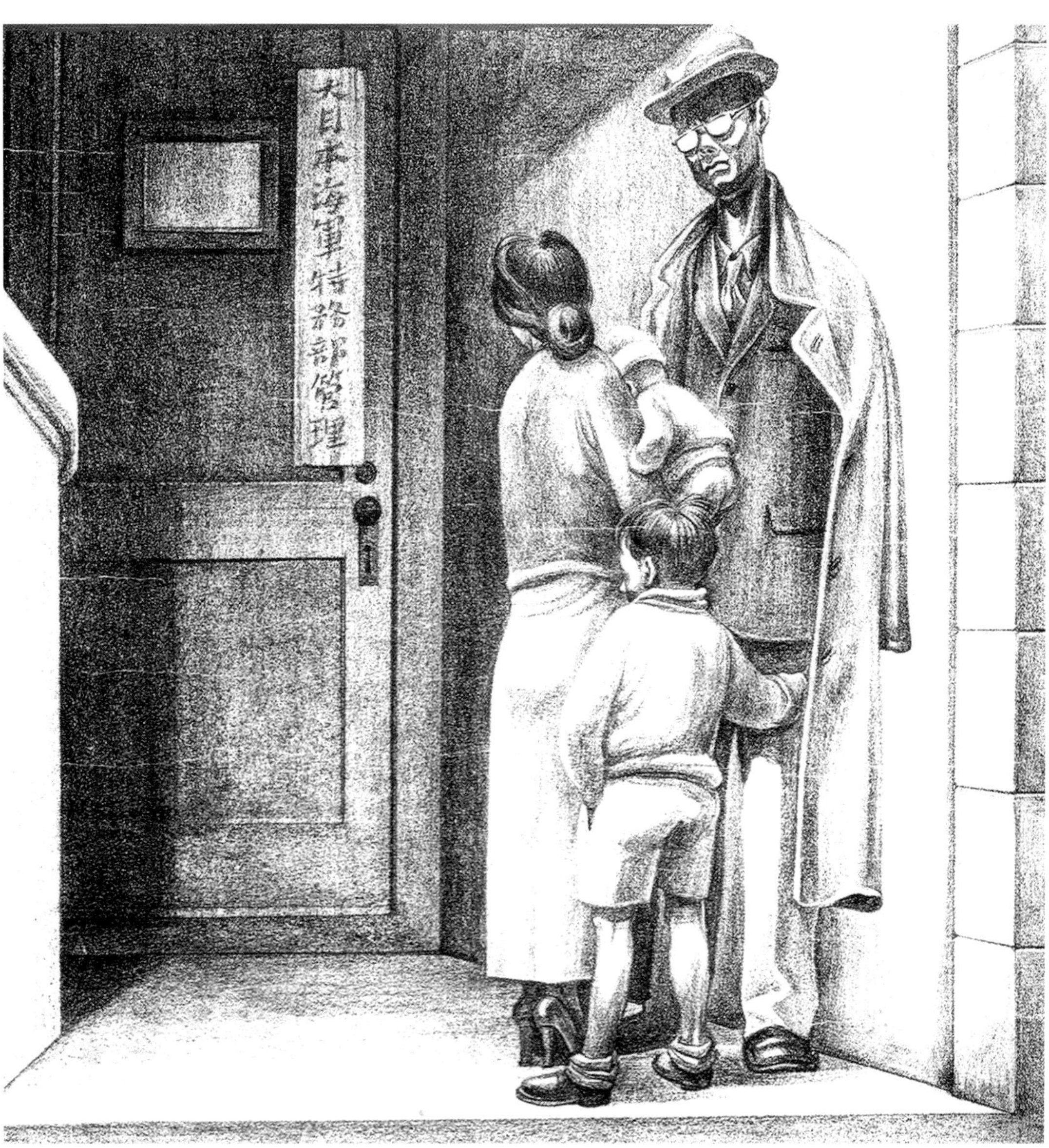

23. A home commandeered by the military in Hong Kong during World War II (1943)

Zhongguo datongmeng). The painting depicts fleeing refugees, perhaps including three generations, who appear lost and badly frightened by the horrors and cruelty of war. The feeling evoked calls to mind the "blue period" of Picasso and his famous painting *The Tragedy.*

During the war, China experienced massive migrations of peoples moving out of the eastern war zones and looking for

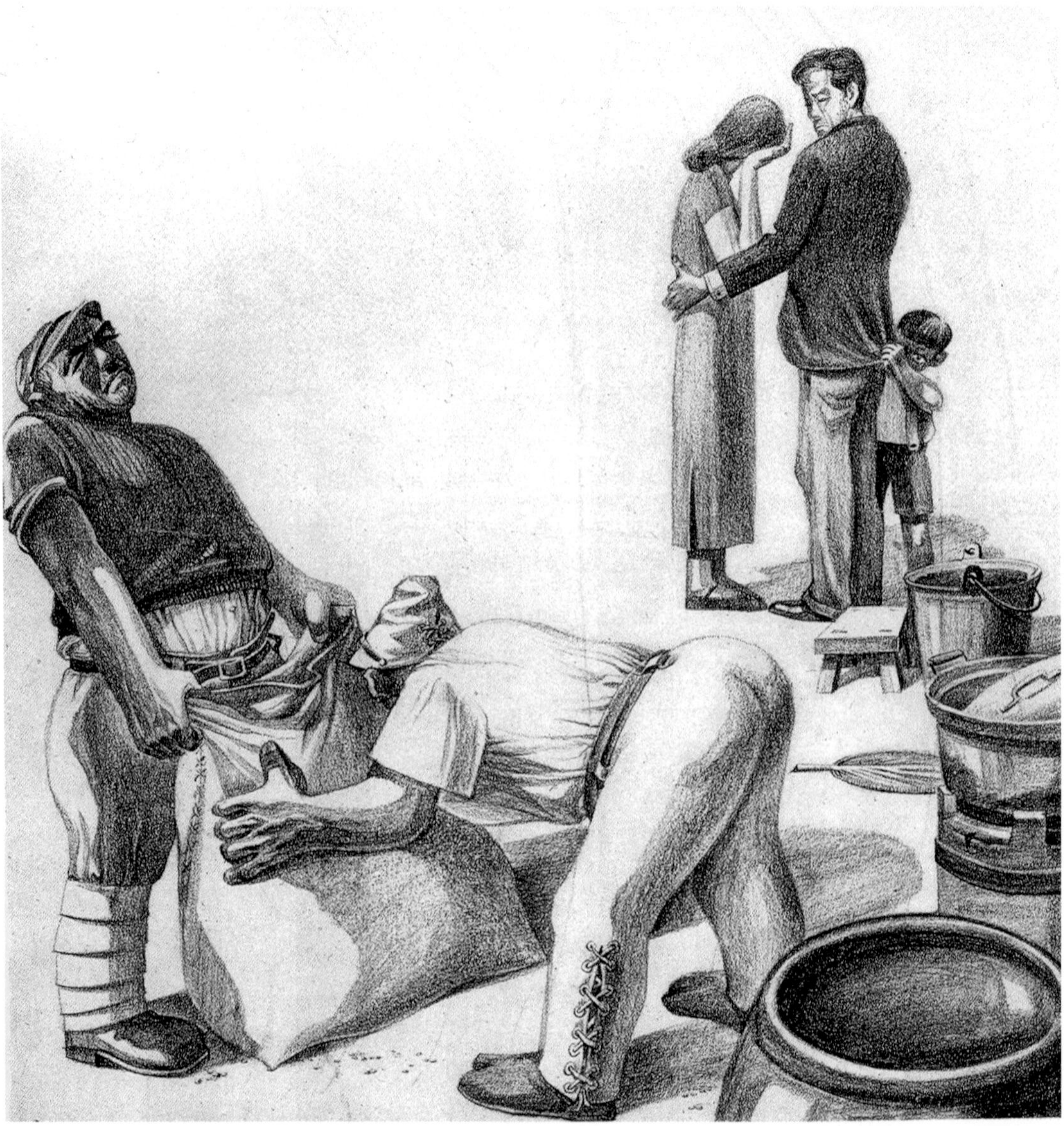

24. Wartime suffering in Hong Kong (1943)

refuge and security further west. In this and other paintings, Xiao Ding was able to channel through his own consciousness the passion and tragedy of the situation and the traumatized state of mind of people. He depicted the raw tensions that inflamed and injured wartime populations, using a visual, emotional vocabulary that his audience was certain to grasp. Xiao Ding continued to publish this and other works

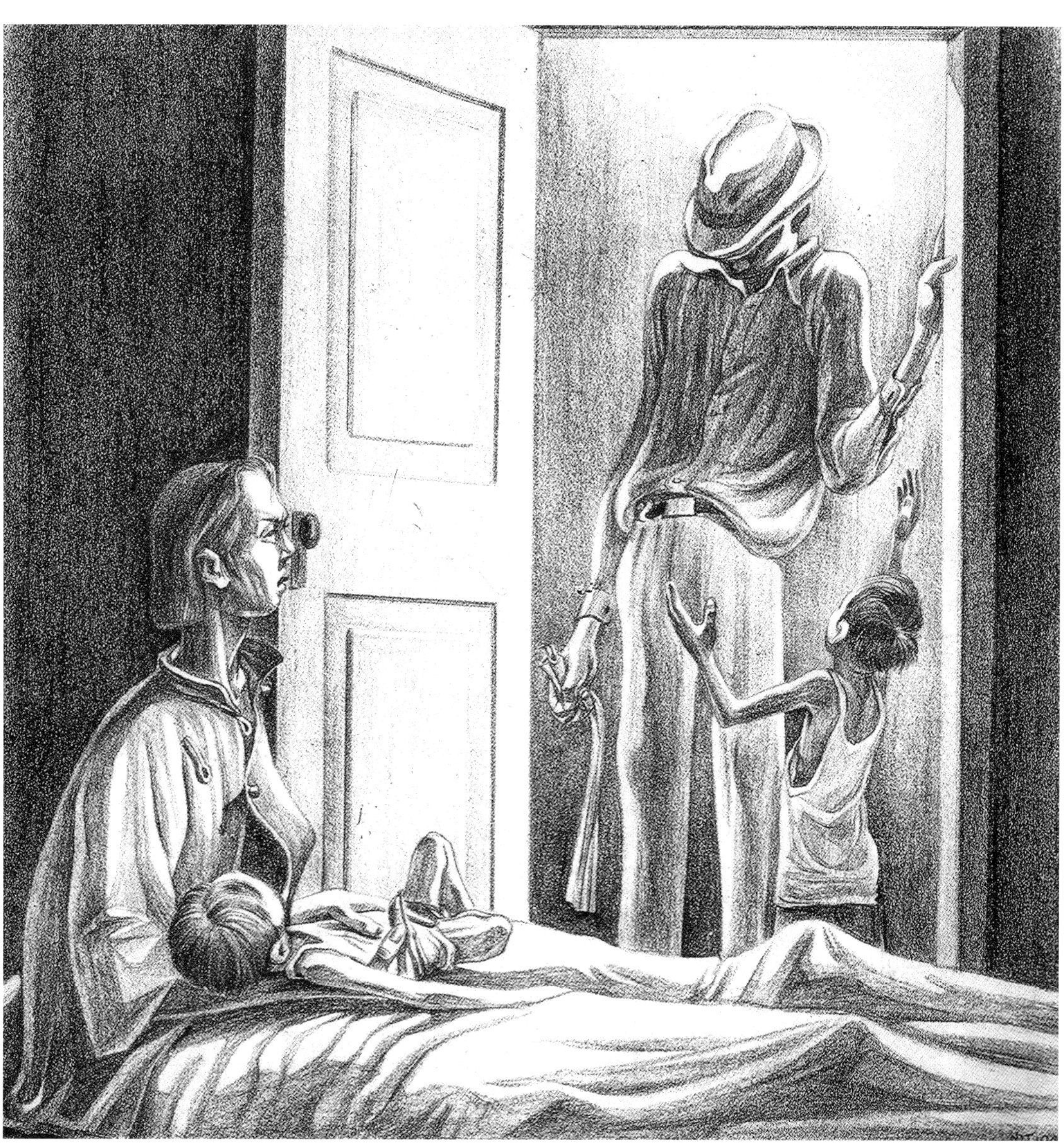

25. *Family hunger in wartime Hong Kong (1943)*

in local newspapers, and to edit the magazine *Young Companion Pictorial*. This magazine predated the similar *Life* magazine in the U.S. Like *Life*, it was rich with illustrations and gorgeous photography, and focused on immediate, real life material, often satirizing profiteers, traitors, spies, collaborators, and their victims (figs. 23–25).

Erliutang Formed in Chongqing

In 1940, Xiao Ding decided to go to China's wartime capital, Chongqing, then the reputed center of anti-Japanese activity. He traveled with his friend and mentor, the playwright, Wu Zuguang, and both found employment there with a local movie company, the China Film Studio, creating costumes and sets.[13] Such good fortune and satisfying work were interrupted, however, by the famous Wannan (South Anhui) Incident of January 1941 when Nationalist troops attacked the Communist New Fourth Army. This clash breached the agreements reached in forming the Second United Front, making conditions for the Communists and leftists perilous, especially in the wartime capital. The Chongqing government soon outlawed its erstwhile Communist partner, thus bringing to an end the two friends' relative security and profitable work on the movies.

Out of work and threatened with arrest or worse, Xiao Ding decided to go to Burma, at least until the situation in China improved. He had a friend in Chongqing whose brother had opened a successful business in Burma. This friend, Tang Yu, a Chinese-Burmese editor of a film magazine, had a very warm relationship with his brother, often receiving funds from him, which relates to an important turn of events regarding Xiao Ding's time in Chongqing.

In late 1941, Tang Yu generously used some of the money sent to him to build a house for his itinerant friends in Chongqing. The simple structure, built from local bricks, had the distinguishing feature of a fireplace, something which greatly pleased Xiao Ding. It happens that the term for fireplace in spoken Chinese is *bi lu*, which can also be understood as Jade House. Having such a pleasing association, Jade House became the chosen name for the new home.

For those living there however, the group home came to be known as the *Erliutang*. This Chinese term is difficult to translate into English. It is derived from a popular folk opera from North Shanxi province called "The Marriage of Xiao'Er Hei," in which one of the characters, *Erliuzi* (Chinese slang for a generally idle man), follows a lazy or bohemian life style. Those gathered in the new house had seen the play and identified with this character. Like him, they did not have formal jobs and still made or found accommodations wherever they went.

Their humble dwelling and the resident salon group gained an elevated status during a visit to Chongqing from the cultural guru Guo Morou. Guo made a point to visit Xiao Ding and the other salon participants, whom he knew well. Seeing the Jade House and its many artistic residents and visitors, he jokingly commented upon what he called their bohemian life style, saying "Since all of you are *Erliuzi*, then this place must be an *Erliutang*," or House of the *Erliuzi*. Sufficiently amused by Guo's christening, Ding and the others wanted to hang a plaque over the hut's entrance with Guo's inscription of the term, *Erliutang*, and his signature. These plans failed as they were unable to locate the appropriate materials.

This incident is described in some detail because it would have unexpected and very unfortunate repercussions for Xiao Ding and his friends. The *Erliutang* designation by Guo Morou seemed to make an indelible mark on the official memory of the Chinese Communist regime after 1949. Some of the signs of the reaction against the artists and writers were already becoming apparent. As early as 1938, Mao Zedong made his views on art and literature known through his speech "The Position of the Chinese Communist Party during the National Struggle." He railed against what he saw as petty-bourgeois attitudes and values rooted in liberalism and Western influences. He instructed Chinese writers and artists to rely on native Chinese subjects, such as stories of peasants and soldiers, or regional folklore, for their art and writings, and to avoid hollow and abstract clichés anchored in the Western tradition. This speech was further amplified in his "Talks at the Yan'an Conference on Literature and Art" in 1943. In those discussions, Mao added to his list of requirements the essential virtue of strict Party loyalty and discipline.

Those artists who had ventured to Chongqing instead of to Mao's kingdom in Yan'an found themselves targeted for correction of their wayward, liberal tendencies. Xiao Ding was not part of the Yan'an circle, and when the Communists came to power, he would find that in the new milieu, he would need more than just apologies to cleanse himself of his "mistaken ideas." As we shall see, that is when the *Erliutang* label came back into play.

Returning to Xiao Ding's trip to Burma: Along the way he witnessed practices common during wartime that became the subject for a series of his paintings. He watched the driver of the crowded vehicle that carried him and others to Burma use endless excuses to levy one fee after another on the hapless passengers. The experience inspired him and he painted a series of works illustrating the various tricks and excuses used by the trip's driver, using the theme "On the road, one stretches one's reach," the latter a euphemism for pilfering. Xiao Ding liked to paint a series of scenes or images, which when shown together tell an interesting story. With this cartoon series (*lianhuanhua*), he succeeded in reworking the ancient tradition of storytelling into a new cartoon format (figs. 26–27). Known collectively as "One Hundred Days on the Eastern River," the paintings appeared in the Hong Kong newspaper *Huashang bao,* and are now held by the Shenzhen Art Gallery near Hong Kong.

Burma was a welcome respite for Xiao Ding. Safe from arrest and with free time to draw and paint, he was able to settle in and enjoy life. He had no regular employment and his expenses were small because he lived with friends. During the three months he spent in Burma, he did not go out much and spent most of his time painting portraits of the Burmese and Indian men and women he met. It was also an opportune time for painting what he recalled from that long trip from Chongqing to Burma.

After three months of comfort and relaxation in Burma, he began to miss the old life in Hong Kong, with its access to current war news and films, and the broad availability of newspapers and journals. He decided to leave Burma by ship and make a stop in Singapore before sailing on to Hong Kong. During his brief visit in Singapore, he happened to come across an old friend, Yu Dafu, who had been prominent in the New Culture Movement (and was eventually murdered by the Japanese). Yu joined him for some drinks

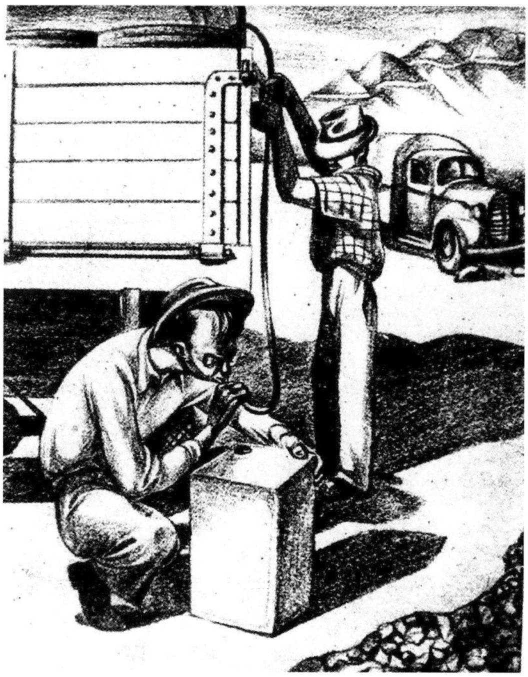

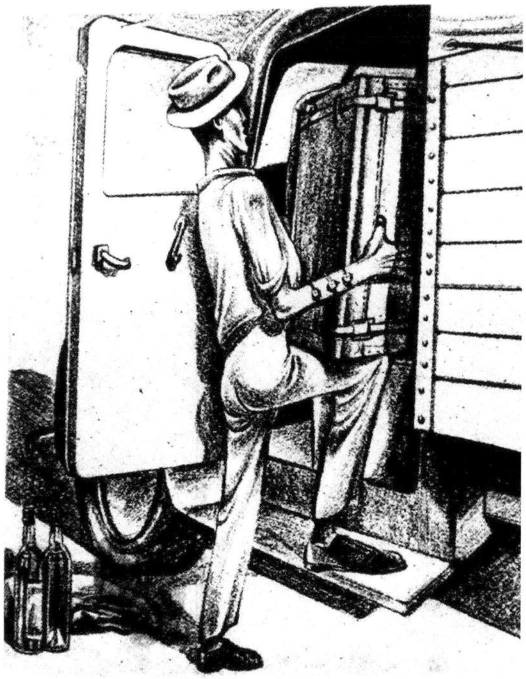

26, 27. Various scams carried out against passengers during Xiao Ding's trip to Burma (1942)

and told him what he knew about the war and of new developments in their mutual cultural circles. Xiao Ding was obviously invigorated by his friend in Singapore, and by the benefits of his brief "vacation" in Burma. After he reached Hong Kong, he began immediately to edit a local newspaper and became active in the Hong Kong Theater Association. His personal contribution to the local theater, which he loved, was to design the many sets for the upcoming new season of plays.

In 1942 Hong Kong fell to the Japanese, making it again necessary to move on. Unfortunately, moving usually included discarding, often by burning, precious things such as books, drawings, letters, diaries, and photographs, so as not to have incriminating evidence on hand if he encountered Japanese or unfriendly forces. After a brief stop in Guilin and a short stay in Chongqing in the company of his artist friends, Ye Qianyu and Xiao Ding went west to Chengdu (fig. 28), in Sichuan Province, and formed an artistic community called the *Ju Yi* group. He was able to derive some income from a teaching position at the Sichuan Provincial Art Academy, which suddenly saw its staff significantly increased by the influx of talented artists from the war zones.

Suffering from poverty and malnutrition, the artists were easy prey to disease, as well as the roving eye of the censor. Several friends were reduced to selling dumplings and peanuts to survive. Chengdu was almost out of range of the Japanese bombing attacks, but the secret police kept a vigilant eye on publishing and any evidence of adverse social action. In his work *Cold Nights*, Mao Dun provides a gripping story of the struggles and hardships of the intellectual classes in Chengdu during the war. The position of the artist or teacher was no longer valued or respected in this war-torn and chaotic country. That of the hustler or profiteer gained the most attention and reward. Figure 29 shows a smug, cor-

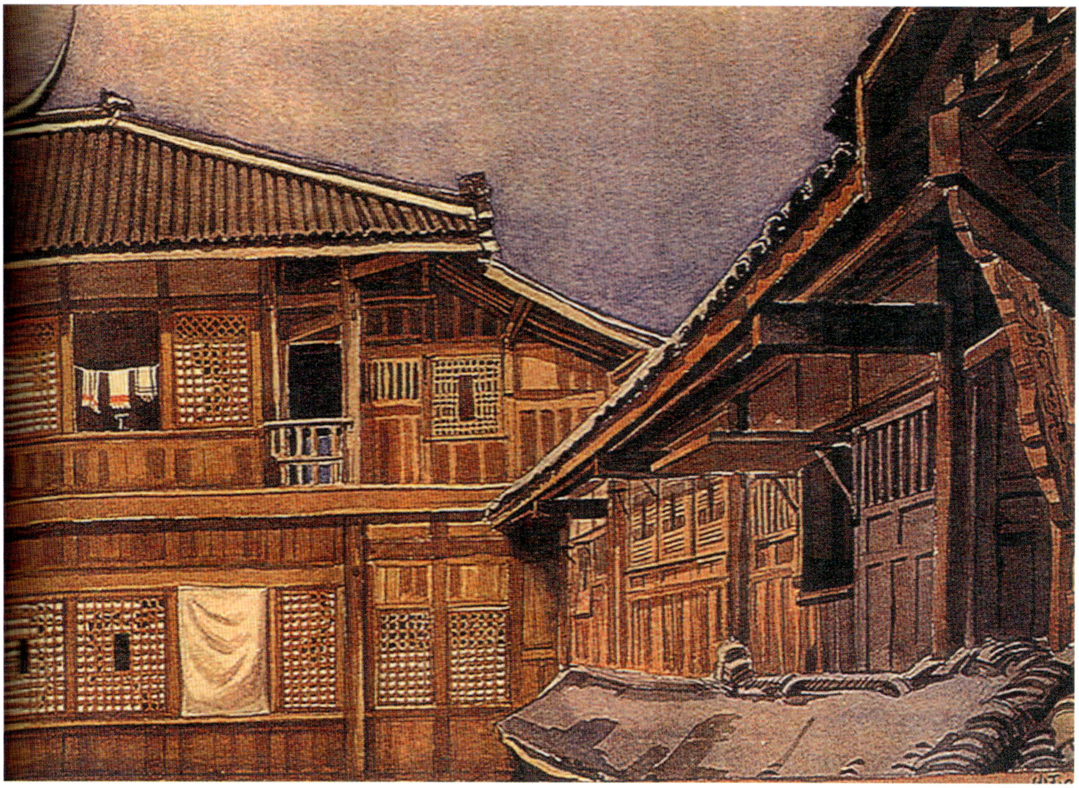

28. Xiao Ding's neighborhood in Chengdu

pulent diner in a Chengdu restaurant who remains oblivious to the malnourished and shabbily dressed figures at his back. The contrast between the dark, shriveled figures and the fat and rosy diner ready to gulp his food, makes for a stark and caustic composition. The emotional content cannot be missed.

A greater degree of freedom of expression greeted those artists who stayed in Guilin, in Guizhou province, and Xiao Ding stopped there briefly after he left Hong Kong. This beautiful and remote city was far away from the prying eyes of the censors, and served as a gathering place and refuge for many artists from Hong Kong and Canton. During the war years, it became known as "The Paris of Free China" and "City of Resistance Culture."[14] Artists and musicians, the latter including the talented violinist Ma Sicong, held concerts and put on

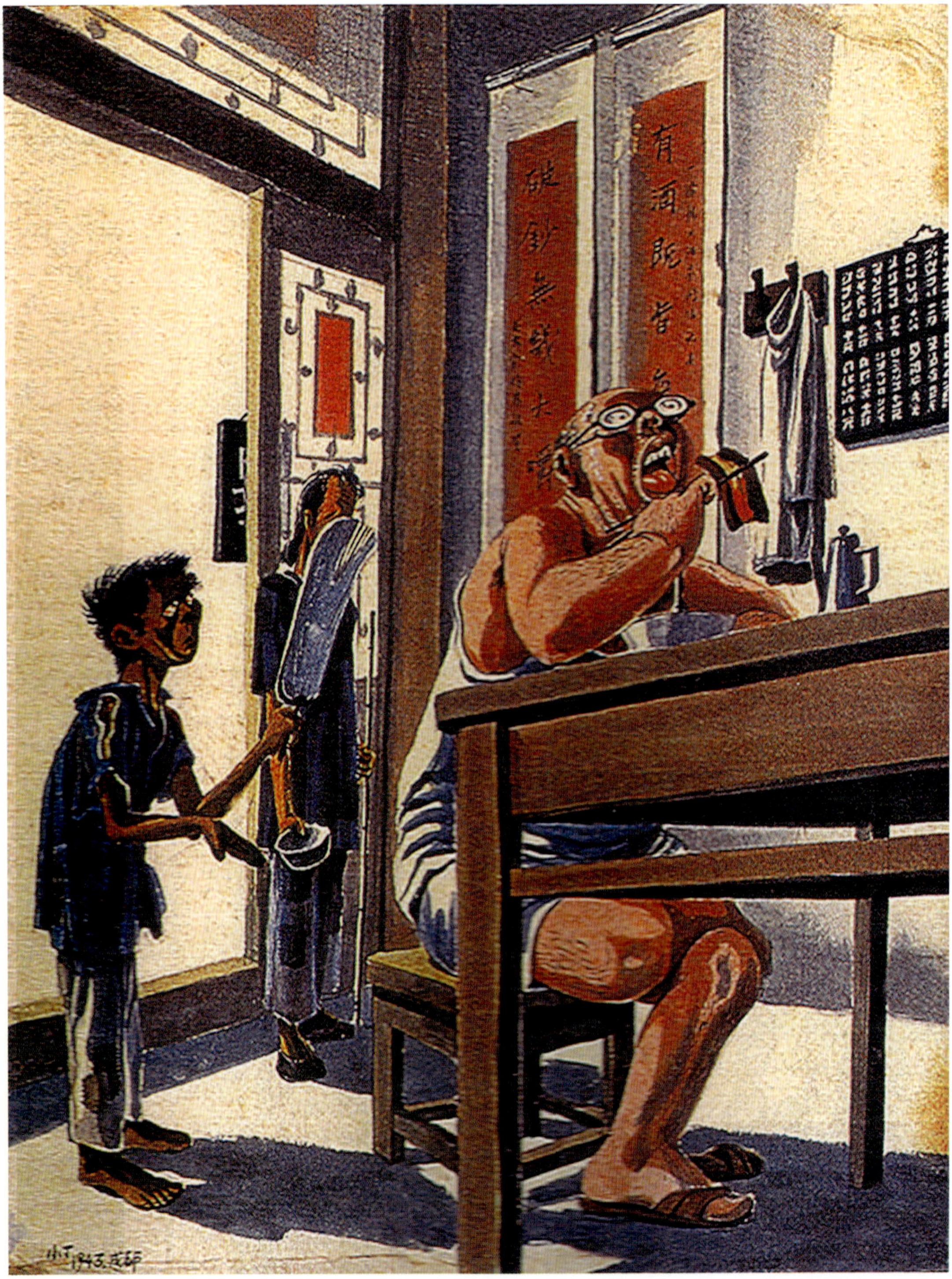

29. A contrast of poverty with greed and wealth, a common sight in Chengdu restaurants (1943)

numerous well attended exhibitions.[15] They included Xiao Ding's paintings of rural life and the anti-Japanese struggle. Mao Dun spent the early years of the war there. The Japanese finally occupied Guilin in September 1944, bringing to an end this flourishing western refuge for writers and artists.

During his years in Chengdu, Xiao Ding found time to venture out into the borderlands of Sichuan Province, and to sketch and paint what he saw (figs. 30–32). The authority on modern Chinese art Michael Sullivan wrote that "it was during these middle years of the war that Xiao Ding matured as a graphic artist."[16] The portrayal of an old peasant woman (fig.

30. Members of the Yi minority in western Sichuan Province (1944)

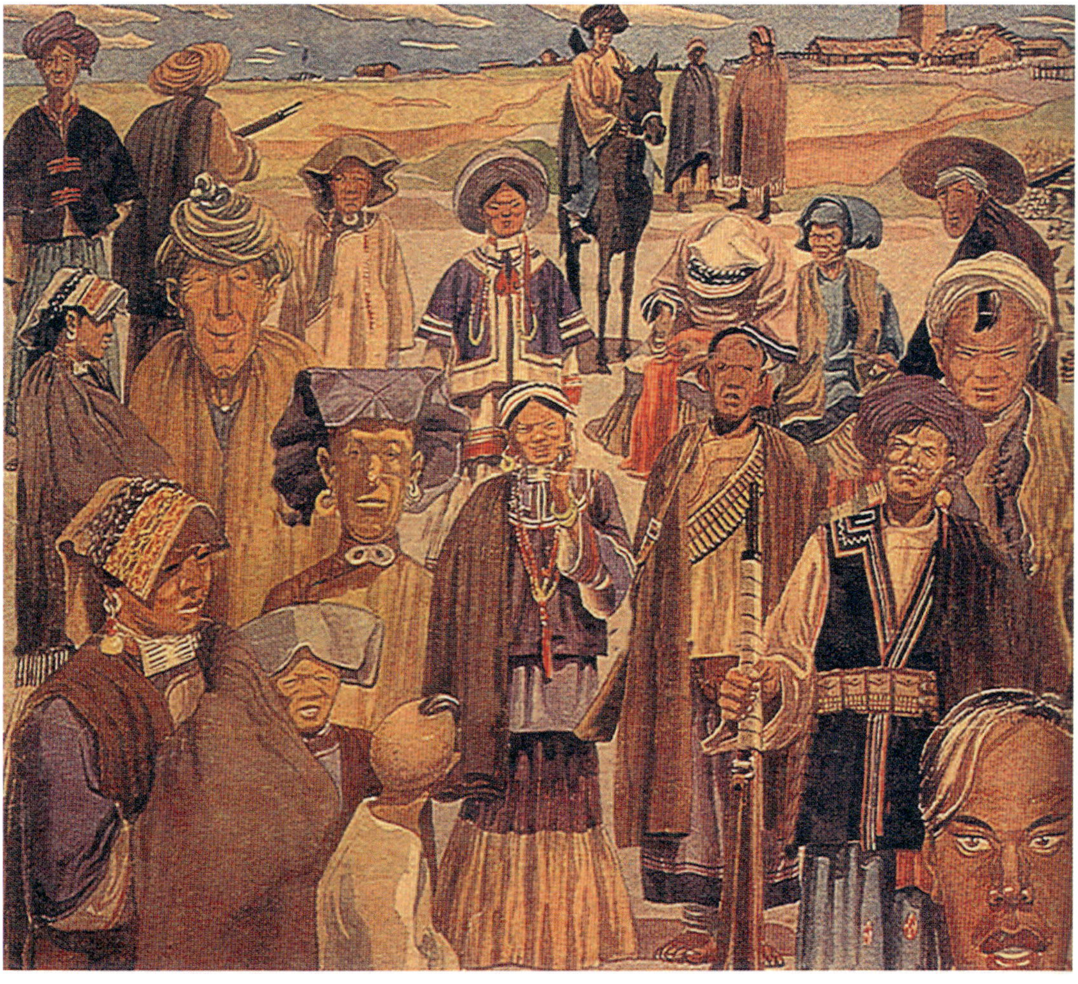

32) probably inspired by what Xiao Ding saw during his walks around the city of Chengdu, clearly shows that development. The expression on the woman's face, with her bent head, makes a connection to the poverty and hardship of the world around her, and allows her image and life situation to emerge

31. Two Yi minority people

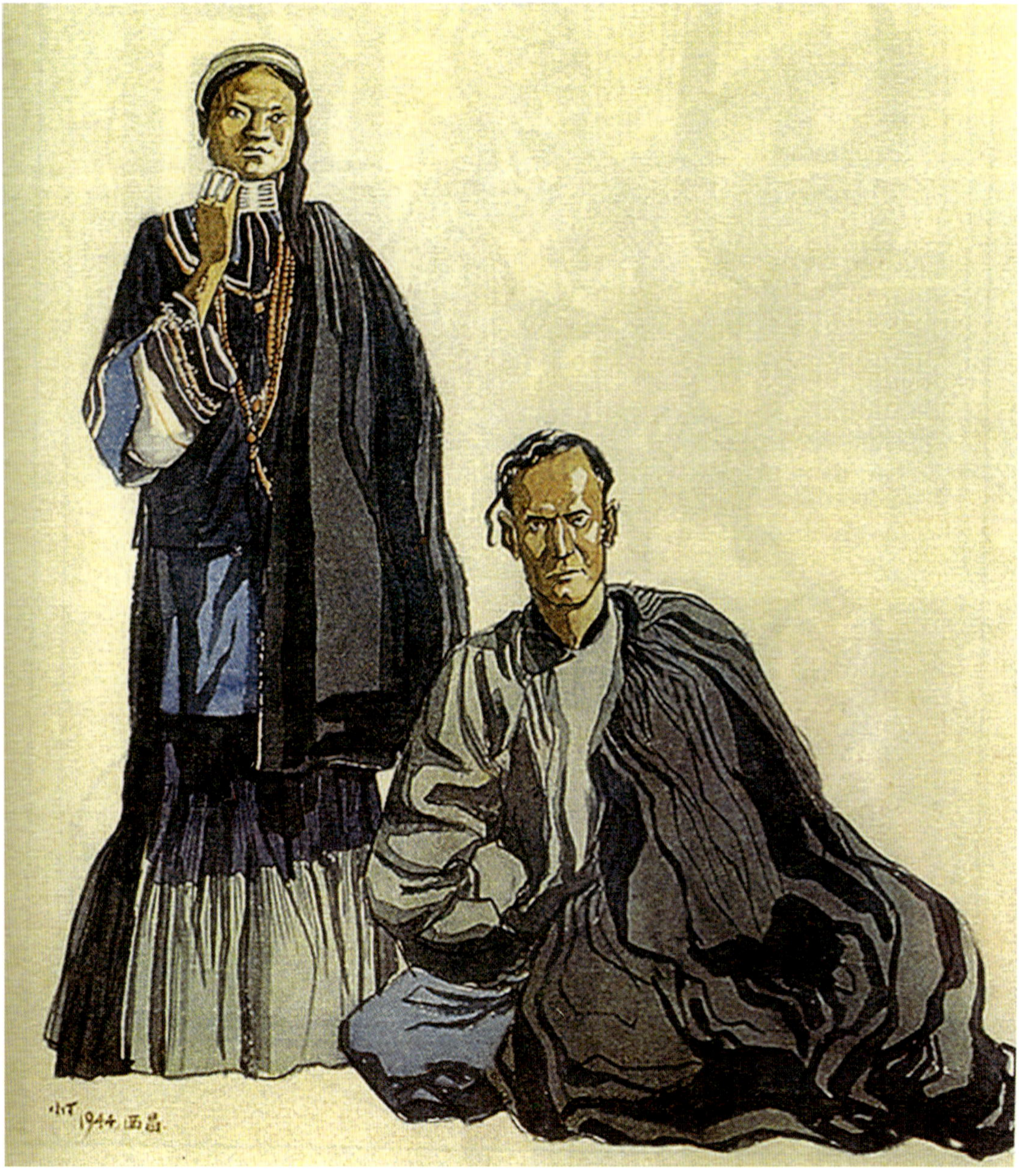

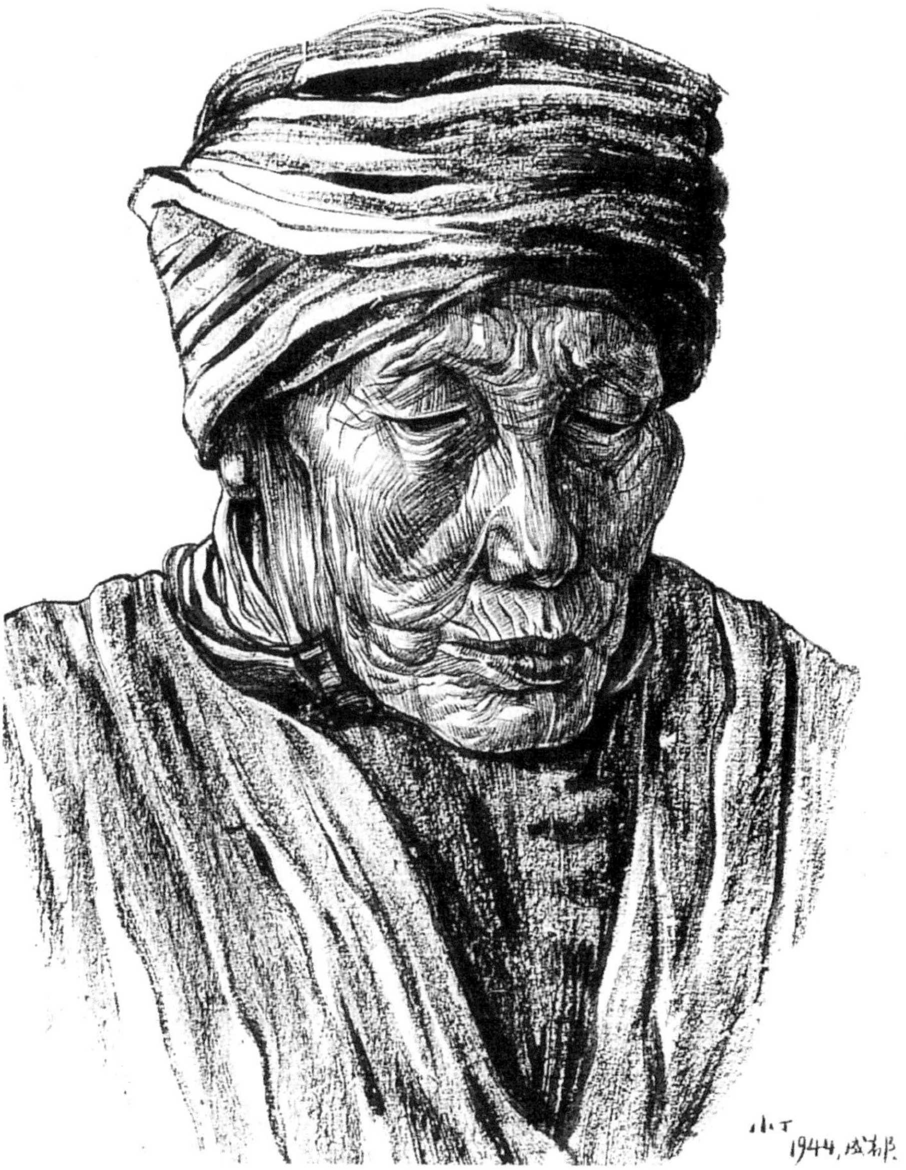

32. Portrait of an old peasant woman in Sichuan (1944)

with a special clarity. Done with Chinese brush and ink, the work takes on the appearance of an engraving, further heightening its effect. Xiao Ding's art of this period clearly expresses his passionate disgust with the social injustices and even atrocities that he finds evident in everyday life.

Xiao Ding's Celebrated Hand Scroll

During the war years, Mao's political influence, including his own brand of censorship of the arts, centered mostly in the territory under his control. Elsewhere, in Chengdu for example, writers and artists gave their full attention to pointing out the oppressive and corrupt nature of the Nationalist Government, with the intention of discrediting the Guomindang. Students demonstrated with huge street banners, some of which bore Xiao Ding's name and image. They had become increasingly convinced that conditions at home were a bigger threat to the people than even the Japanese, and began to advocate this theme in their rallies and other work.

An outstanding example, and certainly his best known work, was Xiao Ding's celebrated satirical hand scroll (*huajie*) entitled *Looking at Images* (*Xianxiang tu*). In this work (fig. 33), he directs his most biting and vitriolic satire at the Nationalist regime, and displays many of his favorite themes. Although choosing the traditional format of the hand scroll, Xiao Ding employs many of his preferred figures to present his critique

33. Ding Cong's hand scroll, Xiangxiang tu *depicts corruption and suffering under the Nationalist regime (1944)*

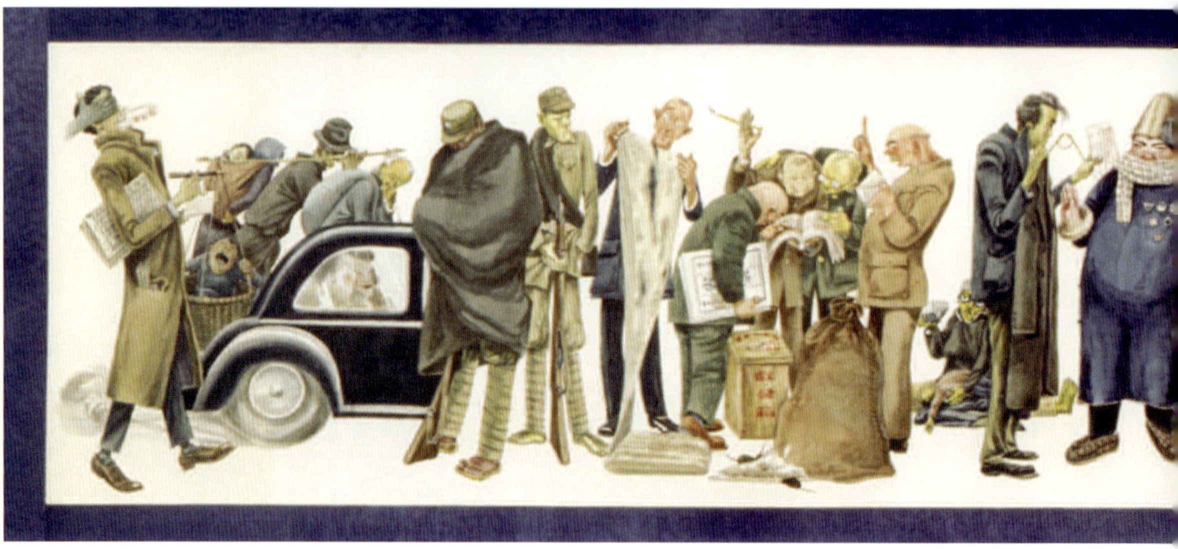

of contemporary waste, profiteering, and corruption. Displayed at an exhibit of the Modern Art Society (*Xiandai meishuhui*) in 1944, it created a sensation. Starting with the image on the right, a cogent analysis of the scroll's contents by Michael Sullivan is as follows:

> It opens with a student, forced to study volumes of useless old lore while his modern textbooks lie idle on the floor. Beside him stands the professor, nursemaid to his pregnant wife and children, who want food, not books. Partially screening the war profiteer counting his gains, two rascals close a secret deal by squeezing fingers hidden in their sleeves. The blind folded artist has painted a dog when he intended a tiger, but five would-be buyers, unable to tell the difference, have attached their red tags to his scroll; the writer's every work, meanwhile, is measured and scrutinized by the huge eye of the censor. The rich man, member of many prestigious organizations, refuses to buy a coat from a refugee,

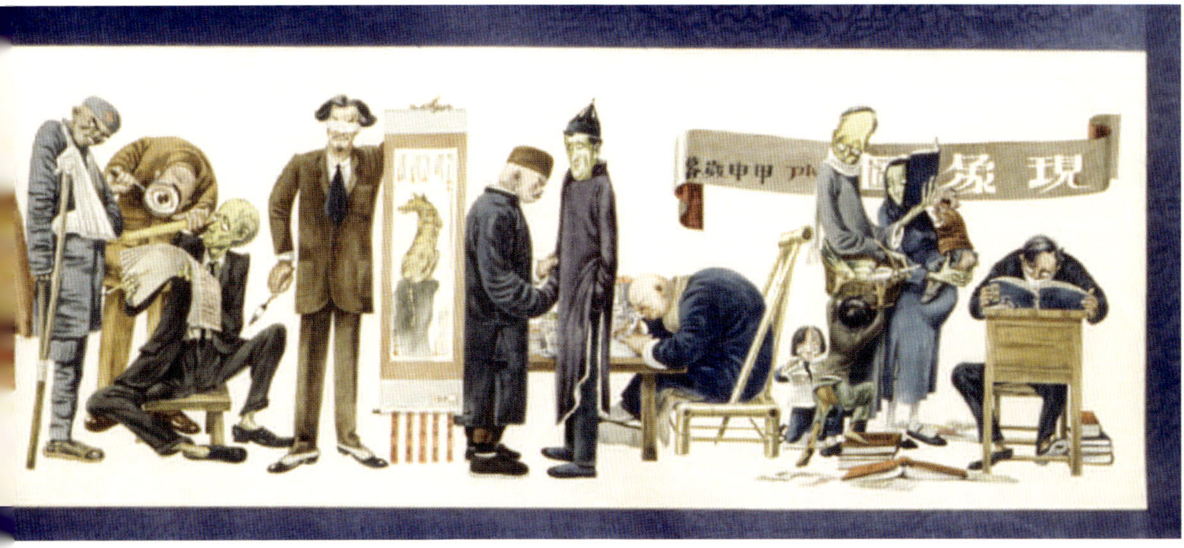

> while the painted woman on his arm holds her nose at the stink of the wounded soldier. Officials haggle over money pledged to feed the poor, while hoarded rice is eaten by rats and cloth rots. Soldiers and refugees crowd the road, while the rich in their limousines drive past unheeding. Finally, the journalist, his pen poised to expose the rot, can speak only through the official invitation stuffed in his mouth.[17]

This work is a devastating exposure of the evils of society under the Nationalist Government. Xiao Ding manages to bring into the work all the sadness and tragedy of the period, and occasionally, a bit of humor, as with the dog painting. It shows the extreme difficulties besetting society at this time, both owing to war and to revolutionary change. The emotions of loss, confusion, and fear, as well as the displays of venality and arrogance, are clearly expressed. It is a panorama of insight into the essence and behavior of this troubled society. There is no doubt that the war years provided Xiao Ding with a remarkable vision and understanding of his coun-

34. The hand scroll Xianshi tu *shows corruption and suffering under the Nationalist regime (1947)*

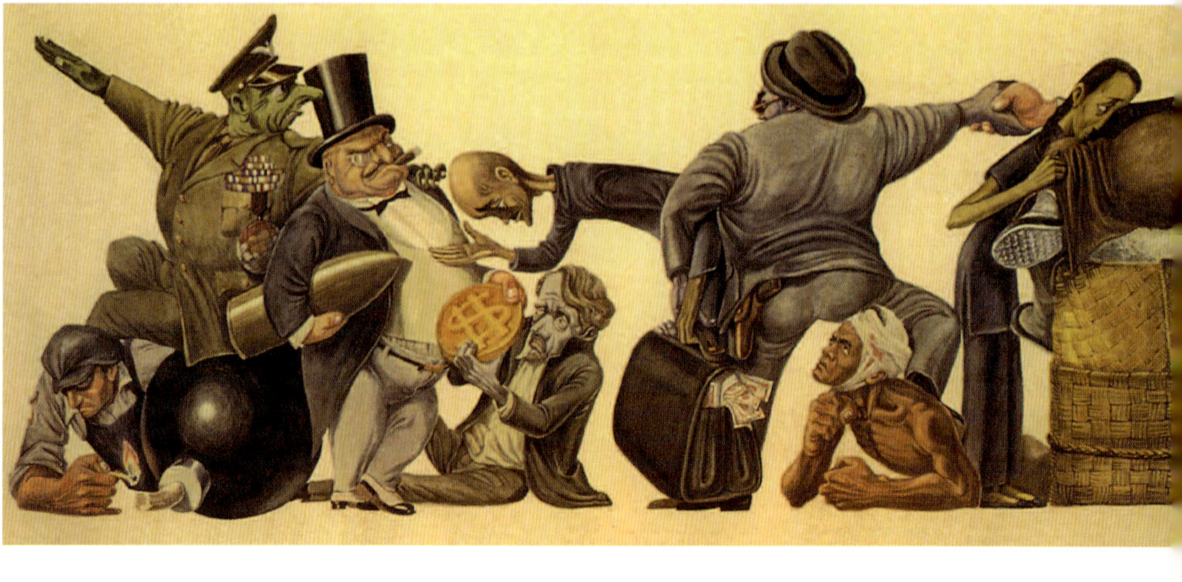

try, and the practiced skill to create such works. The stylistic influences of the Mexican artists and their great wall murals depicting their own society's suffering are also apparent in this work, as is his sense of bitter disappointment with conditions under the Nationalist regime. This *gouache* on paper scroll is held by the Spencer Museum of Art, University of Kansas.

Just three years later (1947) in Hong Kong, Xiao Ding created another satirical hand scroll (fig. 34) with the title, *Picture of Reality (Xianshi tu)*. The war with Japan had ended, but another war, a civil war, was about to begin. As the painting shows, starting from the left, an "Uncle Sam" kind of figure, at Chiang Kai-shek's bidding, is shipping in armaments and other goods while war profiteers are making deals and collecting their gains. Next, the peasant at work in the field is torn from his mother by his forced conscription into army service. The weapons supplied by the United States, rather than serving their intended purpose, were being used against the main enemy, the Communists. The scroll ends with the image of a peasant, getting ready to fire a canon back up the

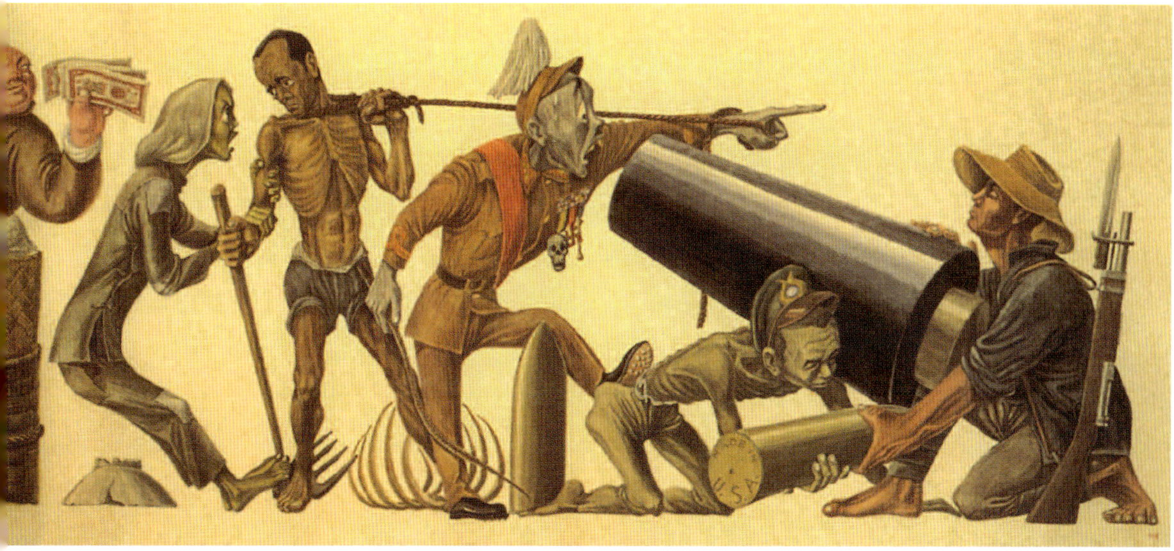

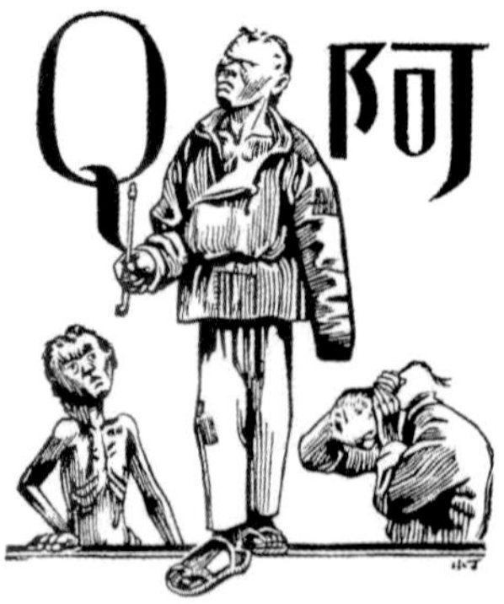

35. Cover of Lu Xun's famous novel The True Story of Ah Q

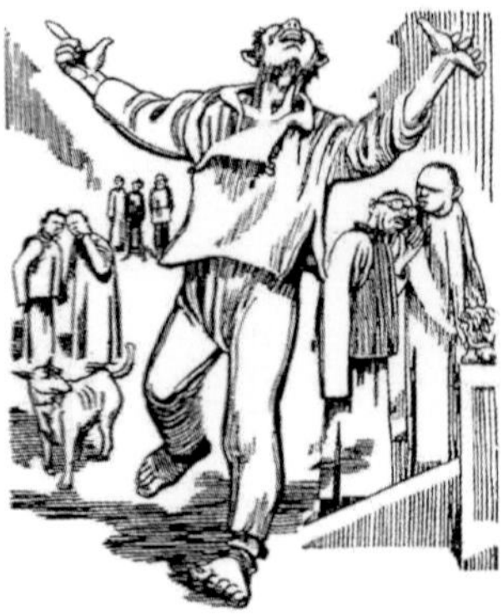

36. An illustration showing Ah Q embracing revolution

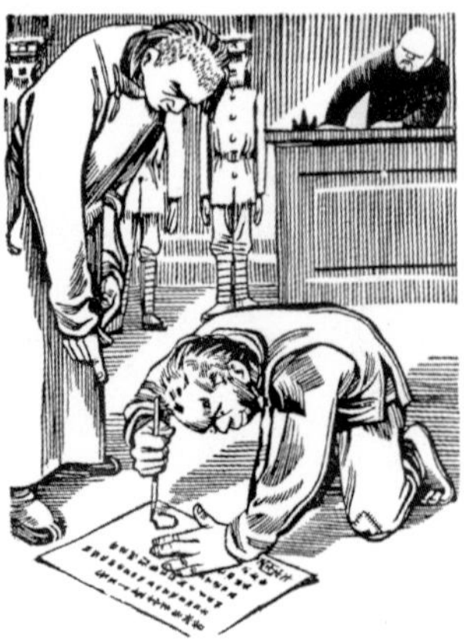

37. Ah Q signing his death warrant with a circle

line, and blow them all to bits. Again, the element of black humor is strong. Also again, the Mexican influence is even more apparent, with the very carefully drawn figures, and the characteristic play of light and dark, highlighting the dramatic storytelling of the scroll.

In 1944, while still in Chongqing, Xiao Ding produced his 20-part serial illustrations of Lu Xun's revealing *The True Story of Ah Q,* which appeared in the *Huaxi wanbao* (*West China Evening Newspaper*). This series of woodcuts (figs. 35–37) also illustrated the book version published in 1945. Ah Q is an ignorant peasant who dreams of revolution and ends up being executed. He continually claims "spiritual victories" in the face of actual defeat and humiliation, suggesting China's unrealistic attitude of cultural superiority to its adversaries, even while submitting to their aggressions. Xiao Ding's illustrations capture the poignancy of this misled and confused figure and his trials, in a crude but powerful and moving manner.

Xiao Ding participated in a major exhibition held at the Sino-Soviet Cultural Association in Chongqing along with Yu Qiangyu, Zhang Guangyu, Liao Bingxiong and others in March 1945.[18] His exhibited works stressed the common theme that the Guomindang was pushing China further into poverty and chaos. Public attendance and support for this charge were heavy at this and other collective exhibits. Another of his Chengdu paintings, illustrated with sprawling and grotesque figures, is his evocative *Hua Lu* or *Flower Street* (fig. 38). Xiao Ding and his playwright friend, Wu Zuguang, visited the bawdy parts of the city in disguise to gather evidence for their art. This scene is of the coarse and heady red light district in Chengdu. The distorted, sometimes elongated faces, portrayed with striking objectivity, give one the experience of being at this place in the company of various social outcasts. The grim story depicted in his

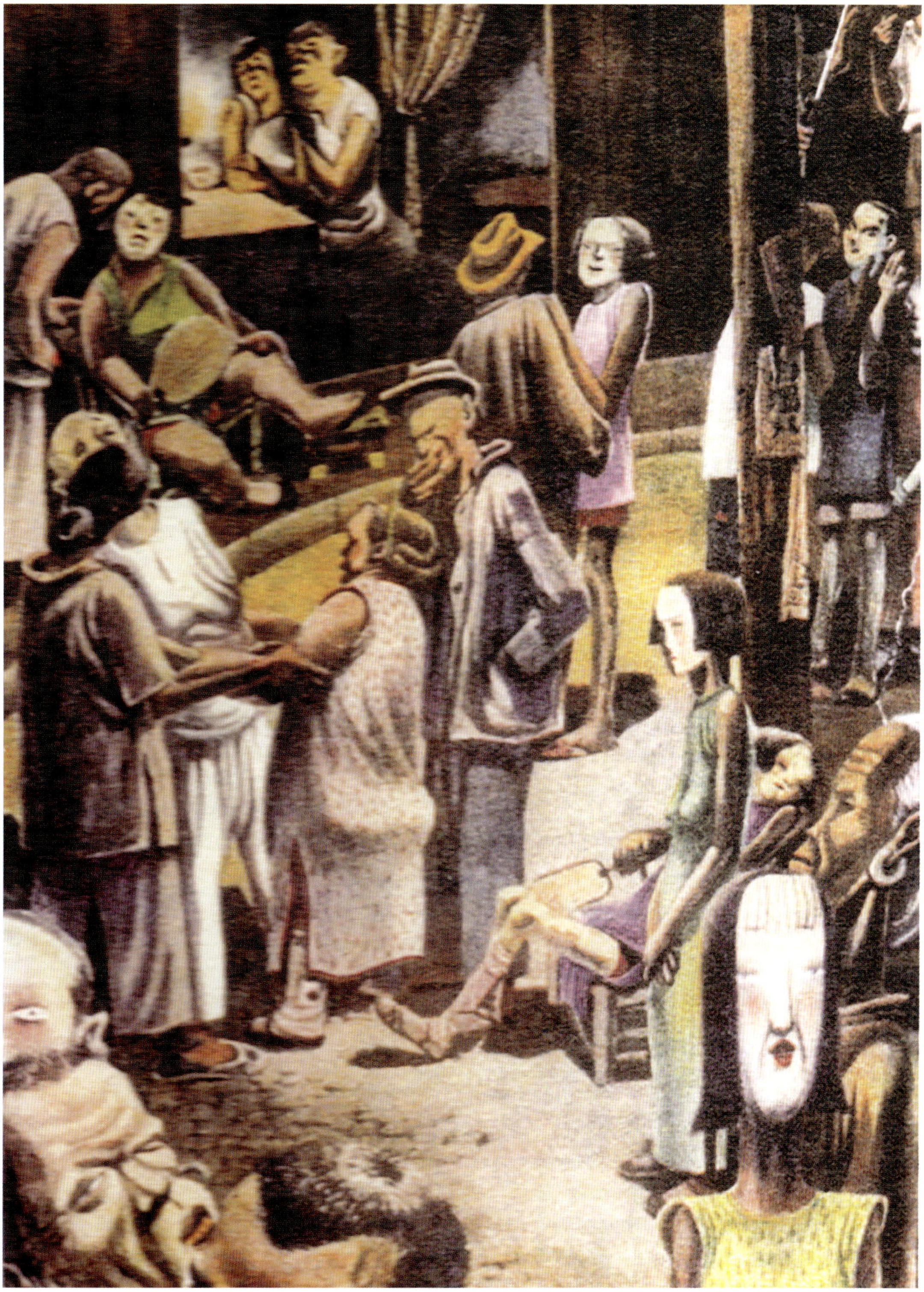

38. The red light district, or "Flower Street" of Chengdu (1944)

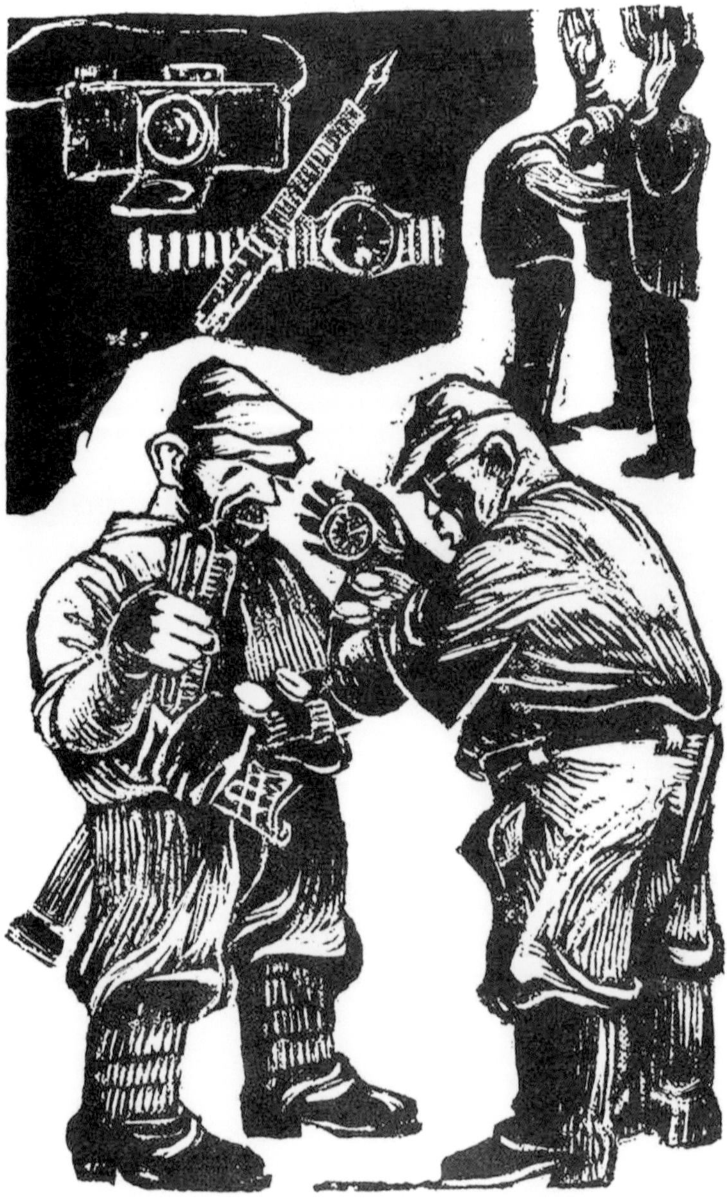

39. Japanese soldiers enjoying the spoils of war

Plunder (fig. 39) expresses with crude intensity throughout the stark composition a chastising message of disgust and ridicule. The technique and mood are completely different from the painting just described.

Working for the Americans

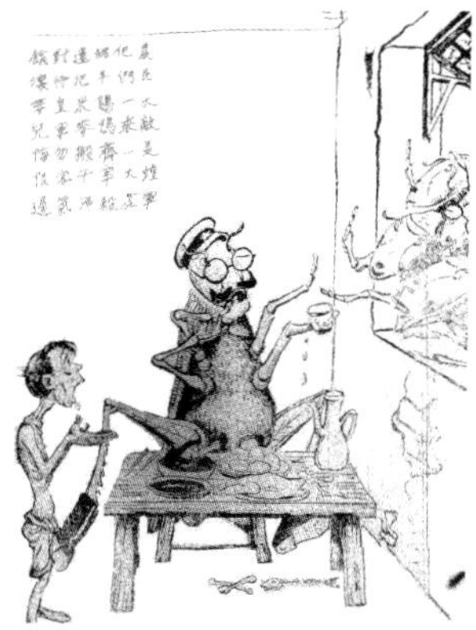

40. Japanese army depicted as locusts (1944)

Paying work was always hard to find for Xiao Ding and the others in his circle. When he was asked by a clandestine unit of the U.S. military in Kunming to produce anti-Japanese posters, cartoons, and other kinds of propaganda, he made the difficult decision to sign on. Dr. William F. Fenn, Dean of the Department of Foreign Literature at Western China University (*Huaxi daxue*) made the introduction. After all, the work was what Xiao Ding loved to do, he needed the money, and it paid well.

In his service with the Americans, Xiao Ding would sneak out at night and search for Japanese posters that were often nailed to trees. He brought these back to his "office" and began the interesting and sometimes amusing work of altering the posters before returning them to the original spot. Usually the alterations involved changing the text in a way that would poke fun at or reflect badly on the Japanese. If the cartoons were his own, he might use an alternate pronunciation of a Chinese character as his theme, the meaning of which would discredit the Japanese. Of course, this had to be done with subtlety, using words and cultural clues that would not be familiar to the Japanese. Another tactic was to reverse or alter a posted Japanese order or instruction to the local population, thus creating a state of confusion. He worked along side American artist William Smith, and journalist Betty McIntosh (fig. 41). Needless to say, the Americans valued his talents and services, and set him to work producing original cartoons and provocative leaflets (fig. 40) that would support their anti-Japanese propaganda efforts. As one might imagine, this five months of work for the United States military became a very serious problem for him later, when he would be accused of being a spy for the Americans.

After the Japanese defeat in August 1945, Xiao Ding was invited by his American friends to come to the United States and work. It was certainly a tempting offer. Once the rejoicing over the Japanese defeat faded and their thoughts turned to the future, the Chinese faced the grim realization that their

41. Xiao Ding with journalist Elizabeth McIntosh and an unknown figure, working for the OSS in flooded Kunming

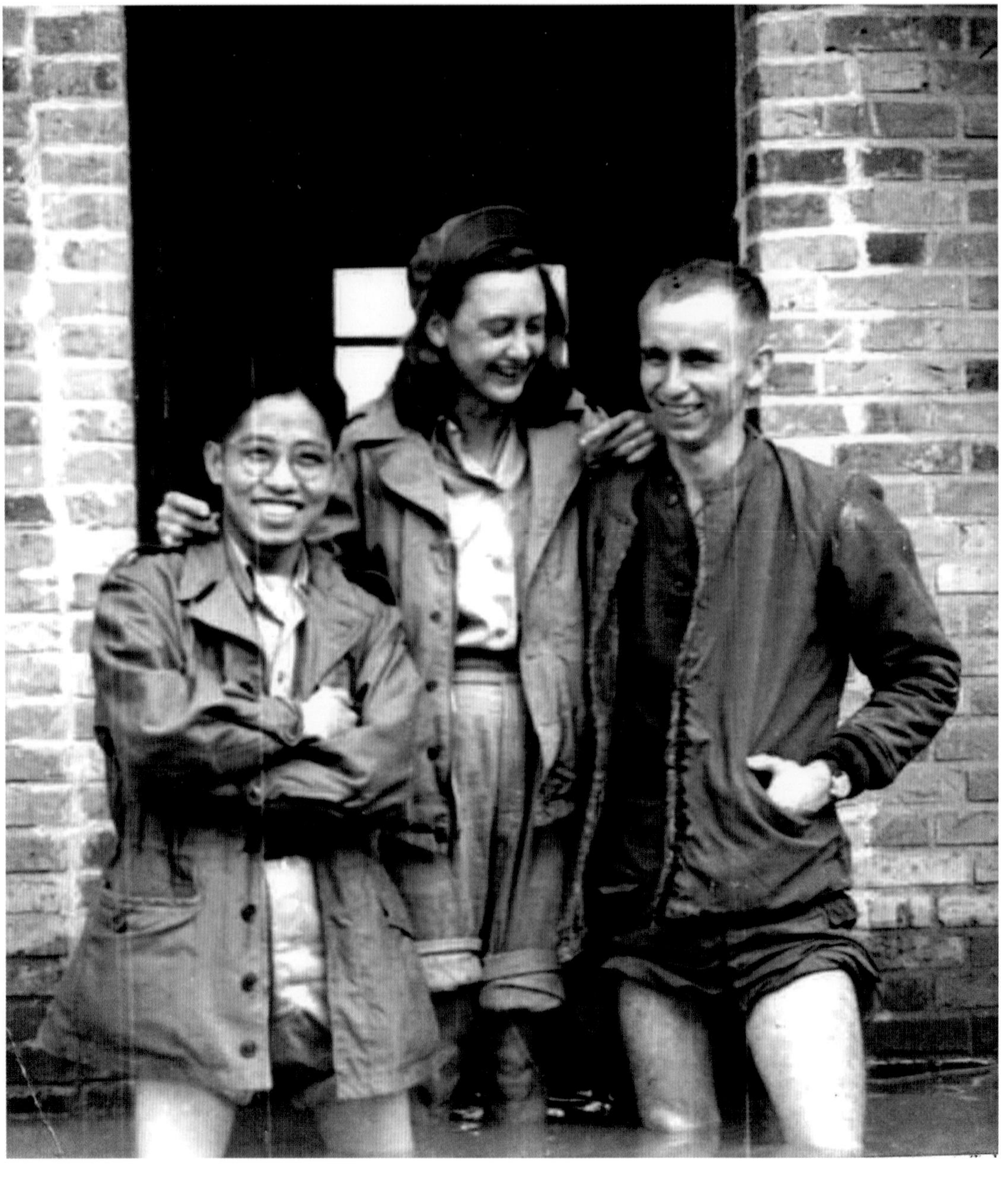

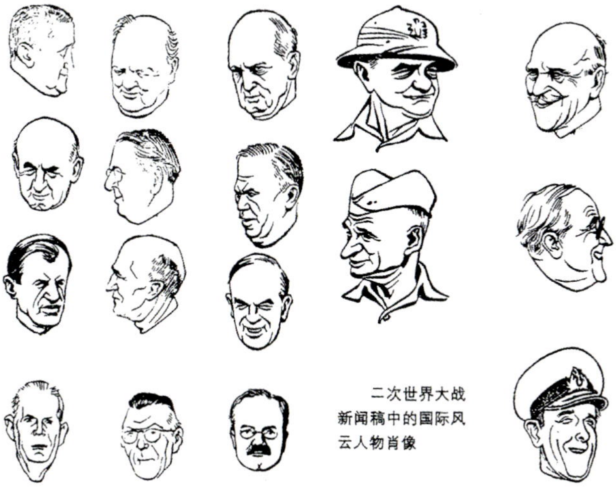

42. *Sketches of Western wartime leaders*

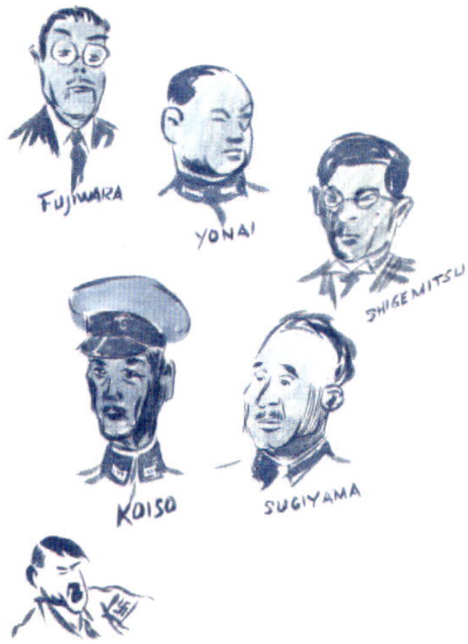

43. *Sketches of enemy wartime leaders*

country was still very much in peril. The domestic conflict between the Communists and Chiang Kai-shek's Nationalist forces showed no signs of abating. Instead, each side could now focus full attention on the destruction of the other. Physical damage to industry and infrastructure, and the massive dislocation of the refugee populations, raised the likelihood of a long and difficult period of rebuilding and healing. With his strong emotional attachment to China, and recognizing the traumatic situation the country was in, Xiao Ding chose to refuse the attractive opportunity, and follow through on his desire to help his country.

Xiao Ding's Art at its Peak

[In these times] the secret police and the people live inseparably together as body and shadow.

—Xiao Ding

Back Home in Shanghai

The war over, Xiao Ding took up residence again in his native Shanghai, along with several other artists. Conditions in the city were bleak. Rampant inflation, caused by failing monetary policies, profiteering, hoarding, and scarcity took a heavy toll on the newcomers (figs. 44, 45). Affordable places to live, groceries, and other basic needs were often beyond their means.

Letters of the period suggest the enormity of the problem. A Canadian woman, married to a Chinese professor, writing of her situation in Shanghai reported: "Rental charged for a one-room

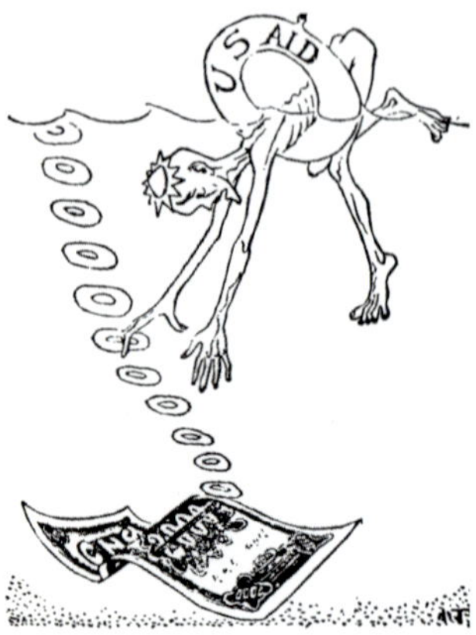

44. American aid to the Nationalists loses value as the currency sinks (1948)

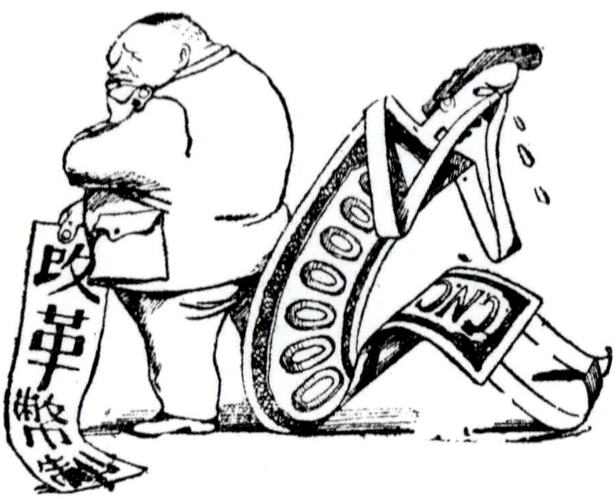

45. Chinese currency cries out for reform

self-contained flat, for which $5,000 [CRB, Central Reserve Bank currency] was paid on in April this year [1945], excluding water, heating, lift and taxes, amounts now to U.S. $25 or at the present rate of exchange $2,500,000."[19]

The cost of coal in winter for heating was prohibitive: "[Coal] is US$100 a ton and Yuwing's [her husband] earnings are just US$10 a month." Survival meant holding more than one job: "Yuwing is teaching in two universities. The sum of the combined salaries at the present rate of exchange amounts to U.S. $40 a month."[20] Finally, even purchases of basic necessities created hardships: "Yuwing tried to buy [a light bulb] but decided the $10,000 CRB was too much to pay for a fifty-watt bulb. We have begun to sell the wormy, rationed rice and second and third grade flour that we had been saving as a last resort."[21] Added to the economic misery were the growing signs of impending civil war.

Xiao Ding and his colleagues mainly survived through the generosity of friends, family, and contacts. A firm commitment to their art and talents helped lighten the hardships they had to bear, while their experience with poverty in the interior provided them with useful lessons on how to survive. They also brought back with them new artistic themes, as well as woodcuts, paintings, and drawings done during that period of western exploration and adventure. The new subjects and styles, based on their observations of tribal groups, minorities, the famous Dunhuang frescoes (Buddhist wall paintings) in the far northwest of Gansu Province, and other treasures, greatly enlivened the more provincial artistic scene in Shanghai, and led to multiple exhibits of their works. Enthusiasm for holding exhibits often outstripped the financial resources available for mounting them, leading to an accumulation of debt. Still, the art scene was invigorating both for the returned artists and the existing artistic culture in Shanghai.

Corruption and Civil War (1945-1949)

As one might expect, the Guomindang had a strong presence in commercial Shanghai. Appalled by the conditions he saw, Xiao Ding was quick to point out in his works the rampant corruption, market chaos, uncontrolled inflation, and abject poverty and unemployment that plagued city residents. He liked to play on contradictions, juxtaposing images of rich and the poor (fig. 46) or the abuser of power and his victim, thereby showing a society in moral decline.[22] He populated his art with corrupt officials, predatory creditors, and abused common people, and his work presented

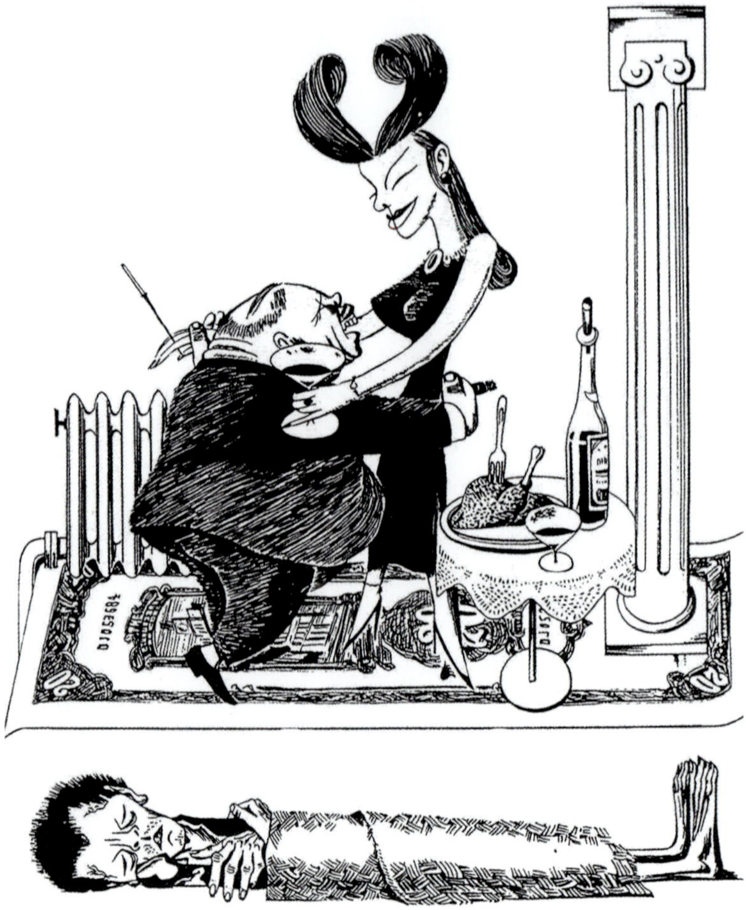

46. An official and his woman wine and dine while others must sleep on the street (1945)

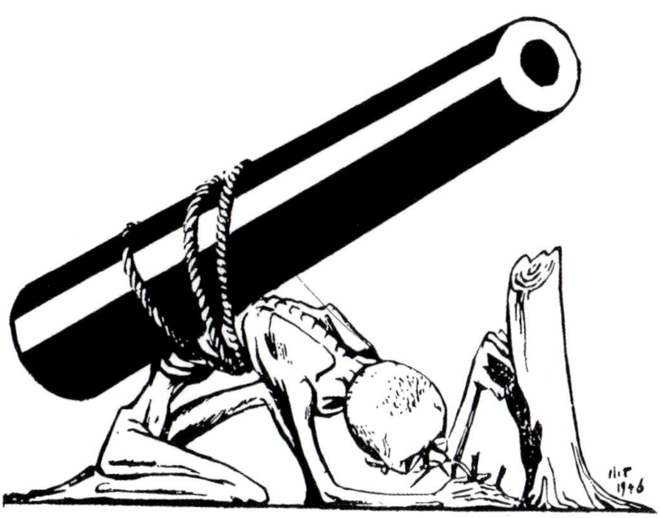

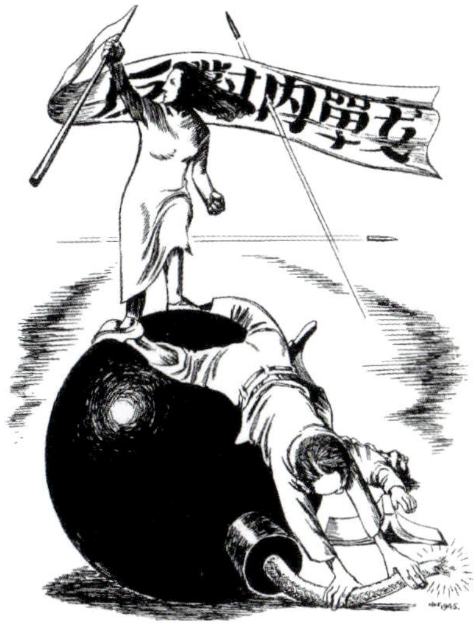

47, 48. The tragedy of civil war (1946, 1945)

real life examples of a lawless society, wrenching poverty, and human tragedy. A more immediate theme was his protest against the civil war that was raging (figs. 47, 48). Had the country not suffered enough?

Xiao Ding still had to avoid the roving eyes of the Guomindang censors, which were even sharper, and certainly more numerous, than in Chengdu. His friends developed a scheme by which they would call Xiao Ding at his office every day. If he answered the phone, they knew he was still safe at work. If there was no answer, they had in mind careful plans for how to rescue him. Living under such conditions made Shanghai people cautious and suspicious, even of friends, as well as anxious and a bit morose, but Xiao Ding continued to create cartoons that condemned corruption, hypocrisy, and pettiness. An especially appropriate image (fig. 49), appearing on the cover of the popular Shanghai publication *Weekly Magazine* (*Zhoubao*) depicts the "Perfect Citizen" under the Nationalist regime: his brain is open for brainwashing, his eyes are shaded by dark glasses, his lips are locked tightly shut, and his hearing is blocked by bribe money.

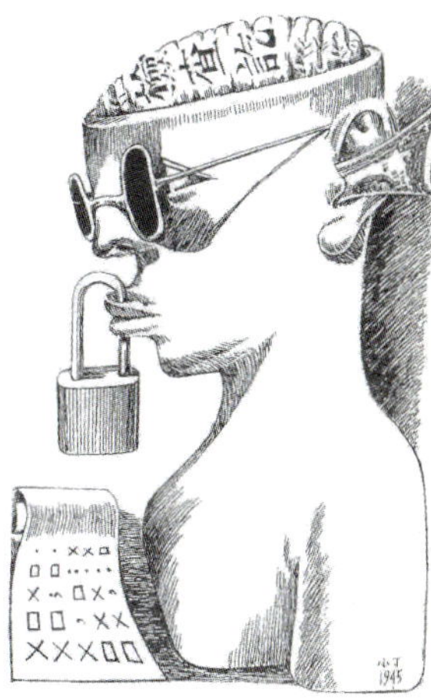

49. "The Perfect Citizen" (1945)

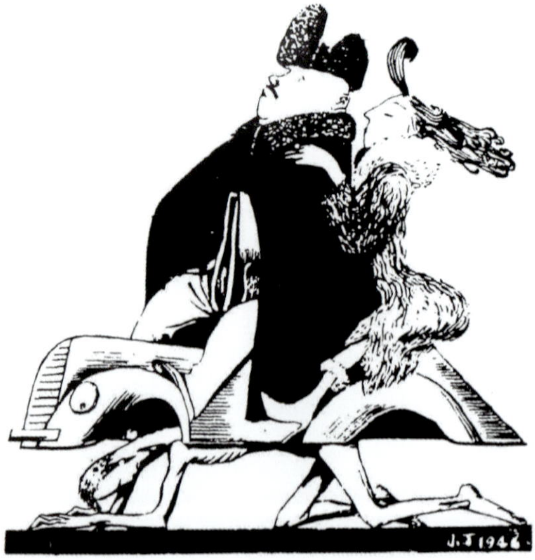

50. Officials in their new cars ride on the backs of the poor (1946)

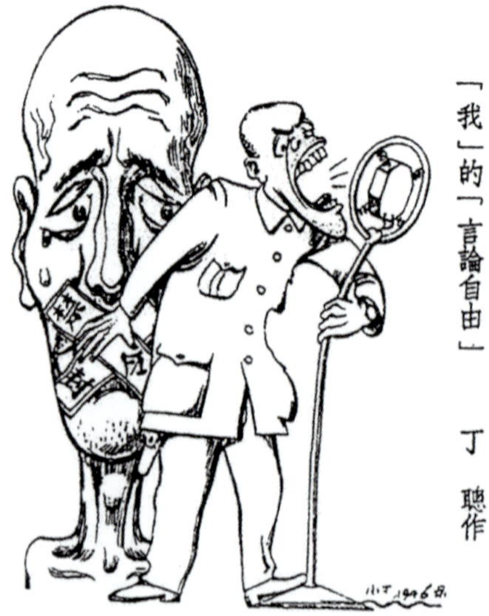

51. "My (so-called) Freedom of Speech" (1946)

Another cartoon titled "A Public Servant" shows an arrogant government official and his bejeweled companion sitting in a car carried by a wizened man below (fig. 50). Instead of serving the people, the corpulent official is riding on the backs of the poor. Like that of the "Perfect Citizen," this powerful image appeared on the cover of *Zhoubao*. In the last issue of this popular publication before it was closed down, Xiao Ding pressed his criticism a step further, producing for the cover a pointed cartoon entitled "'My (so-called) Freedom of Speech" (fig. 51) mocking the government's record of intellectual repression. The angry bureaucrat harangues his audience while the emaciated common man's lips are sealed by the ban.[23]

Xiao Ding provided provocative cover art for three influential leftist magazines in newly enlivened Shanghai: *Democracy* (*Minzhu*), *Culture* (*Wenhua*), and *Masses* (*Qingzhong*). He must have foreseen that the Guomindang would lose little time in closing these magazines down. After viewing just a few issues, the censors focused special attention on shutting down the Communist publication *Masses*, which advocated immediate and comprehensive social revolution. Xiao Ding had also provided provocative cover art for that publication. Hundreds of new journals met a similar fate. Not to be stymied, Xiao Ding continued to make lively sets for stage plays, and to illustrate book covers (figs. 52–55), by many authors already mentioned in this work, including Lu Xun's *True Story of Ah Q*.

Xiao Ding served as art director for a new journal favored in Shanghai cultural circles. Appearing in 1946, *Qingming* (*Spring*), was edited by a respected playwright and typically contained articles reporting on the experiences of the returned artists and writers. It also included translations of important foreign works and thoughtful pieces on various aspects of Chinese drama and literature. Xiao Ding contributed an article displaying his drawings of the minority Luoluo tribesmen of southwestern China. The publication served as a perfect outlet for the artists who had sojourned in western China and were willing to share their unique experiences and observations. It was not a Communist publication and not politically inspired, but this did not save it from the censors, who closed it down after only four issues. The newness of its offerings and the growing apprehension over the likelihood of imminent war no doubt helped kill its prospects.

In the late 1940s Xiao Ding found more opportunities to work with local theater people. Plays were a popular form of entertainment in Shanghai and offered another medium for displaying the new regional themes. As an accomplished artist in theater design, he produced bold and provocative sets, such as one presenting a large Chinese door constructed out of pieces of Chinese money. With the play's chief protagonist entering through this doorway in warlord dress, Xiao Ding was able to support the play's theme of venality and exploitation of the common people.

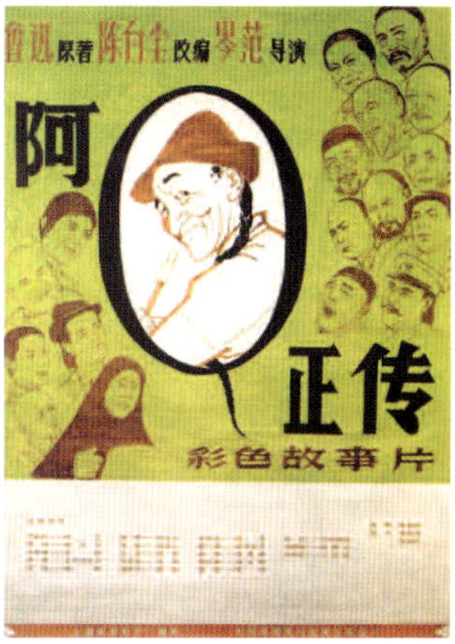

52. Book cover for the novel, Ah Q

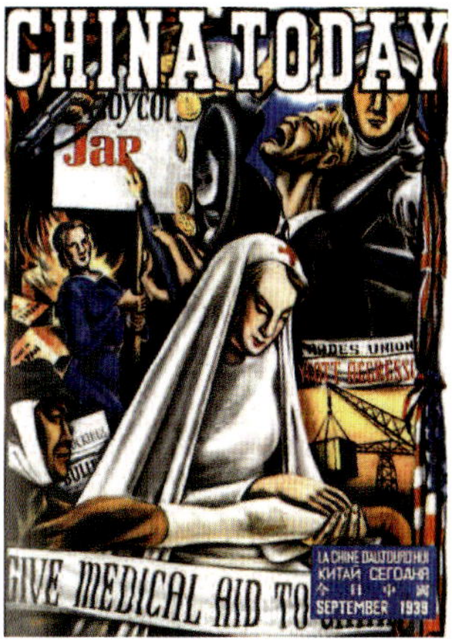

53. China Today *magazine cover*

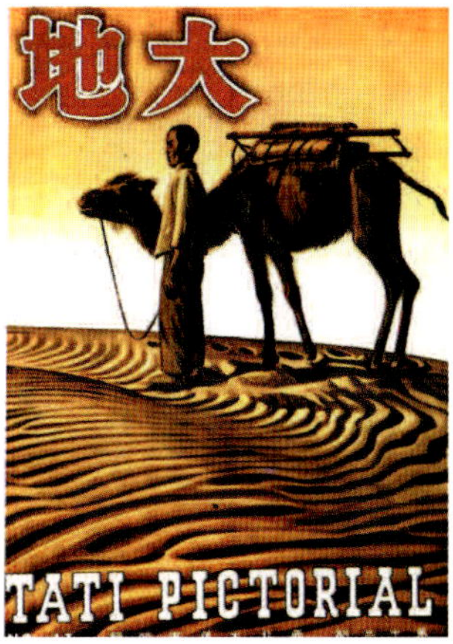

54. Big Country *magazine cover*

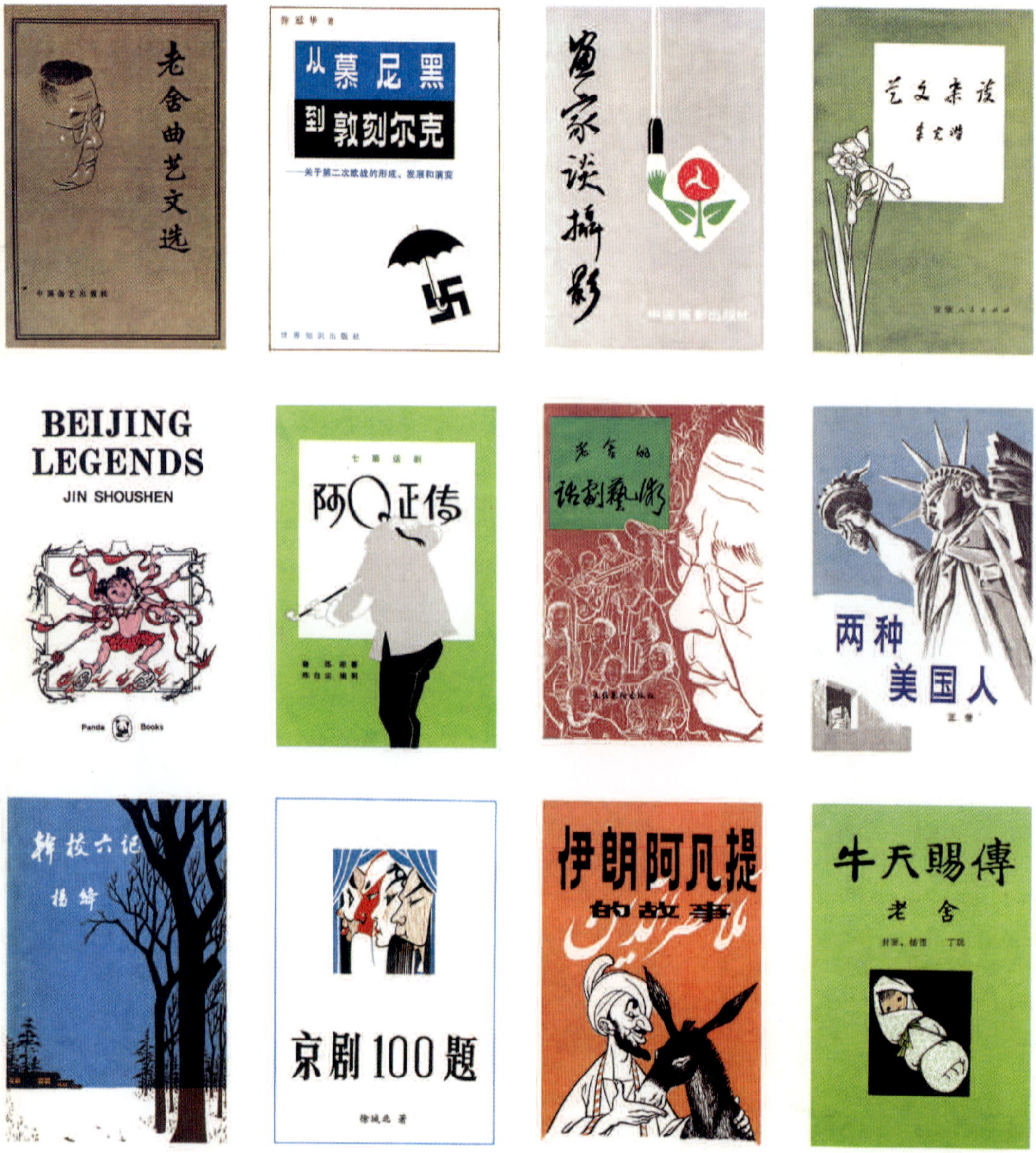

55. *Various book covers by Xiao Ding*

"The Promise of Democracy" (fig. 56) is a haunting image depicting the deceitful manipulation of individual hopes. In it the towering official figure holds out to the younger generation a promise of democracy, while holding behind his back a tall hat sending a very different message, one of a dark future. In some of his art, Xiao Ding worked with scenes or

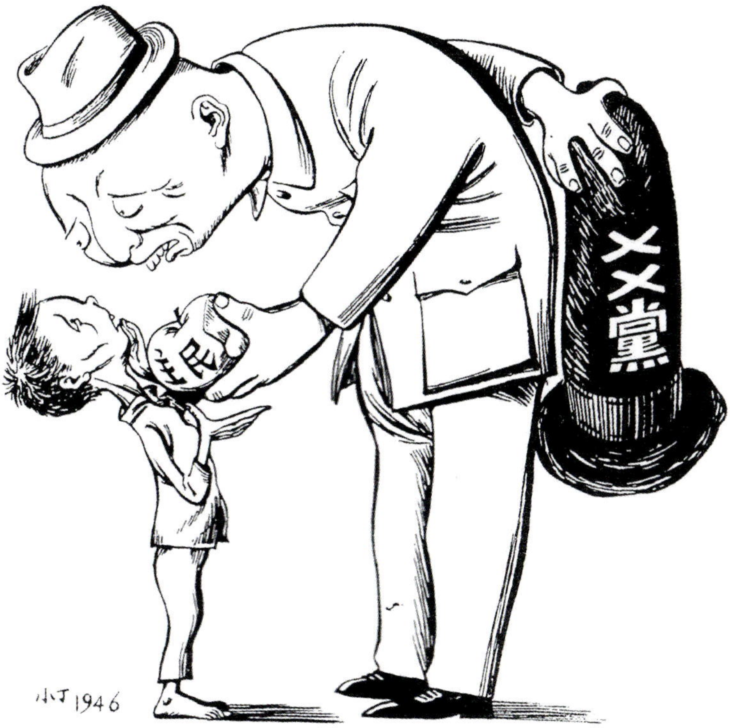

56. "The Promise of Democracy" (1946)

figures from the past, and placed them in a negative, but current and similar context. In this manner he hoped to avoid direct or official accusations of political dissent. To any such accusation he could respond innocently, "What could be political in my depiction of a historic tale?" The same strategy could be applied with current art themes that were merely suggestive, but not directly political: "Where is the politics?" Xiao Ding's designs for the stage were in high demand within the theater circles for his sardonic evocations of widespread discontent.

The New China United

The Chinese Civil War ended with Chiang Kai-shek retreating with his defeated forces to the island of Taiwan while Mao's forces began the challenging work of setting up a new government in Beijing (figs. 57, 58). The Communist Party sent representatives to Hong Kong to invite talented writers and artists to return to China and contribute to its development. Those who accepted the government's plea boarded a ship and sailed north to Tianjin and Beijing. As late as 1948, the Nationalist Government in Nanking (now Nanjing) had made a similar bid for support from the same talented group.[24] Those who accepted made their way south to join the dwindling Guomindang ranks, soon to depart for Taiwan.

At the time, Xiao Ding resided in Hong Kong with his artist friends, who with him had fled from persecution in Chongqing in 1947. The Guomindang had his name on a blacklist because of the unfavorable images he had painted of Chiang Kai-shek's government in his famous hand scrolls (see figs. 33, 34). Typical of the uncertain and confused political

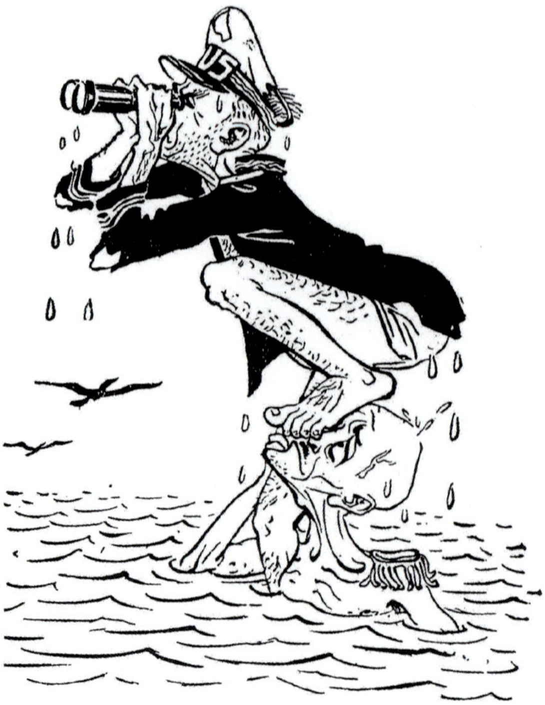

57. American admiral stands on a Nationalist's shoulders to look at mainland China, now lost. "Tell me, what do you see?" (1954).

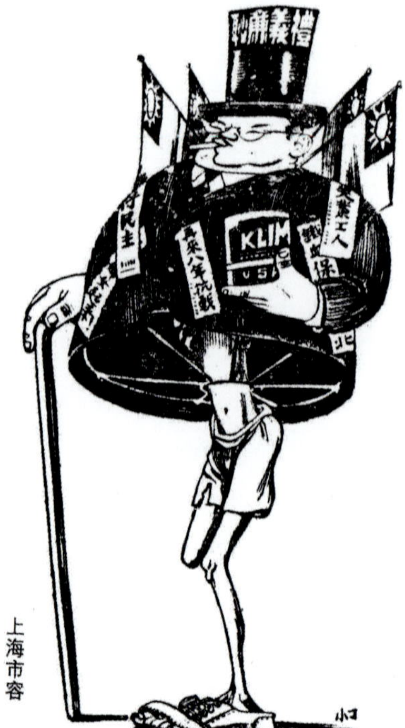

58. A caricature of the city of Shanghai

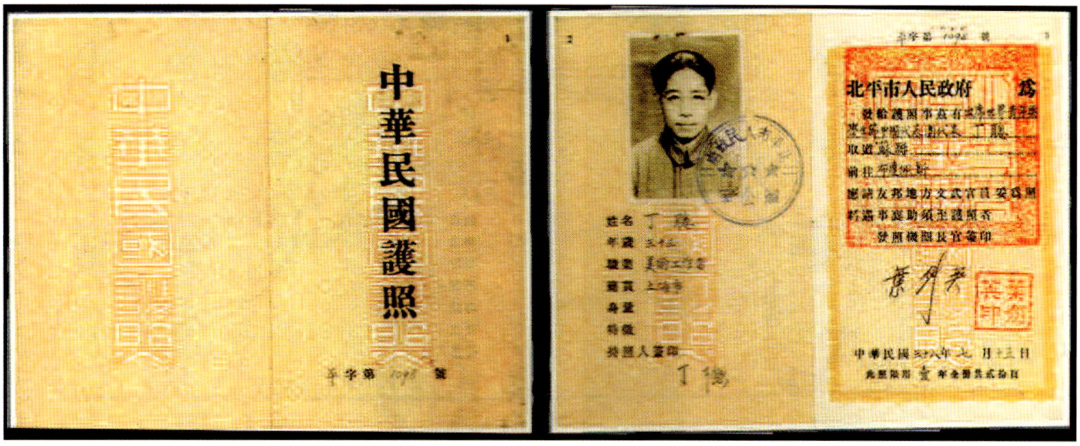

59. Nationalist passport used by Xiao Ding

climate, Xiao Ding was at the same time on a "protection list" sent to Hong Kong by the Chinese Communist Party underground and signed by Zhou Enlai. Filled with optimism and anticipating welcome and support, he left Hong Kong for Beijing. He was soon selected to join a delegation of Chinese artists attending an International Youth Festival in Hungary. This trip abroad was complicated by the fact that his new home government still lacked an official name and recognition, and no passports were yet available for travelers. Needing some kind of travel documentation for the trip, he found himself, ironically, traveling on a "Republic of China" passport (fig. 59), signed by the key Communist Party leader and Beijing Military Chief, Ye Jianying. It wasn't until his delegation stopped in Moscow that Xiao Ding learned that a new government, the People's Republic of China, had been formed in October of 1949. On October 1, Mao Zedong had exclaimed to an enormous and cheering crowd gathered for the occasion on Tiananmen Square that: "The Chinese people have stood up."

For Xiao Ding and his circle, the early years under the new government were full of hope and enthusiasm. A great sense of relief came with knowing that the Japanese had been defeated, the imperialists banished, and a newly "united

60. Scenes of the New China with perfect families of workers and peasants (1961)

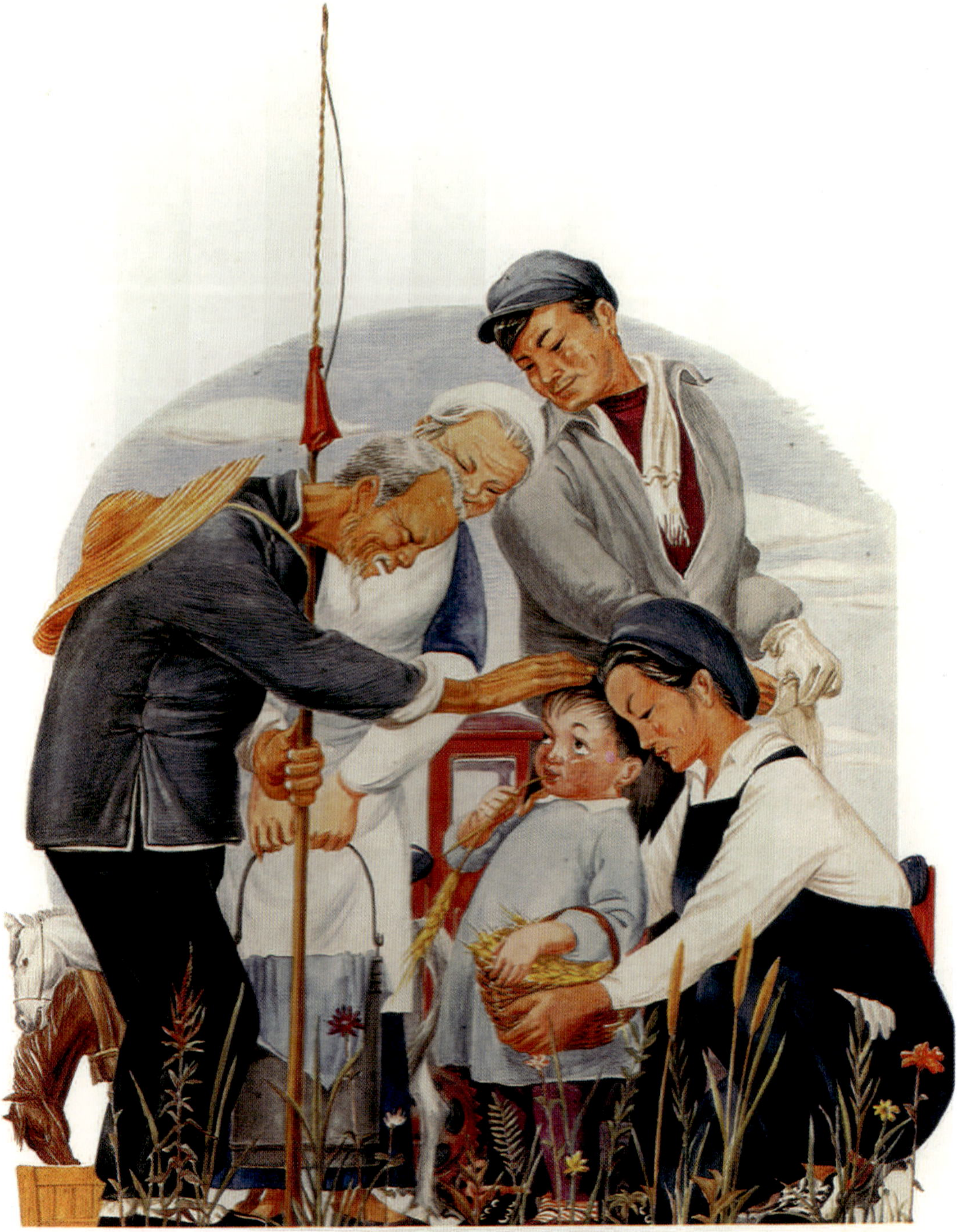

country" established. A later series of paintings (figs. 60–66) captures the upbeat sentiment of this period. They present idealized scenes of rural life in China, including perfect families made up of healthy and handsome workers and peasants, smiling as they perform rural chores, and enjoying well-deserved relaxation after a hard day's labor. The sturdy bodies, smiling faces, and bright colors bring to mind the work of the American artist Norman Rockwell, whose artwork Xiao Ding did know and admire. They also reflect the Socialist Realism favored by China's Russian mentors.

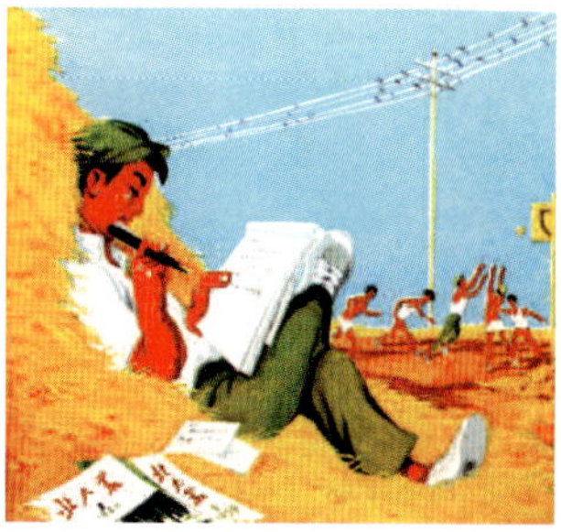

61. Writing a letter home

Unfortunately, the initial euphoria gradually dimmed when it became apparent to Xiao Ding that he would not be engaged in full-time artistic endeavors, as he had hoped, whether teaching or continuing to paint and draw. Instead, he found himself assigned to a demanding management position as the assistant editor-in-chief of an official publication, *People's Pictorial* (*Renmin huabao*). He had to start this periodical from scratch, hiring the staff and handling daily operations. This publication was to become China's newest and most authoritative propaganda magazine, aimed at generating themes and material for the various social movements that the Party sponsored. Meeting the strict requirements and oversight responsibilities occupied most of Xiao Ding's time. With the little personal time he had left, he had to continue his service as a leader of the Chinese Communist Youth League. Once again, his passion for drawing and painting would have to be set aside. There was one bright spot during this period. Xiao Ding's younger sister succeeded in introducing her forty-year-old bachelor brother to his future wife, Shen Jun (English name June). The two married on December 31, 1956, without ceremony except for enjoying a dinner at home with a close friend, the writer Feng Yidai.[25]

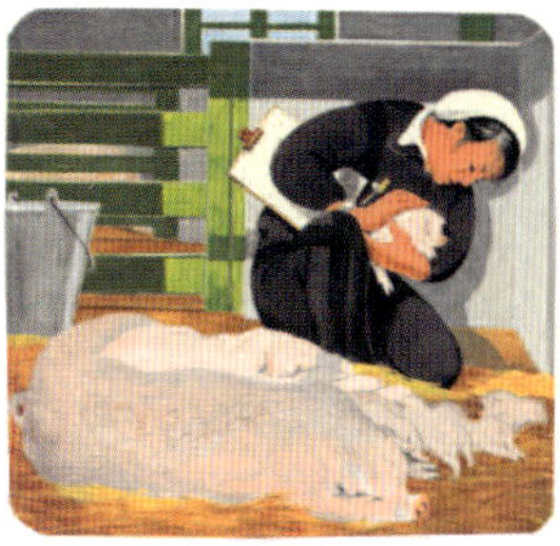

62. Girl tending pigs

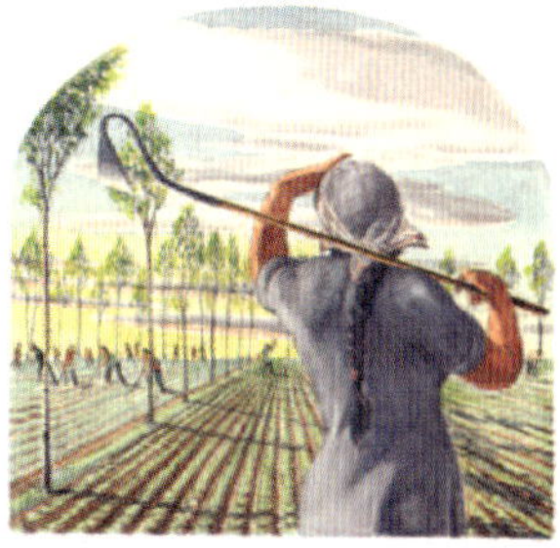

63. Idealized farm work

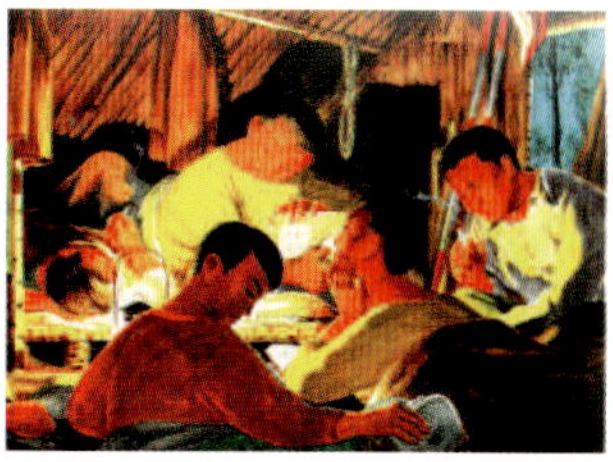

64. Family gathered around the radio

Xiao Ding's talents had reached their peak during the 1940s. However, from 1950 until 1956, his prospects for fur-

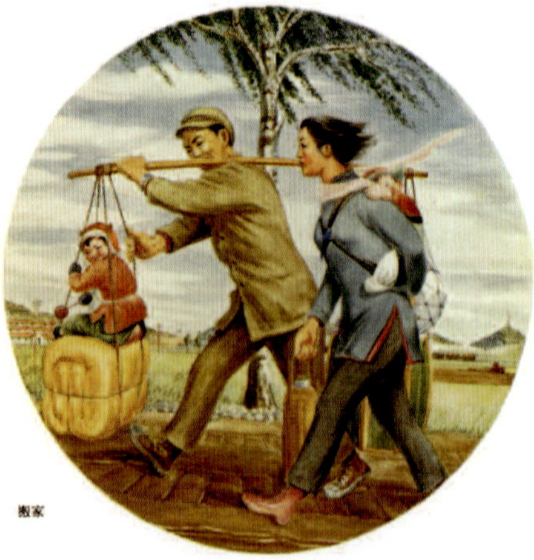

65. *A happy family in the New China*

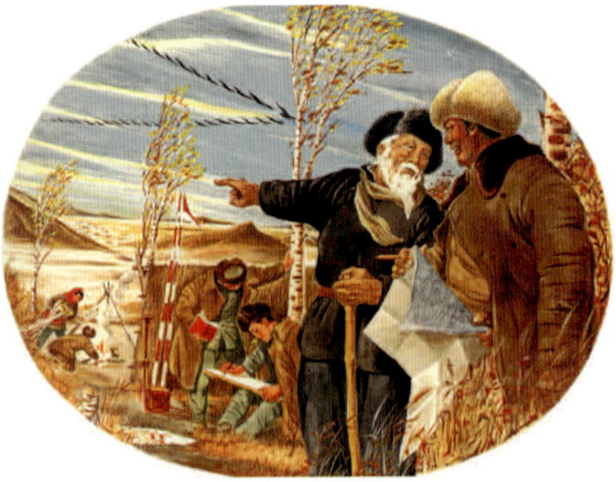

66. *A Rural prospecting team*

ther growth and development seemed bleak under the new regime. Being part of the Chongqing circle and not the more dominant Yan'an group surrounding Mao and other top leaders, kept him outside of the dominant artistic circles in Beijing, tending to marginalize him. There was also the problem of his service with the American military. Xiao Ding had had no opportunity to explain to government officials the nature of his wartime relationship with the Americans, especially with its military intelligence department; he was unable to prove he had not been a spy for them. Because of the chaos of the war years, he had no photographs or documentation to explain his actual position, and no one to verify his duties and activities at that time. This problem emerged again with the surge of patriotism brought on by the Korean War. A somewhat related problem involved his younger sister, who lived overseas. Nationalism had reached such a peak in China that what might seem like a minor "infraction" (his sister's foreign residence) was seen as a major indicator of potential disloyalty. All of this combined baggage did not bode well for his future prospects.

Mao Attacks the Arts

While the magistrates are free to burn down houses, the common people are prohibited even to light the lamps.
—Chinese proverb, often quoted by Xiao Ding

Even with the establishment of the new China, Mao Zedong continued to be uneasy about the depth of loyalty to him and his programs among intellectuals and artists. He expected artists and "mental workers" to make generous contributions toward the work of reconstructing China. Furthermore, they had to apply their talents in service to China in strict accordance with Mao's thought and direction. National meetings of literature and art workers spelled out the directions to be followed. Organizations such as the Central Academy of Fine Arts, operating under the watchful eye of the new Ministry of Culture, gathered artists and writers at all levels into a web of control. A campaign of political reeducation, intended to remold thinking and to rid cultural organizations and their members of "bourgeois elements," was a priority. Western influences, especially Western modernism, were taboo, and the arts and artists from the Soviet Union became the models and mentors for Chinese artists and writers. The wave of nationalism and patriotism churned by the Korean War only helped turn the country inward and effectively slammed the door on the West.

Xiao Ding was just one of the cosmopolitan, independent artists who would be harshly affected by these trends. He made an uneven start in the new regime by making unpopular suggestions for the campaign to reconstruct China. Especially troublesome was his negative evaluation of the merits of having Soviet advisors in China, especially since these experts enjoyed an elevated status within Party circles in Beijing. During his recent stop in Moscow with the youth festival delegation, Xiao Ding had had an opportunity to meet and learn about Soviet plans and guidance for China. He concluded from that experience that the Soviet ideas might have been useful in the Soviet context, but were not at all suitable to China, which he claimed the advisors did not understand. His insistence that they were quite wrong in their recommendations for China was not welcomed by the Party elite. All things Soviet were currently in fashion among the leading Beijing cadres, putting Xiao Ding's ideas outside the community, making him something of a heretic.

Art to Serve Politics

The Yan'an group, who had worked closely with Mao and were guided by his thinking, set the new direction and ground rules for the arts in China. Its central axiom was that the purpose of art was to serve politics, and all those who followed or practiced the arts should accept and promote this official policy line. Party cadres, charged with implementing Mao's dicta, would come to exercise a decisive role in artistic organizations and programs.

In the course of this policy implementation, a clear pattern emerged whereby a period of officially encouraged, relative openness and freedom would be followed closely by a reigning in, or period of harsh repression. This carrot and stick pattern was unmistakable in the workings of the Hundred Flowers Movement (1956–57), which started with a burst of creative output, but was abruptly followed by a period of stifling "adjustment." In 1956, Zhou Enlai gave an important speech welcoming "healthy criticism" of the government by intellectuals, encouraging the "blooming and contending" of various schools of thought. Artists were encouraged to get out of their studios, join the peasants in the countryside, and learn about the role of art in class struggle. Pressure was on to study and apply Marxism to real conditions using revolutionary themes such as the heroic exploits of the People's Liberation Army, the great feats of labor heroes, and the productive lives of the ever smiling peasants. Many artists and intellectuals, however, used the new cultural and intellectual freedom to explore ideas outside of the ways of understanding and approaching problems advocated by the Party. This was where trouble began; the Party had not counted on protests against its core principles, such as holding the Soviet Union as model for economic progress, or obvious policies, such as the banning of foreign literature. Some students and intellectuals went so far as to question the legitimacy of Communist Party rule.

The unexpected wave of criticism of the Party's political and cultural leadership that arose during the Hundred Flowers Movement caused the Party to respond with a firm counterattack; a harsh rectification campaign to correct the faulty trends was instituted. The flowers began to wilt in 1957 as the Party launched the Anti-Rightist Campaign, which selected artists as a primary target. Throughout his life, Xiao Ding had resisted any attempts to control his artistic work and thinking. The complete abolition of individualism, now demanded by the Party in order to cement a solid mass following, was something he could not stomach. The Party agenda was to build its web of control, centered on Mao Zedong and his revered writings. It required that Chinese society experience a complete reorganization so that no loose ends would escape its control. Even thought processes were

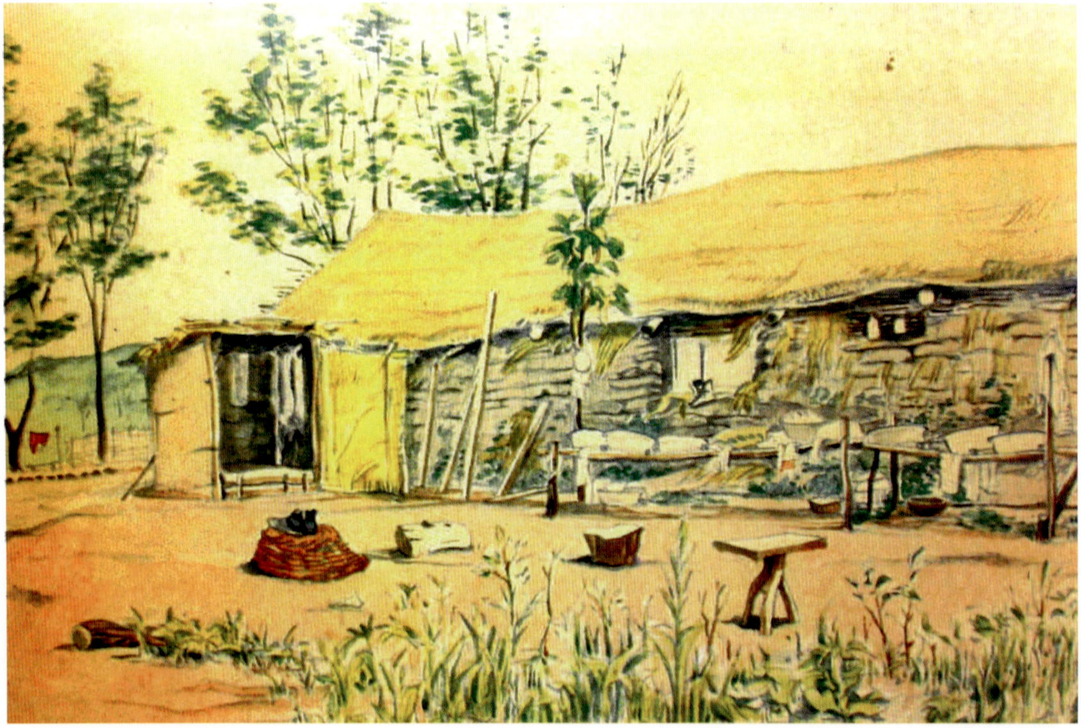

67. *Xiao Ding's dwelling in Beidahuang*

fair game to be reformed; people could be "re-educated" to align their thinking to match the "correct" position of the Party on all matters. Party units attached to organizations of all kinds were to act as the engines to mobilize the masses around the Party's set goals. This was not an atmosphere in which Xiao Ding could operate safely or for long.

One group targeted in the Anti-Rightist Campaign were the lazy and corrupt "bohemian" cadres who contributed nothing to China's strengthening.[26] As an example of such self-indulgence and uselessness, the Party created a stereotypical image based on that of the *Erliutang* artistic group that Xiao Ding had belonged to in Chongqing in the 1940s. Of course, this was greatly to Xiao Ding's detriment, as well as to the others in that circle. Even in implementing this harsh rectification campaign, however, the Party's methods were laughably bureaucratic. In June 1957, for example, the Party ruled that every work unit must identify five percent of its membership as "bourgeois rightist intellectuals," *even if there were no artists or writers in the unit* (emphasis added).

Exile in the Northeast

Labeled a "bourgeois rightist," Xiao Ding's fate was to endure endless struggle sessions in which he became branded a non-person. He was sent to Beidahuang, a farming area in the northeast of China, near the frigid border with the Soviet Union; there he lived in a stable and took care of horses (figs. 67, 68, 71, 72). A literal translation of Beidahuang is "great northern wilderness," suggesting a Chinese Gulag, which in fact it was. Before leaving Beijing for the countryside, Xiao Ding desperately wanted to visit his wife, who was

68. Inside the dwelling (1958)

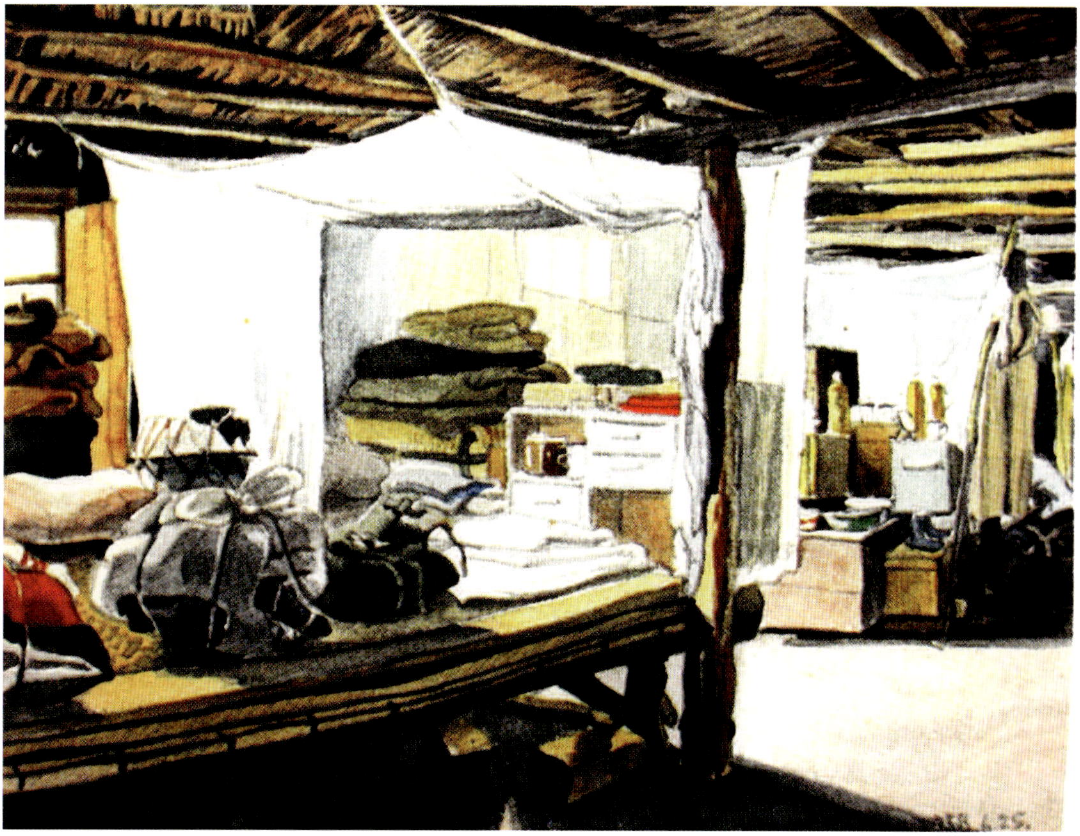

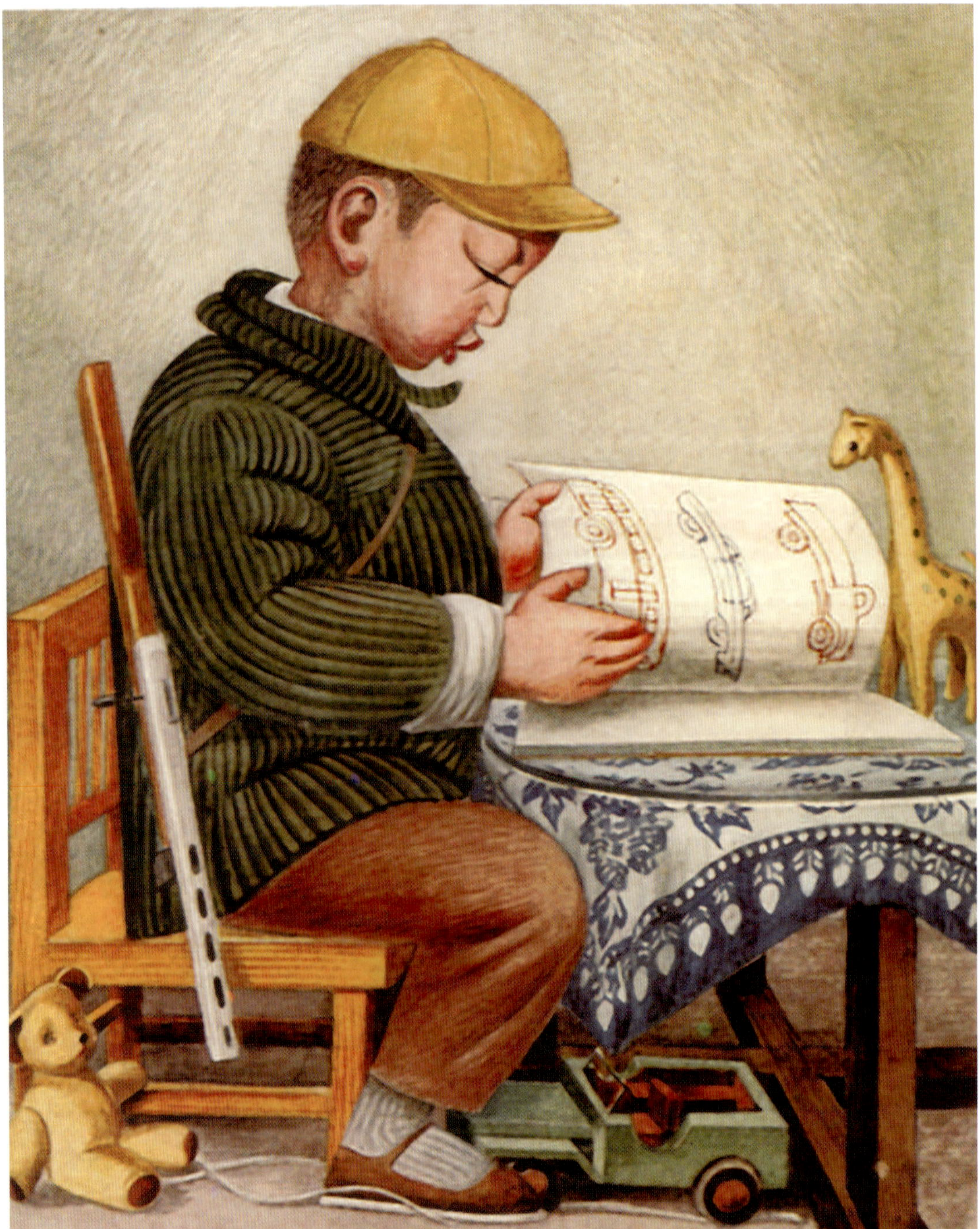

69. *Xiao Ding's son at age four*

in the hospital giving birth to their first child. The authorities, however, denied his request to visit her; he was not to be reunited with his family until his son was three years old (figs. 69, 70).

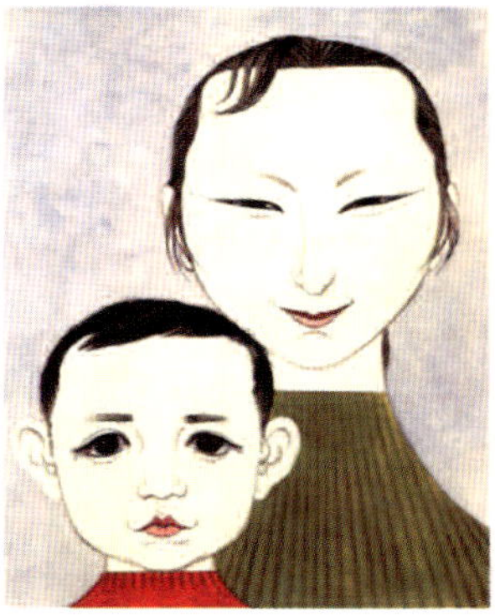

70. Xiao Ding's wife, Shen Jun, and their son

Xiao Ding's situation deeply depressed him because he believed that he had worked hard for the Party, and yet somehow, he became labeled as anti-Communist. At low points he even wondered if the Party was right and that he had done something profoundly wrong. These self-doubts followed extensive brain washing that he other artists and writers had to suffer, and the bogus confessions he was forced to make over and over. Xiao Ding later was to say that he could withstand the pain of the struggle sessions, but his own perceived sense of the injustice of his situation was what tormented him most.

Xiao Ding was assigned heavy work on the farm—cutting trees, building a peasant's house, planting rice, and doing

71. Outside the dwelling (1958)

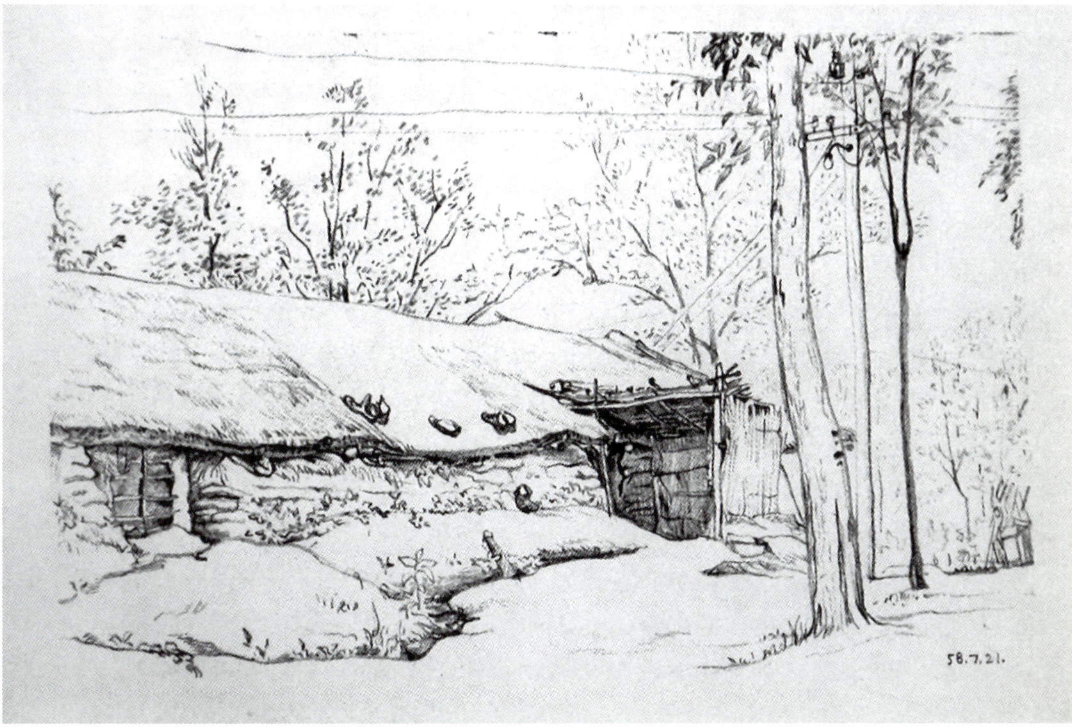

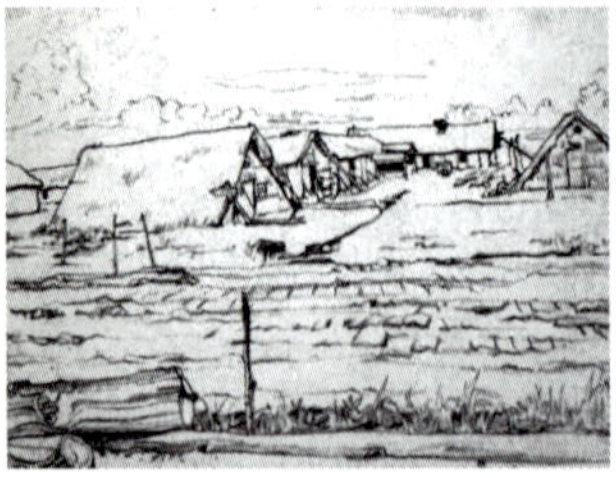

72. *Xiao Ding's neighborhood in Beidahuang (1958)*

other farm chores. His only real pleasure came during labor breaks, when he might sneak out and sketch scenes of local peasants and their activities, or paint in secret from memory after others went to bed. He felt fortunate to have this modest creative outlet to preserve his sanity (figs. 73, 74). Later during his exile, Party officials decided to start a local magazine, called *Beidahuang* after the region, and assigned Xiao Ding, under various pseudonyms, to produce and illustrate it with cartoons and drawings.

Unable to find a suitable local printer for the new magazine, Xiao Ding requested permission to travel by train to a city where he knew the chances for finding one were better. What happened during his journey gives a sense of the insidious atmosphere of this traumatic period. After receiving permission to travel, he happened to meet a group of young people

73. *Local elementary school children (1958)*

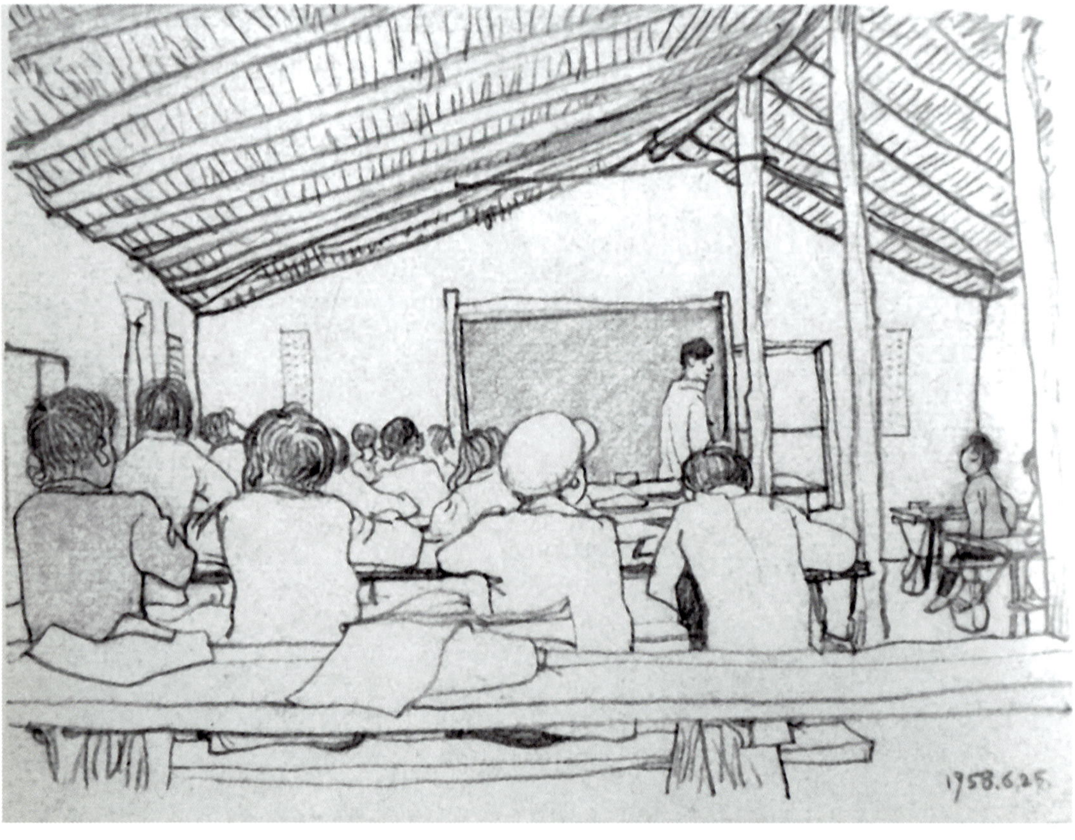

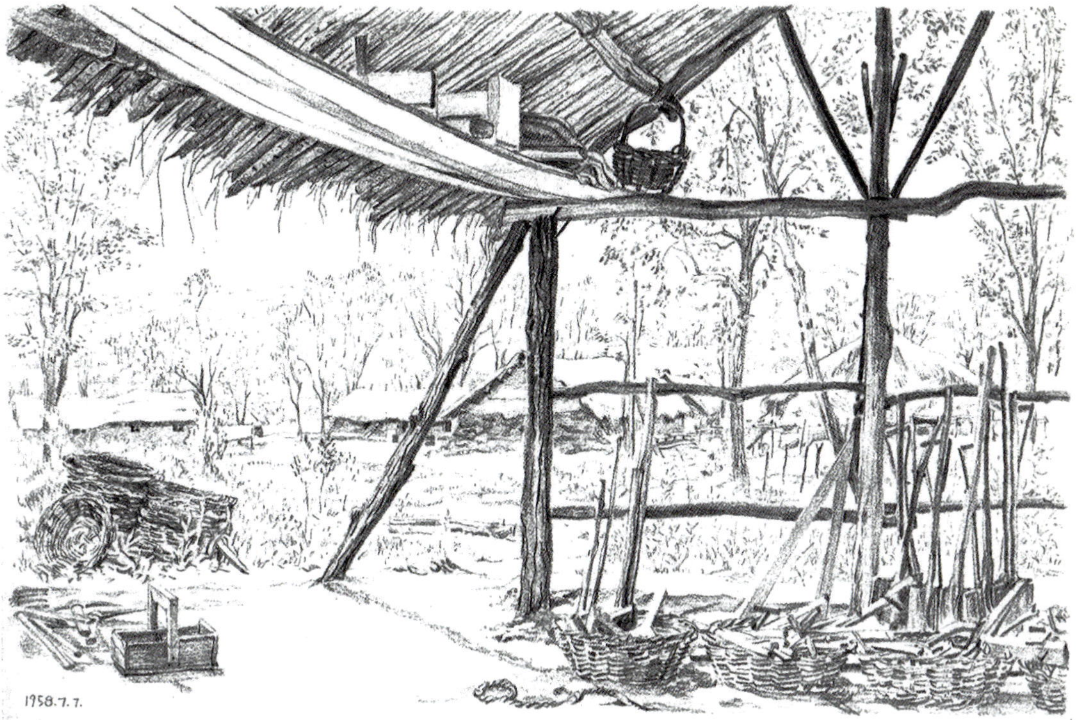

74. The stable (1958)

on the train whom he found lively and congenial. Having few opportunities to enjoy such spirited and informed company back on the farm, he invited the group to dine with him. To Xiao Ding's way of thinking, they simply enjoyed a pleasant meal together, but when he returned to the farm, he found himself in trouble again. Members of the group had reported to the authorities that in the course of their time together, Xiao Ding had "eroded their spirit" with his talk and actions.

Out of Work in Beijing

In 1961, Xiao Ding was moved to Beijing, where he was unable to find work. With his bad "rightist" background, no employer wanted to give him a position. In one way, this worked out in his favor, as he was able to use his abundant free time to finish paintings he had started back in the country. He painted portraits of local peasant family members and

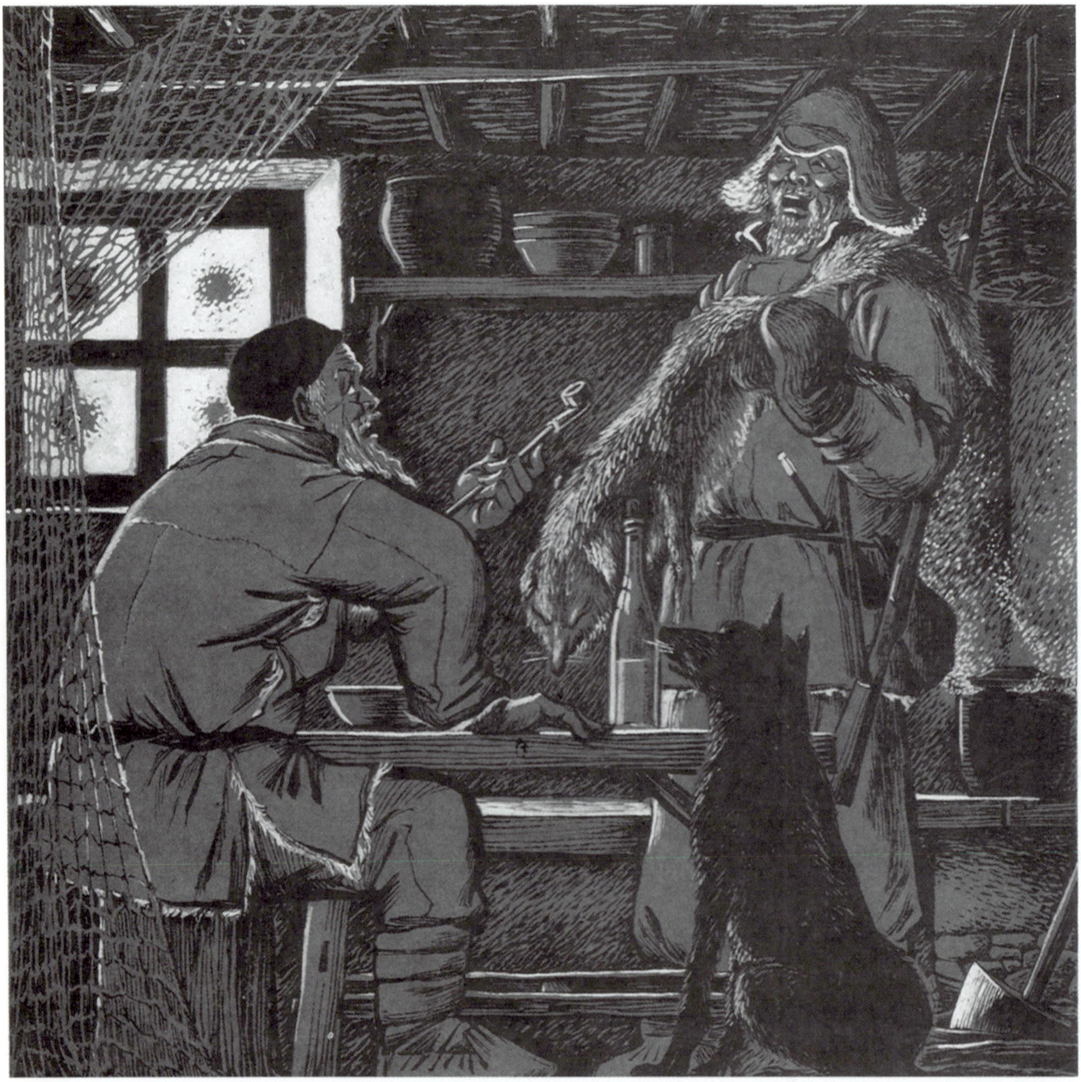

75. *Inside a peasant's house (woodcut print)*

their neighbors, as well as other interesting rural sights he was able to recall (figs. 75–77). His work drew heavily on folk traditions and themes such as peasant drawings, paper cuts, and even rural New Year's pictures, and favored the woodcut as a format. This period was a welcome respite from the trauma and hard labor of the past years.

In 1962, Xiao Ding was one among hundreds of thousands of branded "rightists" officially exonerated. This marked the beginning of another political swing toward a period of relative moderation, during which the Party admitted grievous errors committed during the Great Leap Forward (1958–60). That radical campaign had aimed at organizing all the peasants into People's Communes, and then mobilizing them to establish productive rural industries. The new directive was "to smelt good iron" while minding the pigs and tending the crops. But the iron produced was of low quality while crops went neglected, and lower cadres were reluctant to report truthfully to their superiors until it was too late. The tragic outcome of this campaign soon emerged in the guise of widespread famine, ravaging the countryside and taking more than thirty million lives. In the economic chaos that ensued, Soviet aid and support lost all credibility and the Russians departed.

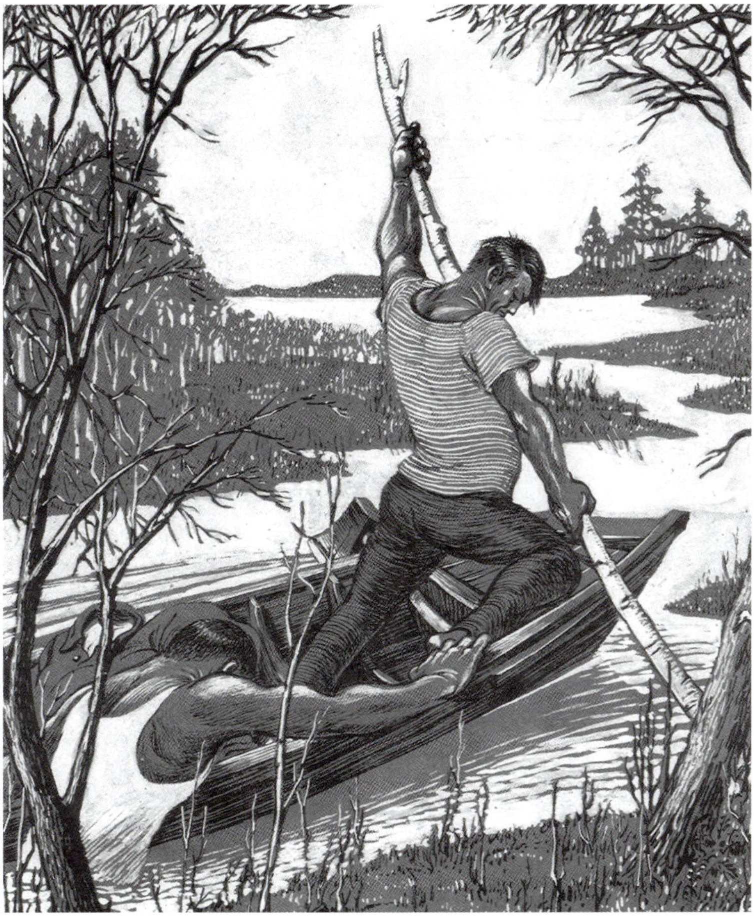

76. Workers poling a boat upstream (woodcut print)

During the interval of relative freedom that followed the failure of the Great Leap Forward, Xiao Ding approached the International Bookstore (*Guoji shudian*) in Beijing with a proposition: he could help them advertise their books by using some

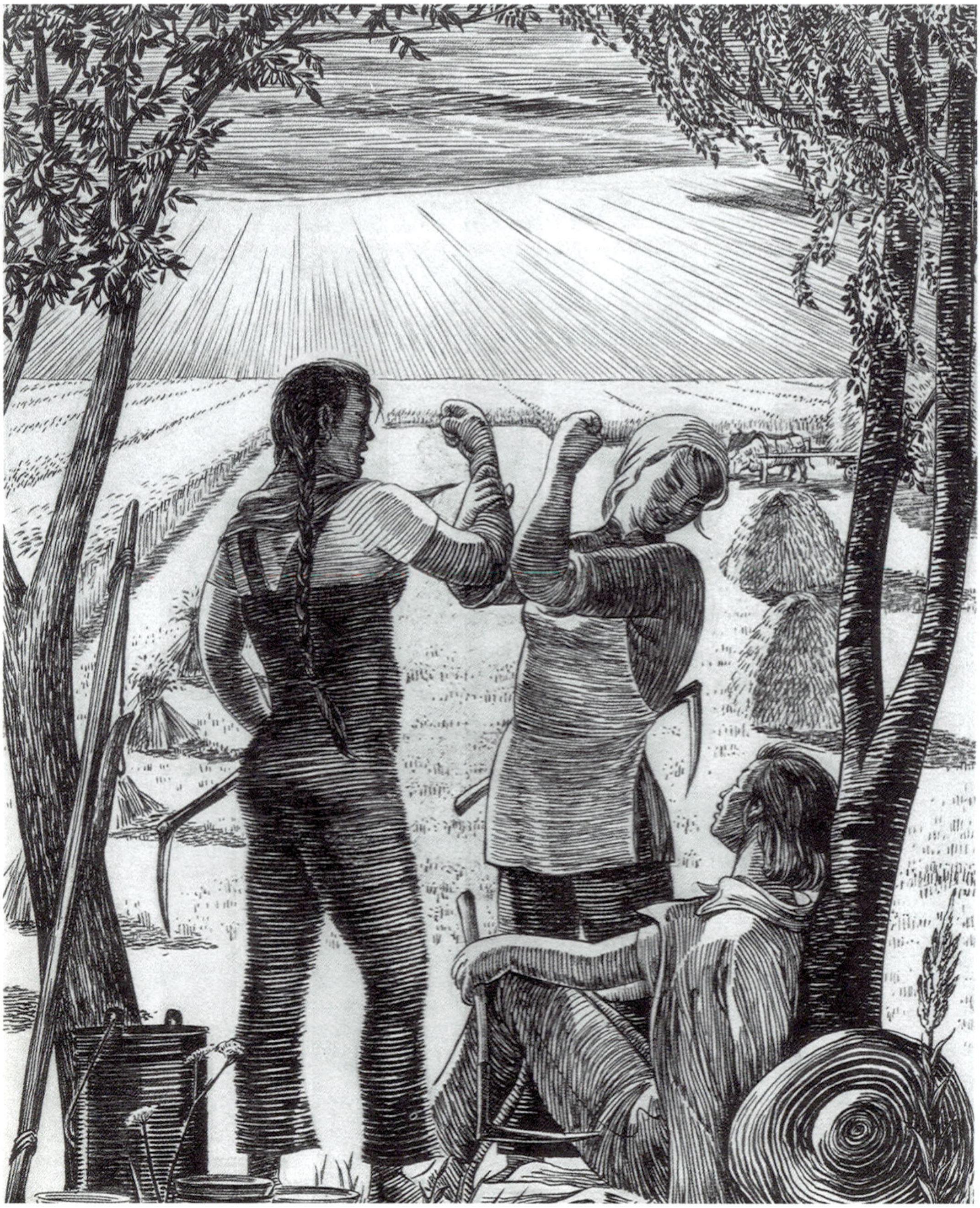

77. *Comparing strength (woodcut print)*

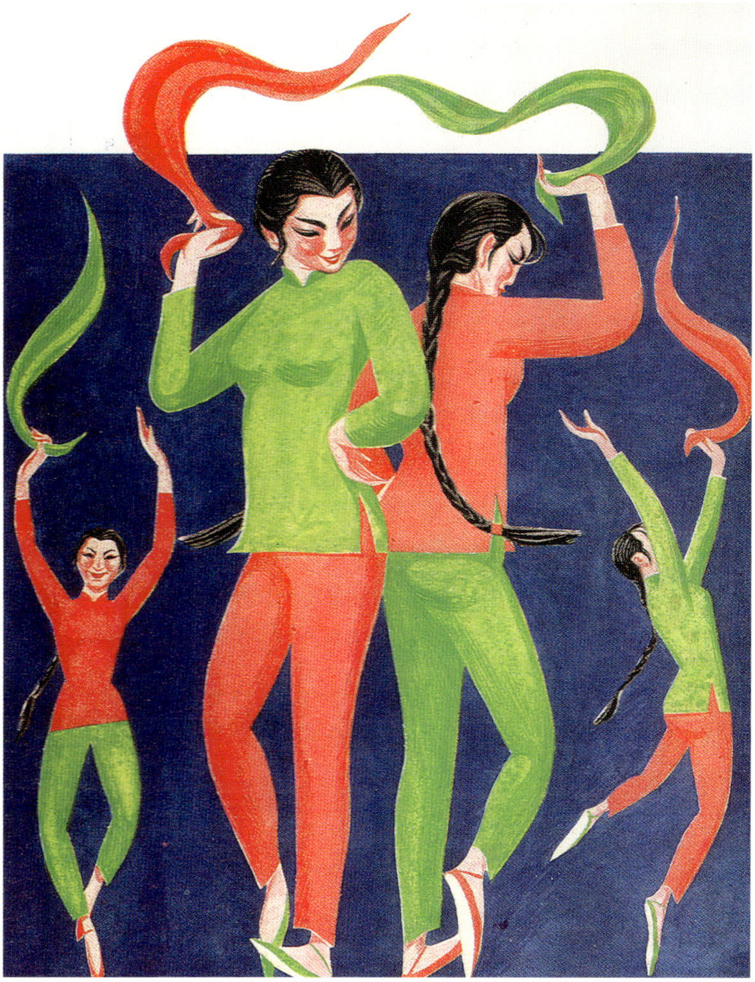

78. "Welcome, Spring"

of his art work. His offer was accepted and he put to good use the money earned by arranging a family gathering in Zhejiang province, the first in three years. The next family gathering would not take place until 2004, when his son returned from the United States. While enjoying this rare family gathering in the home town of his dear friend Yu Qianyu, the Dings recalled that in 1956, when they were married, they did not even have a proper bed for their wedding night. In a light-hearted mood, they had an amusing picture taken of themselves, now many years older, regally ensconced inside an ornate Chinese bed, posing as honeymooners (fig. 79).

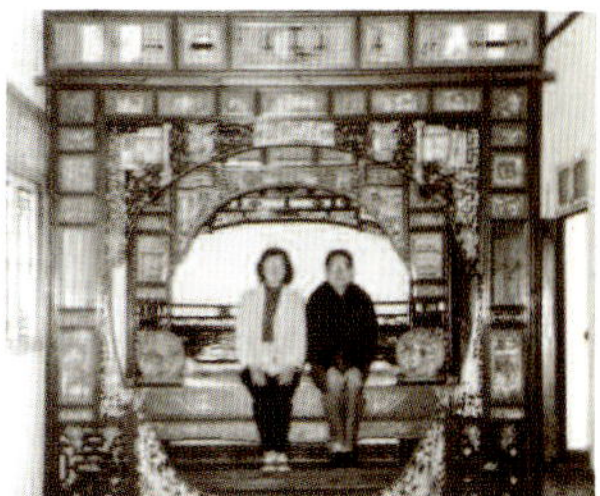

79. The Dings imagining the honeymoon they never had

The Cultural Revolution

Xiao Ding often noted that although the Guomindang censors had been vigilant and worrisome, he found the Communists even more formidable. In the 1960s, he became embroiled in one of the most bizarre and cataclysmic political upheavals of modern history, China's Great Proletarian Cultural Revolution. Lasting ten years, from 1966 to the death of Mao in 1976, it proved especially destructive for those in the arts and literature. As an indication of the devastation, during a brief period of "red terror" lasting from August through September 1966, approximately 1,772 were murdered in Beijing; in Shanghai, in September 1966, there were 704 suicides and 534 deaths; and in Wuhan, 62 suicides.[27]

Mao Zedong personally masterminded this campaign, which he promised would "create great disorder under heaven." It was driven by his continued suspicion and mistrust of the leading Communist Party cadres, especially those at the top of the hierarchy and ensconced in a large bureaucracy in Beijing. Mao felt these fears confirmed when he was attacked for the failures of the Great Leap Forward at a major Party plenum. Not satisfied with the chilling results of the subsequent Socialist Education Movement and its Anti-Liberalism Campaign of 1964–65, he decided to respond more decisively. As explained in one of the key documents of the Cultural Revolution, drafted by Mao, the new campaign was aimed at "Those representatives of the bourgeoisie who have sneaked into the party, the government, the army, and various spheres of culture, and [who] are a bunch of counter-revolutionary revisionists."

Typical of Mao's approach, the campaign emphasized mass mobilization of widespread and violent support, driven by class struggle between the bourgeoisie and proletariat. It started in Shanghai, with an attack on a play which Mao saw as making a veiled criticism of his Great Leap Forward policies. Top Communist leaders became central targets of the campaign, often only through implied guilt based on their associations. Even veterans who had served the Communist Party for decades became "freaks and monsters" and had to be purged. When attempts were made to moderate the campaign, Mao mobilized the Red Guards to "bomb the headquarters" under the slogan "to rebel is justified." Inspiration came from Mao's "Little Red Book" of revolutionary quotations, which by 1967 numbered 350 million copies in print.

Zealously pursuing their mission to destroy Mao's enemies, Red Guards dragged leading cadres from their homes, made them wear dunce caps, and subjected them to public "struggle sessions," which for some was too much to bear. One senior leader, who committed suicide, first saw his children expelled from school and his wife paraded in the streets and exposed to public ridicule. Teachers suffered abuse from their students and were labeled "scum of the party, scum of the people." Artists saw their lifetime work desecrated, destroyed, or stolen. As rampaging Red Guards rummaged through the homes of cadres, looting and destroying collections of books and art, the People's Liberation Army was called to intervene and reassert control. In the city of Wuhan, violence escalated to the point that an uprising in opposition to the Cultural Revolution eventually pitted Party members against the PLA. Violent clashes occurred in cities around the country, as well as in Beijing, and included the sacking the British Embassy compound.

Some leaders acted quickly to avoid the approaching onslaught. Guo Morou, then President of the Chinese Academy of Sciences and senior cultural leader, stated bluntly that all of his writings, according to "present day standards," were "poisonous weeds" that should be burned. Others could not avoid the onslaught. Liu Shaoqi, second in command after Mao, became a main target of attack for corrupting the Party through his alleged revisionism. Mao labeled him "China's Khruschev," who would subvert the Chinese revolution and lead the country on the path to bourgeois capitalism and revisionism. President Liu became an icon of evil in the Cultural Revolution, someone who stood in the way of Mao's Brave New World. He had to go, so Mao managed to have him officially relieved of all of his posts and expelled from the Party at a major Party plenum meeting. Ill and lacking medication, Liu died in prison in 1969. His wife was publicly humiliated as "a capitalist roader" at a massive public rally and held in prison for twelve years.

Xiao Ding Attacked Again

Xiao Ding did not escape the terrors of this period. In May 1967, the Ministry of Culture was abolished and a group called the Arts and Literature Group of the Chinese Cultural Revolutionary Group took over under the leadership of Mao's wife, Jiang Qing. In 1968, artists and writers were forced to leave their urban lives and "go down" to the countryside for re-education.

The first direct attack on Xiao Ding appeared in the official "throat of the Party," the People's Daily (*Renmin ribao*) on September 19, 1967. As before, Xiao Ding came under criticism not only for being an artist and intellectual, but also for his work with the American military during the war years. He was accused of denying a core tenet of Mao's ideology when he criticized Mao's core commitment to the slogan: "Red over Expert." Xiao Ding opposed this preference for the ideologically pure over competence and skill saying that "no layman can lead a professional."

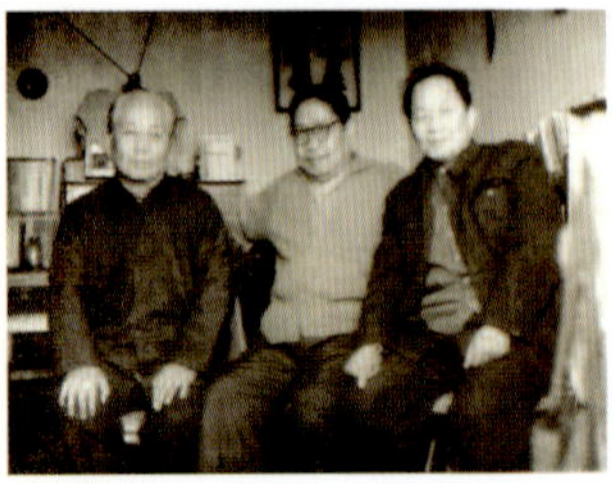

80. The Erliutang *group in Beijing, including from left: Wang Zuguang, Xiao Ding, and Huang Miaozi*

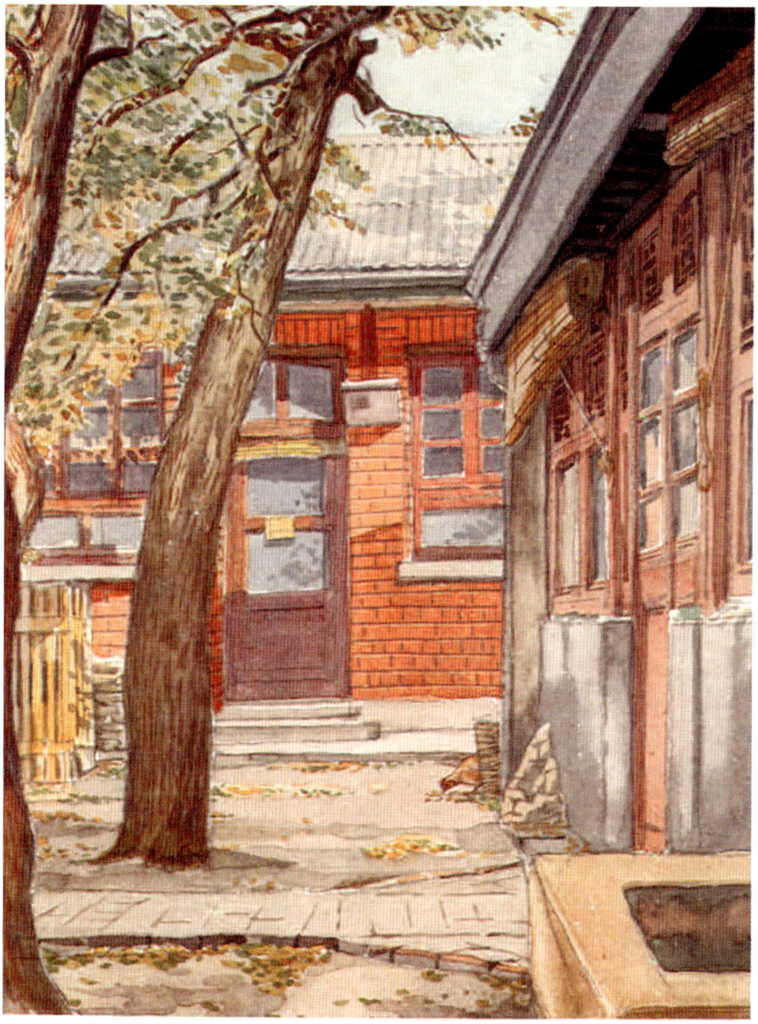

81. Xiao Ding's home in Beijing

An equally important sin was Xiao Ding's membership in a Beijing incarnation of the *Erliutang* (fig. 80). During the late 1950s, the Beijing home of his playwright friend, Wu Zuguang, had become a gathering place and stopover for artists and intellectuals visiting or living in Beijing. Again, the name *Erliutang*, Guo Morou's humorous appellation for the group dating from the Chongqing years, caught the attention of the Party, who had employed it as a label for lazy persons living a decadent lifestyle and promoting revisionism.[28] In 1964, Mao had already expressed his dim view of the Beijing bureaucracy, seeing it as a resting place for lazy cadres. To

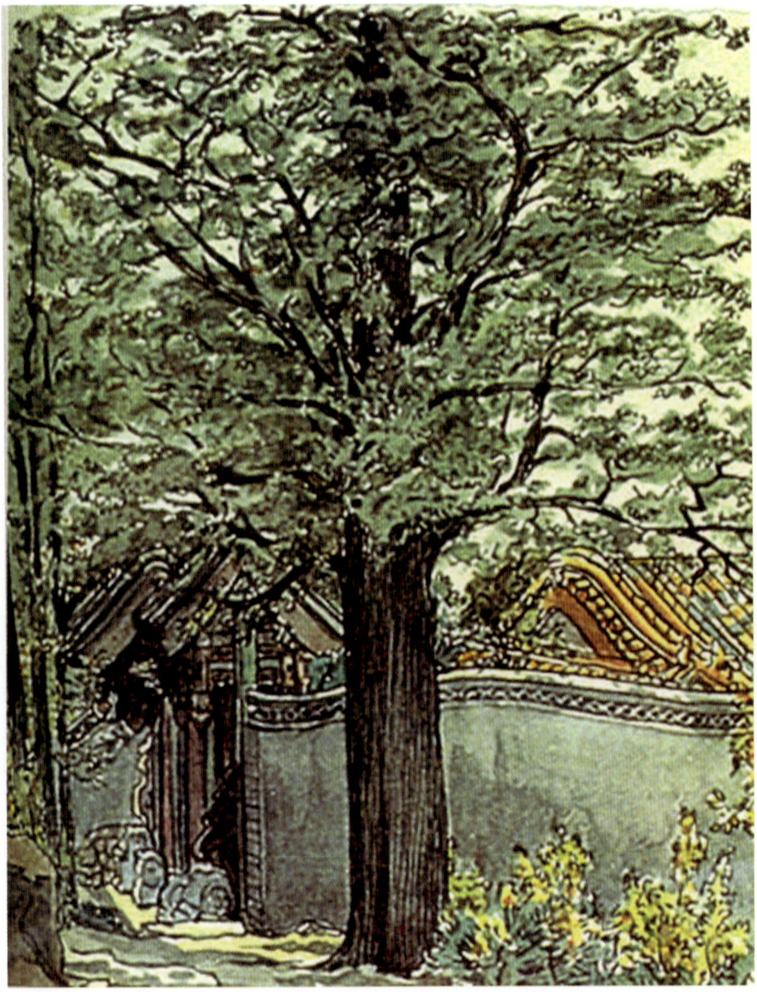

82. Summer Palace grounds in Beijing (1)

underscore his disdain, Mao described laziness as "one of the sources of revisionism." Armed with this weighty pronouncement from Chairman Mao, the Red Guards had all they needed to take on Xiao Ding and his colleagues associated with the *Erliutang*. They were accused of being spies for the Guomindang, idlers who ate fancy food and drank excessively. They were cheats and liars who attacked the government's agricultural policies and, "throwing shit on Mao's ideology," wanted to establish Western capitalism. The most damning accusation was equating *Erliutang* with the Hungarian Petöfi Club, whose membership included intellectuals who had agi-

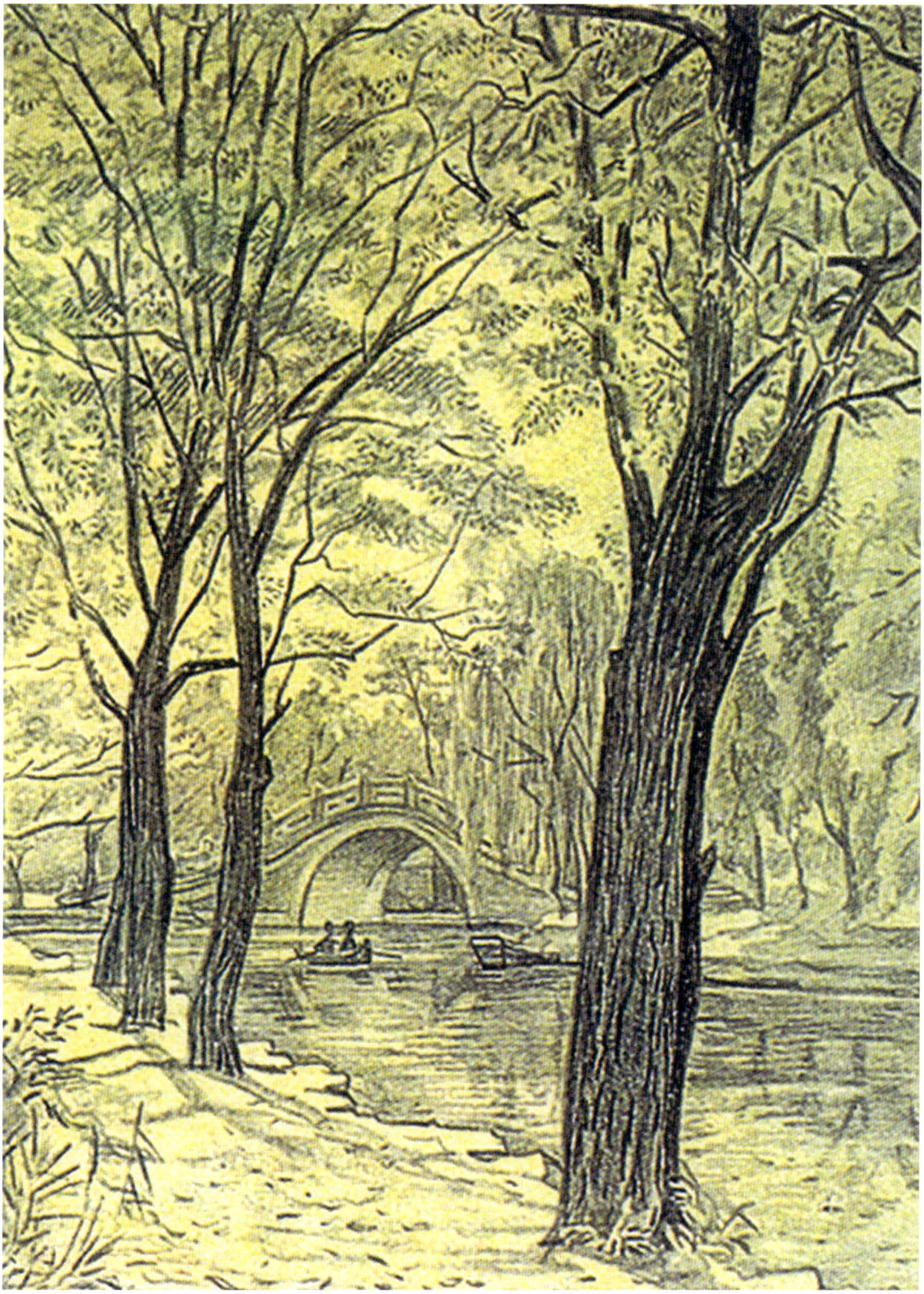

83. Summer Palace grounds in Beijing (2)

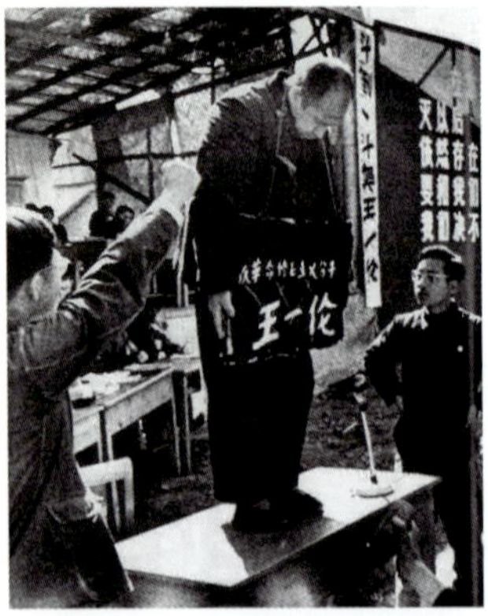

84. An official from northeast China "struggled" in a way Xiao Ding described as his own experience

tated the public to revolt against the Communist government of Hungary in 1956. Xiao Ding and other group members faced the serious charge of trying to "change the color" of the Party from red to white.[29]

Xiao Ding was removed from his position at the China Art Institute after being told that the authorities wanted to "upgrade" him. He was later dragged through the street in huge public humiliation sessions, with papers glued to his back reporting his alleged crimes, and a tall dunce cap on his head (fig. 84). He was forced to stand for hours in the notorious "airplane" position, which involved bending forward from the waist with arms extended outward. After several more beatings and struggle sessions, and with no money or income, Xiao Ding was sent to the countryside to work as a swineherd. He was moved several times, his last location being a May 7 Cadre School near Beijing, where re-education of errant cadres took place. An example of the outlandish criticism he received is that that pigs in his charge always became too fat. He recalled wanting to reply that at least the pigs could not betray him as some of his co-workers had. His duties included serving as veterinarian to the animals under his care. If a goat gave birth during the night when no specialist was available, he would have to assist in the birth and be responsible for a good outcome. Most painful during this time was the farm's prohibition against his having any materials or opportunity to paint or draw. His days were filled with hard labor and constant struggle sessions during which he would have to write endless confessions of his fictitious crimes. During his exile caused by the Anti-Rightist Campaign of 1957, he at least could look forward to some moments in the day to paint and rejuvenate himself mentally.

The depressing inhumanity of this period was emphasized by the official use of public ridicule, the branding of veteran writers, artists, and intellectuals as traitors and humiliating them in public. Some were unable to bear the pressure and while incarcerated, and with no other recourse to end their suffering, placed chopsticks in their noses and banged their head against hard surfaces, driving the implements into their brains to commit suicide.

A painful personal experience for Xiao Ding, and another example of this officially sanctioned inhumanity involved his ailing wife, Shen Jun. Also sent to the countryside, but to a different location, she was discovered to have a stomach tumor that needed immediate surgery, permission for which required her husband's signature. However, the military guards at the farm refused to allow Xiao Ding's permission to go to Beijing, a trip needed to attend to the matter. The reason for this refusal is telling of the heartlessness and ignorance of those in charge. The year was 1972, when U.S. President Richard Nixon was preparing to make his celebrated visit to China. The official accusation was that Xiao Ding still worked as a spy for the United States, and if allowed to come to Beijing, might try to exchange state secrets with Nixon or his staff. His visit to Beijing would thus endanger the Chinese state.

Once again the charge that Xiao Ding was a traitor had been dredged up to be used against him. He had colluded with the enemy, the United States, and that was that. Left unsaid, of course, was how his cartoons had been an important contribution to the U.S.-China war effort against the common enemy, Japan. There is no question that his work for the American military cost him dearly in later life, and took a heavy toll on his emotional well-being during the Cultural Revolution.

In addition to forcing Xiao Ding to constantly confess to his own errors, his persecutors also tried to get him to incriminate his friends. They knew he was celebrated in cultural circles and had many friends, probably many who shared his seditious views. His shrewd response to their prying was to agree with his tormentors that so-and-so was a bad person and probably had done many bad things—but, Xiao Ding would say, "he had never told me anything about them." This usually infuriated his keepers, who would then beat him until he was bloody and unconscious. None of his friends revealed anything negative about Xiao Ding, but some of his co-workers succumbed to the heavy pressure. They would fabricate wild stories to please their interrogators, which made his life even more difficult.

So many sad stories were related during my interviews with Xiao Ding, I felt compelled to ask him how he was able to survive such treatment, and to maintain his sanity, while many of his friends did not. He was very passionate in his reply. He said simply, "I had a clear conscience." He believed that he had always followed the Party's programs and served his country well. He stressed that his "inner heart was very calm" because he knew he was right; he had done nothing wrong. When dragged into struggle sessions to make confessions, he agreed to whatever accusations were made, over and over again, but he knew they were just lies. His mind was not confused by doubts, allowing him to eat and sleep well and thus preserving his health and allowing his survival. Others could not maintain such mental clarity and composure and found themselves doubting their own integrity, fearing that they must have done something terribly wrong to deserve such cruel treatment. Such self-doubt could lead to tragic ends, such as the suicide of writer Lao She, who drowned himself in Taipinghu on August 24, 1966.

Following the establishment of the new regime in 1949, veteran writers, artists, and intellectuals often found themselves in conflict with the Party that had come to power. The common ground that existed in the 1930s and 1940s had been lost when the regime insisted on the primacy of politics, loyalty, and discipline over free artistic expression. Further, the new, mainstream thinking about literature and art provoked sharp divisions in opinion regarding the current social and political situation. Those like the *Erliutang* followers found themselves in direct conflict with the political leadership. Although the early years of the PRC were part of a transitional period, which partially explains the disagreement between those in literature and the arts, and leaders responsible for the political, economic, and social well being of the new country, this sudden and deep divergence remains an important topic for research. For intellectuals and artists like Xiao Ding, the rich tapestry of China's great tradition was in tatters, and its replacement or renewal through a new cultural renaissance had yet to be realized.

The extremely violent period of the Cultural Revolution was over, but the "cleansing of the class ranks" continued until the death of Mao in September, 1976. Even in the face of economic chaos and the loss of life, Mao still felt that it was necessary to finish the job. The new "revolutionary committees," formed from Party, PLA, and representatives from the masses, were put in charge of this work and began filtering out class enemies. A person, or more often a rival, might be persecuted as retribution for a previous dispute or perhaps by someone simply wanting to prove her or his revolutionary credentials. The crimes cited might be based not on a recent infraction, but on an interpretation of some historical event. Xiao Ding's crime was "belonging to an underground studio" in the 1940s. He could not be dismissed from the Party because he had never joined, but like others, he could be sent to the countryside to perform hard labor, which as we have seen was his fate. Using figures just on the rural population, 36 million people were persecuted, sometimes murdered, tortured, or made to suffer hard labor as acts of retribution.[30] In Shanghai and surrounding counties, 64,000 persons had been "dragged out and struggled."[31]

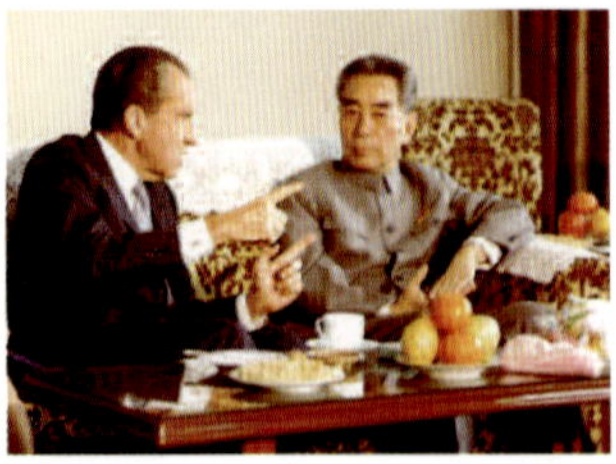

85. Zhou Enlai meeting Nixon on his 1972 visit to China

The role of the PLA in the Cultural Revolution began to concern Mao, who urged the military to return to their barracks and limit their activities to military affairs rather than become involved in civil matters. During the late 1960s, clashes with the Soviet Union on China's northern borders stoked fears that war was imminent. Mao thought China should "play the U.S. card" and get to work on building a more professional PLA to face the perceived outside threats. A major setback regarding his plans for the military was the sudden and shocking defection of his clearly identified heir apparent, PLA chief Lin Biao, who had flown out of China with his wife and son on September 13, 1971, supposedly headed for the Soviet Union, but instead crashing in Mongolia. Mao was able to put his defection to official use, casting Lin Biao as the new scapegoat for all leftist crimes, and the PLA's influence in top circles diminished with his demise. Zhou Enlai and other moderate leaders now saw an opening for rehabilitating desperately needed veteran leaders, and to start enabling China to participate in the world community. Zhou is said to have protected artists and intellectuals to the extent politically possible. He also played a prominent role in the Nixon visit (fig. 85). In October 1971, the People's Republic of China was voted into the United Nations; the Nixon visit took place in February 1972, and Japan replaced its recognition of Taiwan as representing China in favor the mainland by establishing relations with the PRC in September 1972.

The fortunes of the radicals Jiang Qing and the rest of the Gang of Four began to decline as a thawing of the political climate progressed. With Lin Biao gone, Zhou Enlai diagnosed with cancer, and Mao in increasingly poor health with no designated successor, the question as to who would lead China was pressing. Mao finally had to turn to Deng Xiaoping, whom he called to Beijing with instructions to guide the

86 (opposite). "Sooner or later the back door opens." The "back door" refers to evading the system to get what is wanted (1981)

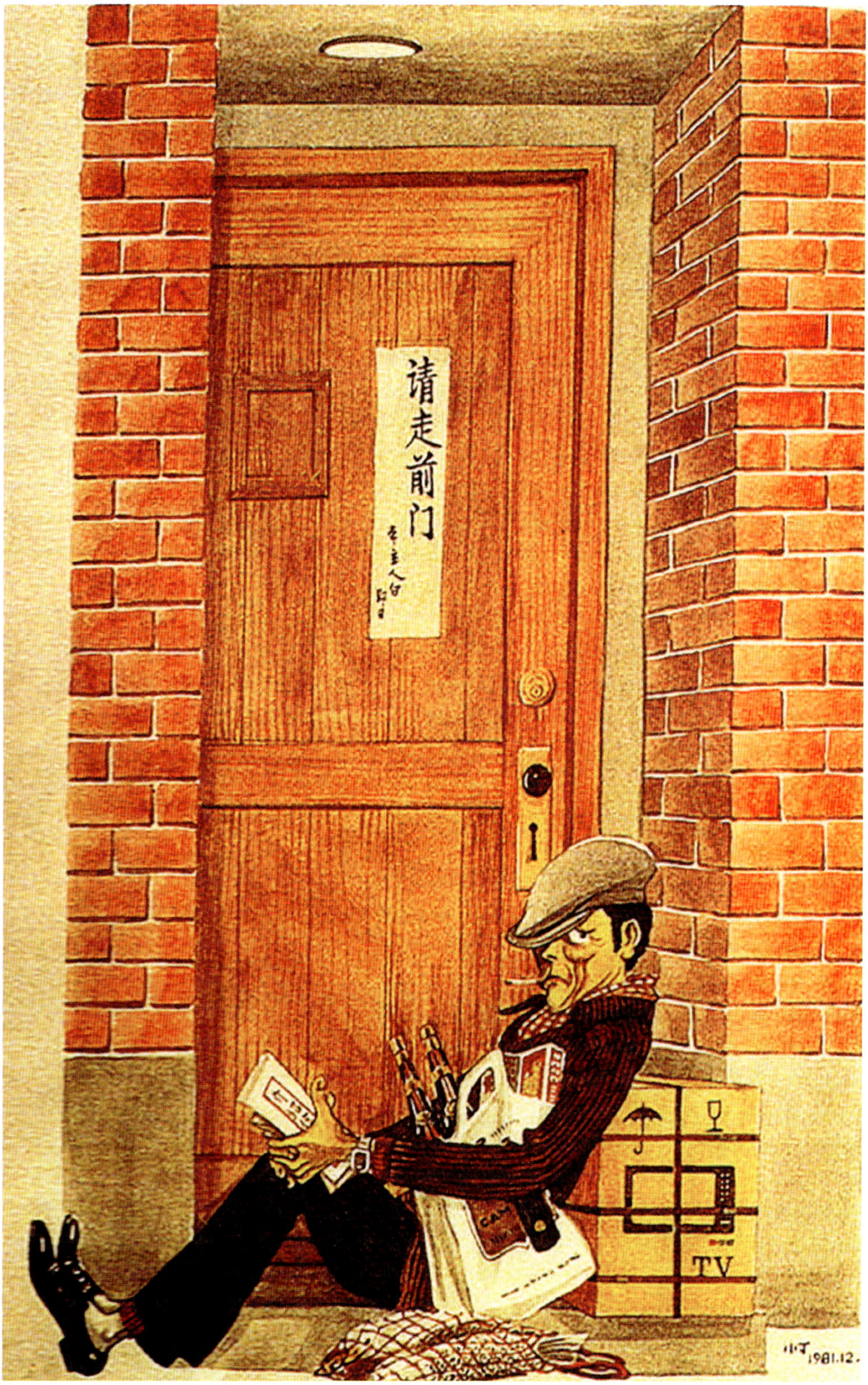
请走前门
TV
小丁 1981.12.

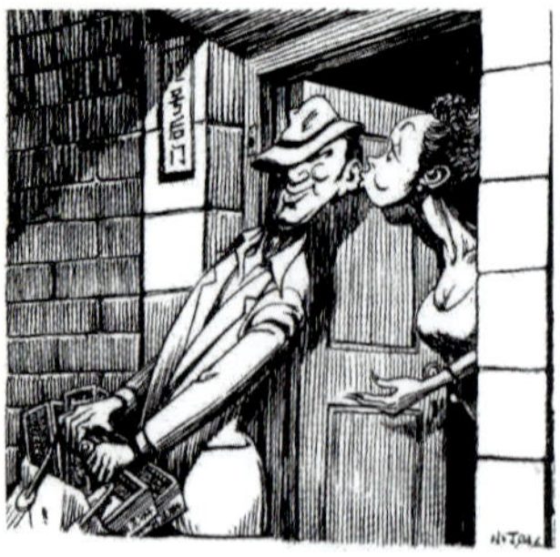

87. "When you need something, don't bother with collecting cigarettes or liquor, call in advance with just money"

ravaged economy. Previously criticized as the "Number 2 Capitalist Roader," Deng had been sent down to work as a fitter in a factory in Hunan Province that repaired agricultural machinery.[32] Deng began the work of restoring order to the economy in March 1973, and rehabilitated other Party cadres to help him with the effort.

This did not, however, end the machinations of the radicals, who still saw Zhou Enlai as the main obstacle to their wielding increased influence. Zhou's familiarity with the *Erliutang* group inspired Jiang Qing and others to make this "counter-revolutionary" group a special target for their venom. They intended to attack Zhou indirectly by making a strong case against this group of artists and intellectuals. Xiao Ding was especially vulnerable because he had a warm relationship with Zhou, the only central leader he knew personally. In the summer of 1973, the Gang launched a new campaign targeting Lin Biao and Confucius, employing the time-honored critical tool of using historical allegories to criticize the present situation. Its allusion to the Duke of Zhou strongly suggested Zhou Enlai, and by making a link to the already pilloried Lin Biao, they were able to confirm the charges of the corruption of elites and their indifference to the plight of the common people.

In the meantime, Xiao Ding remained in the countryside on a labor farm. The authorities called him a "complicated person," who still bore watching, and assigned a guard to keep an eye on him. From his perspective, Xiao Ding noted the moral decline in the country that came in the wake of the Cultural Revolution, especially in the 1970s, after the movement's more violent stages. Fear and suspicion remained widespread among the population and using private connections to attain personal ends, whether revenge or gain, became the norm. Offering bribes in exchange for favors was the accepted method. The Chinese expression for how one gained admittance to college or found employment or won a promotion was literally by "going through the back door." Lack of civility and absence of any culture, even traditional culture, made for a drab and mean public existence. These observations would provide good subjects for Xiao Ding's cartoons during the 1980s when he could again practice his art (figs. 86–89).

When Zhou Enlai died on January 8, 1976, an astonishing outpouring of grief and sadness emerged spontaneously around the country. In Beijing, the mourning focused on the laying of wreaths on the Monument to the People's Heroes in the middle of Tiananmen Square. The public reaction to the government's attempt to mute the response to Zhou's death and mount attacks against Deng Xiaoping, backfired and became what some have called the First Tiananmen Inci-

88. "I never take bribes" (1986)

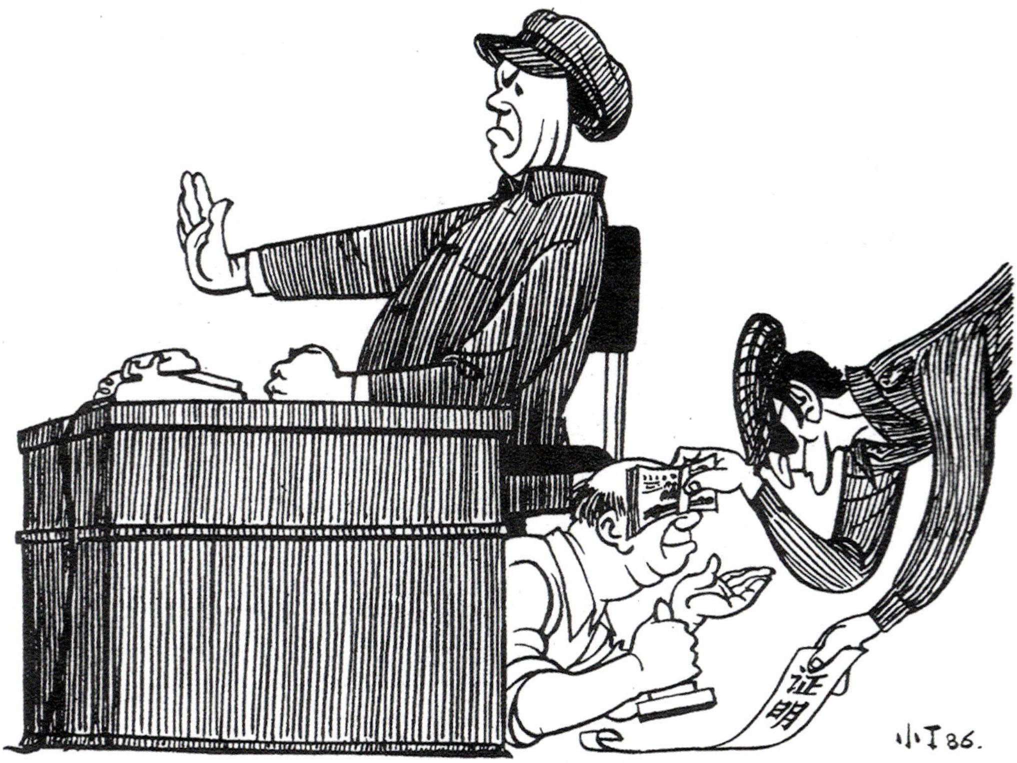

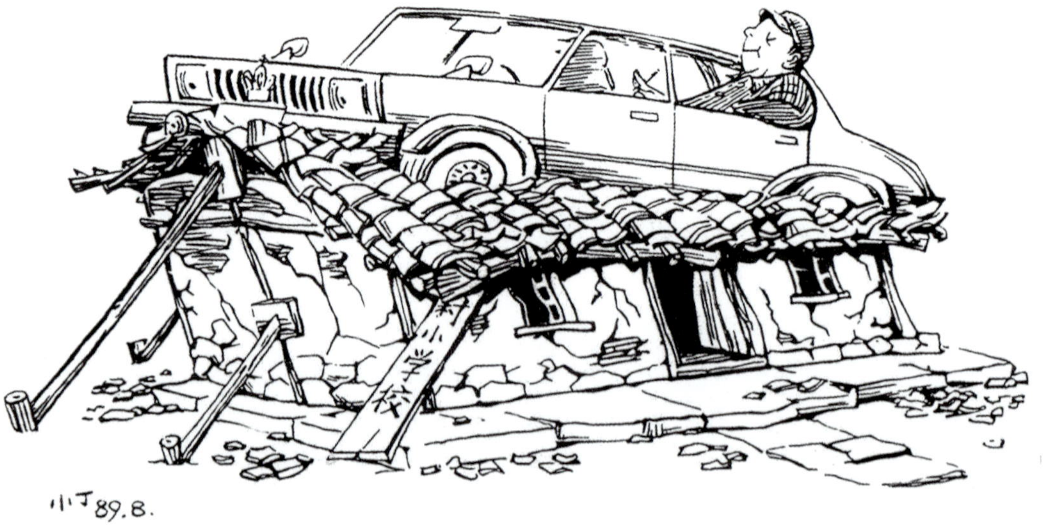

89. An official spends money for an elementary school to purchase a car that he intends to be chauffeured

dent, with two million people gathering on the square, some even daring to attack Mao Zedong directly.[33] Once again, the Gang of Four blamed the *Erliutang* for creating an uprising in Tiananmen like that done by the Petöfi Club in Hungary. One Gang of Four member charged Deng directly as being China's Imre Nagy, just as Zhou Enlai had earlier been similarly charged. It appears that membership in the *Erliutang* was routinely expanded to accommodate new scapegoats as they were needed.

The Tiananmen demonstrations and laying of wreaths ended without violence, but in their wake, Deng would be blamed for the disruptive behavior. Some ten thousand persons around the country found themselves arrested for participating in similar local demonstrations. The Gang of Four told artists and writers to support this reaction and strongly condemn the Tiananmen events with posters and paintings supporting their position. Xiao Ding, of course, would play no role because he was still condemned to re-education and labor.

Rehabilitation and Return

My health and body are not very free in responding to the rapidly changing times, but my heart is always in harmony with my people.

—Xiao Ding

Following in rapid succession in this confusing and chaotic period of China's modern history were several momentous events. Mao Zedong died on September 9, 1976. In less than a month, the members of the Gang of Four were arrested and the Great Proletarian Cultural Revolution came to an end, its demise officially proclaimed at the Eleventh Chinese Communist Party Congress held in August, 1977. Hua Guofeng, who as Mao's second chosen successor had received his personal endorsement that "with you in charge, I am at ease," soon found himself isolated and supported with only mediocre talent at his disposal to handle his enormous responsibilities. Real power soon shifted to Deng Xiaoping, the only person with sufficient ability and experience to guide the country through this stormy period. In January 1972, Deng traveled to the United States to mark the occasion of the normalization of US-China relations. He then participated in the rehabilitation of victims of the Cultural Revolution, including Liu Shaoqi, previously dubbed "China's Khruschev." Members of the Gang of Four were put on trial from November 1980 to January 1981, with hard sentences meted out. Finally, the verdict on the disastrous consequences of the Cultural Revolution appeared in July of

1981 in the Party's authoritative *Resolution on Party History*. Of course, Mao's role could hardly go unmentioned in such a key document, but he also could not be totally discredited by it. The Chinese Revolution and the Party would only suffer by their obvious association. Instead, Mao was cast as a tragic hero, who made leftist errors, but who was still a great proletarian revolutionary hero.

Xiao Ding Exonerated

By 1979, nearly all of the artists and writers who had suffered disgrace and punishment during the Cultural Revolution were rehabilitated. Xiao Ding received official pardon in the *People's Daily* on August 19, 1979, which presented a complete reversal of the official position regarding the *Erliutang* group. Along with eight others active in the arts, film, and literature, Xiao Ding's good reputation was restored; the group was deemed to be no longer anti-Party, and even capable of making important contributions to China's future. Still undaunted, Xiao Ding had his own plans for the future, and it could not have given much comfort to the regime:

> My generation has had very rich experiences; in World War II, we escaped from place to place without food, and after Liberation, we were educated by the CCP. We feel a strong sense of responsibility to say something, to satirize."[34]

Leading up to this reversal of his fortunes in 1979, Xiao Ding had been living in the National Art Institute, which was soon to host an exhibit of 600 paintings to celebrate the new atmosphere of cultural freedom. Xiao Ding helped to mount the paintings, but had none of his own works available to exhibit. Still unsure of his status, he started to work on illustrations for a book by Lu Xun, thinking that this type of work might be a safer choice than drawing cartoons. When a physical examination confirmed that he suffered from high blood pressure, he was able to get two weeks vacation, during which time he completed the illustrations.

In 1979, Xiao Ding was finally released from the ban on his cartoon work, but that came as a grim reminder that he had now lost more than twenty years of his professional working life. For Xiao Ding and the others of his circle, that painful thought of lost creative opportunity was hardest to erase from memory. This sad realization, however, seemed to spur anew his creativity. After 1978 he published more than thirty collections of his work, in English, German, and Japanese.

Fear Lingers in the 1980s

The ability of artists and intellectuals to free themselves mentally of the nearly total control which the Party had exercised

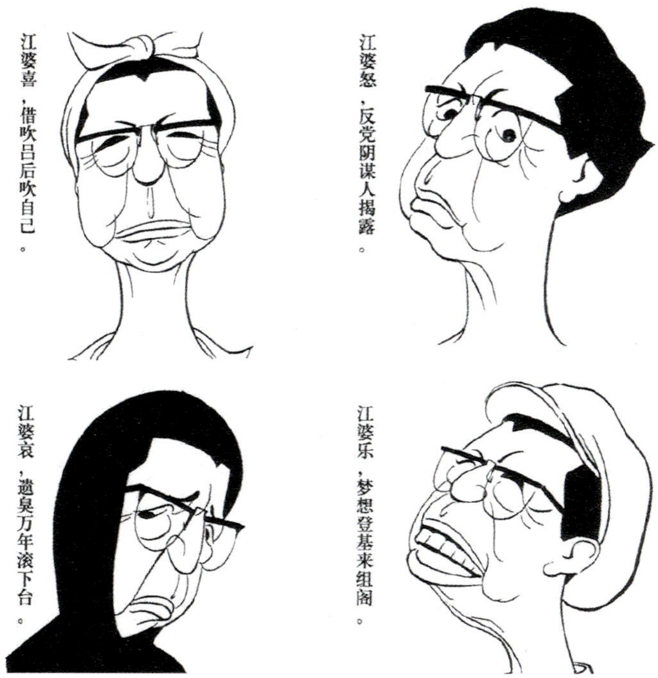

90. Various expressions of the notorious Jiang Qing (1977)

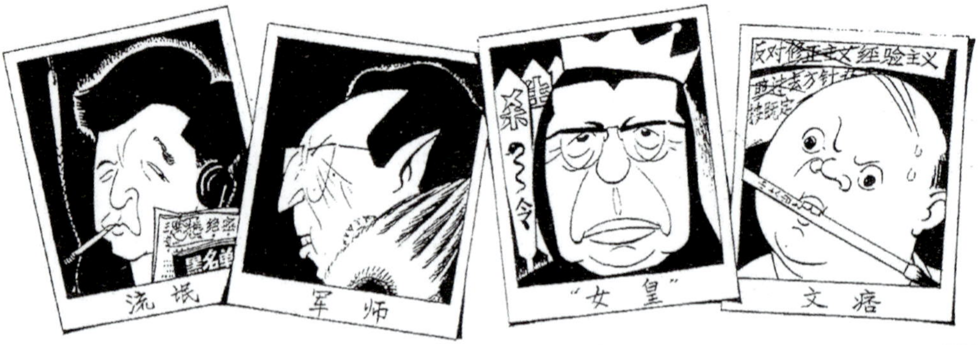

91. Caricatures of the Gang of Four, who led the Cultural Revolution: the rogue, Wang Hungwen; the strategist, Zhang Chunqiao; the empress, Jiang Qing; and the literary pretender, Yao Wenyuan (1976)

over their lives came slowly at first. Fears lingered as they began to create again, with each having to decide which medium or subject was safest. Having lived with constant harassment and fear of arrest, they were plagued by images of the "big brother" that might suddenly reappear to ruin their lives. Nevertheless, their pent up desire to write again, paint again, and be heard again won out. The 1980s saw an astonishing outburst of creativity that became known as "Peking Spring." One of Xiao Ding's first projects resulted in a series of satirical cartoons depicting the machinations of the hated Gang of Four. He gave special attention to the artists' nemesis, the "White-Boned Demon," Jiang Qing (figs. 90, 91). Even though Xiao Ding had had little opportunity to practice his skills in recent years, he was quite bold in his characterization of his new themes. The inspiration and energy he seemed to derive from these odious subjects poured forth in striking portrayals of their facial expressions and their easily recognizable notorious behavior.

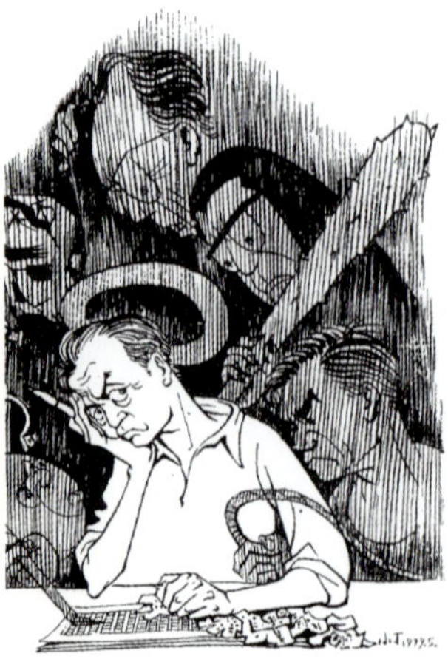

92. "It is hard to forget the past beatings, whips, and endless self confessions under the Gang of Four" (1979)

Even though the Gang of Four was already under official arrest and public attack, one always had to wonder whether the warm winds blowing from Party Central would shift again to an icy, Siberian cold. As his work shows (fig. 92), the specter of the Party's critical gaze remained difficult to escape after so many years of harsh treatment. Those who had been persecuted still lived with vivid memories of being beaten,

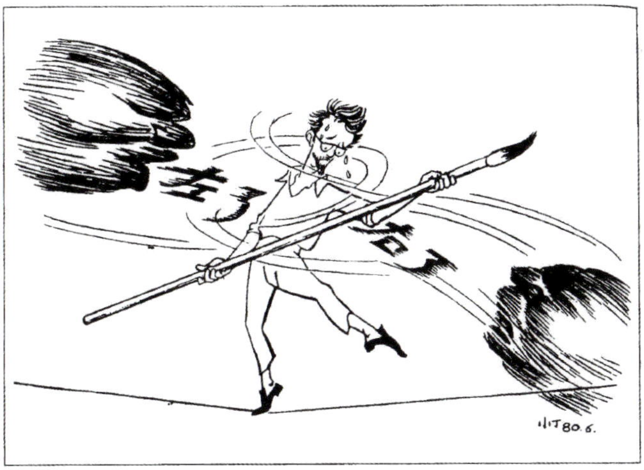

93. *"Writing is a dangerous profession; one must be careful to first test the winds to see which way they are blowing" (1980)*

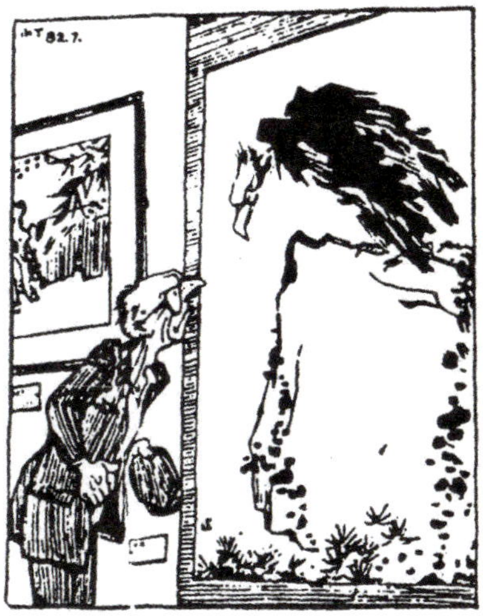

94. *"We see what we want to see in pictures"*

whipped through the streets, and made to wear dunce caps in ceremonies of public humiliation. Creating anything for publication, whether written or visual, remained a potentially treacherous path because the winds of censorship so frequently shifted; one had to be expert at sensing when the political winds might suddenly change direction (fig. 93), and consequently how one's work might be interpreted (fig. 94). Treading carefully, even the government censors had to make absolutely sure that all "barbs"— criticism or negative comments about the government or its policies—were completely removed from the writer's or artist's work (fig. 95).

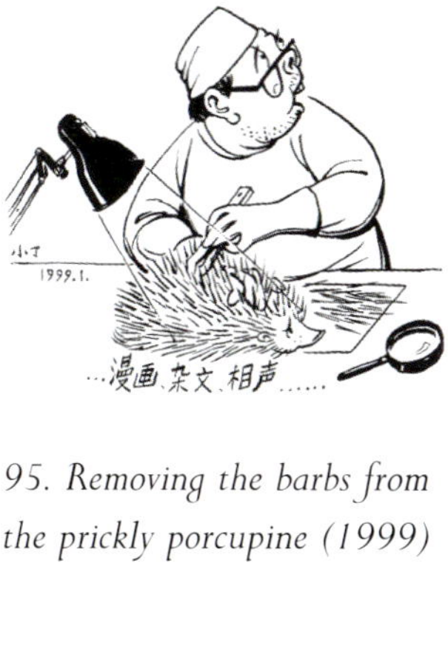

95. *Removing the barbs from the prickly porcupine (1999)*

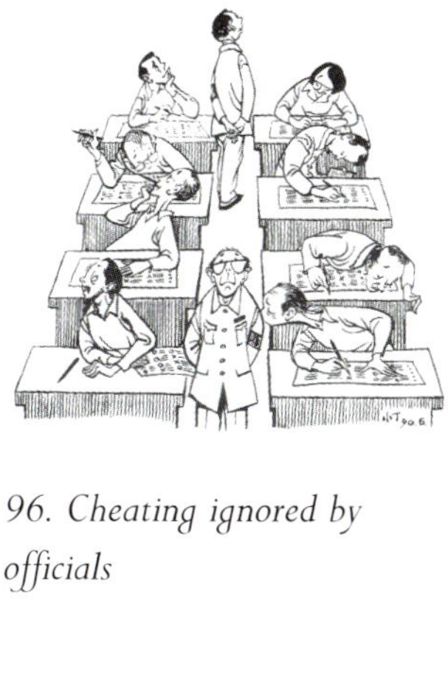

96. *Cheating ignored by officials*

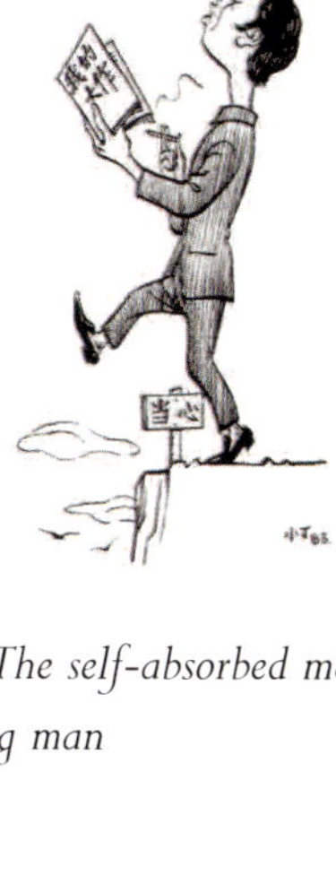

97. *The self-absorbed modern young man*

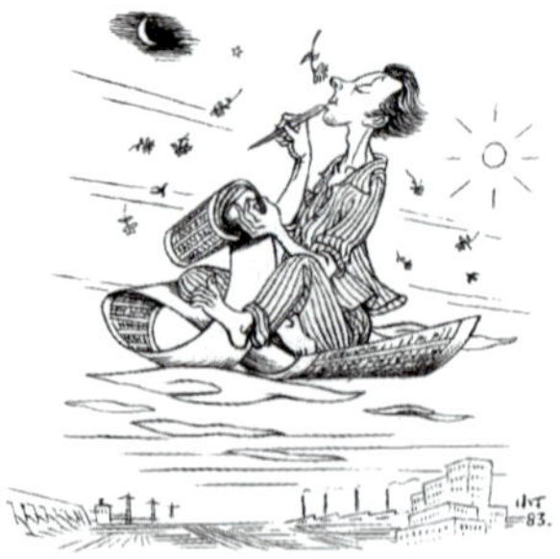

98. Intellectuals out of touch with the real world

Meanwhile, the age-old and still common problems of official corruption (fig. 96) and a general indifference to it (fig. 97) hampered attempts to improve society. Wary of the dangers of social activism, many intellectuals remained aloof and out of touch (fig. 98), while the Party's position on all matters was limited to what was officially approved (fig. 99), making it unable to effect any real reform.

The important literary journal *Reading* (*Dushu*) had frequently published Xiao Ding's work, beginning from the journal's inception in 1979 until Xiao Ding's health no longer permitted him to make regular contributions. In a 1986 cartoon commemorating the first one hundred months of *Dushu's*

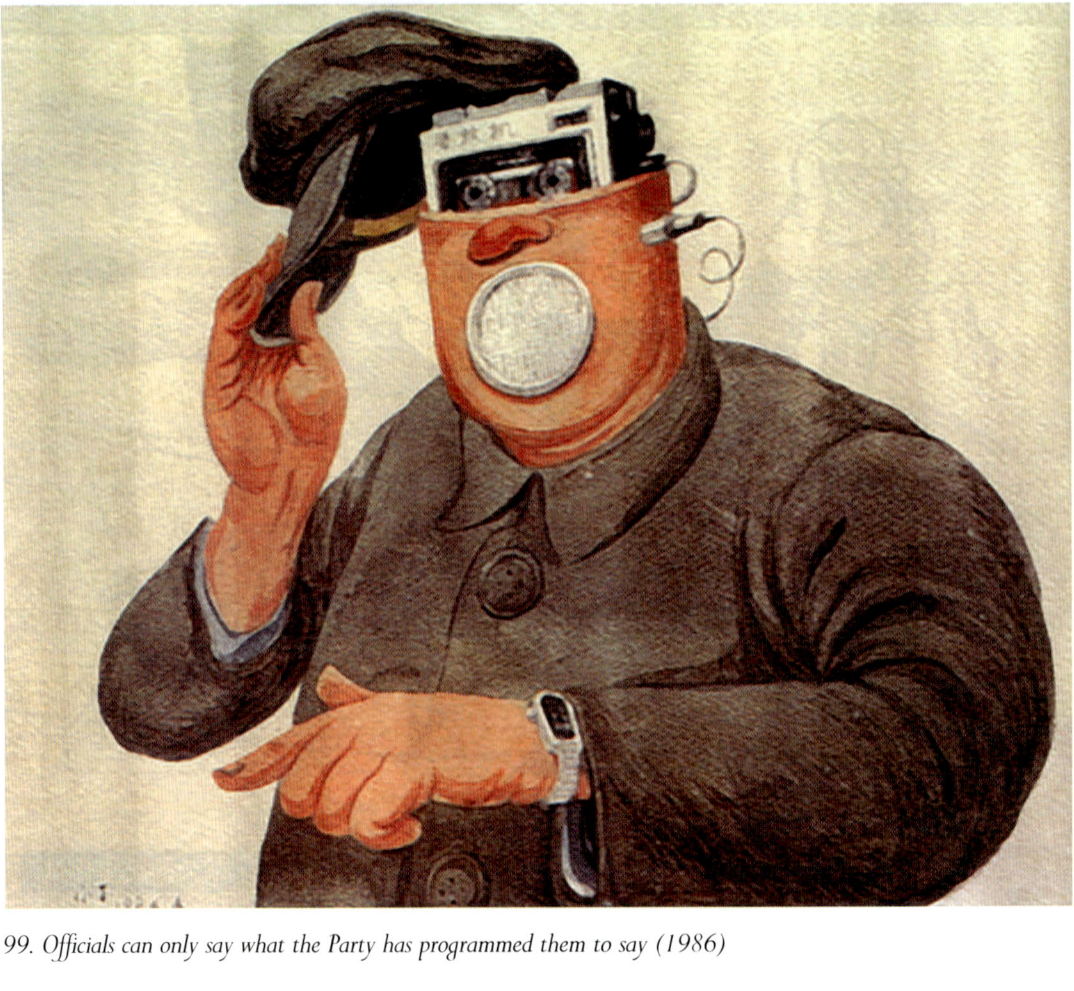

99. Officials can only say what the Party has programmed them to say (1986)

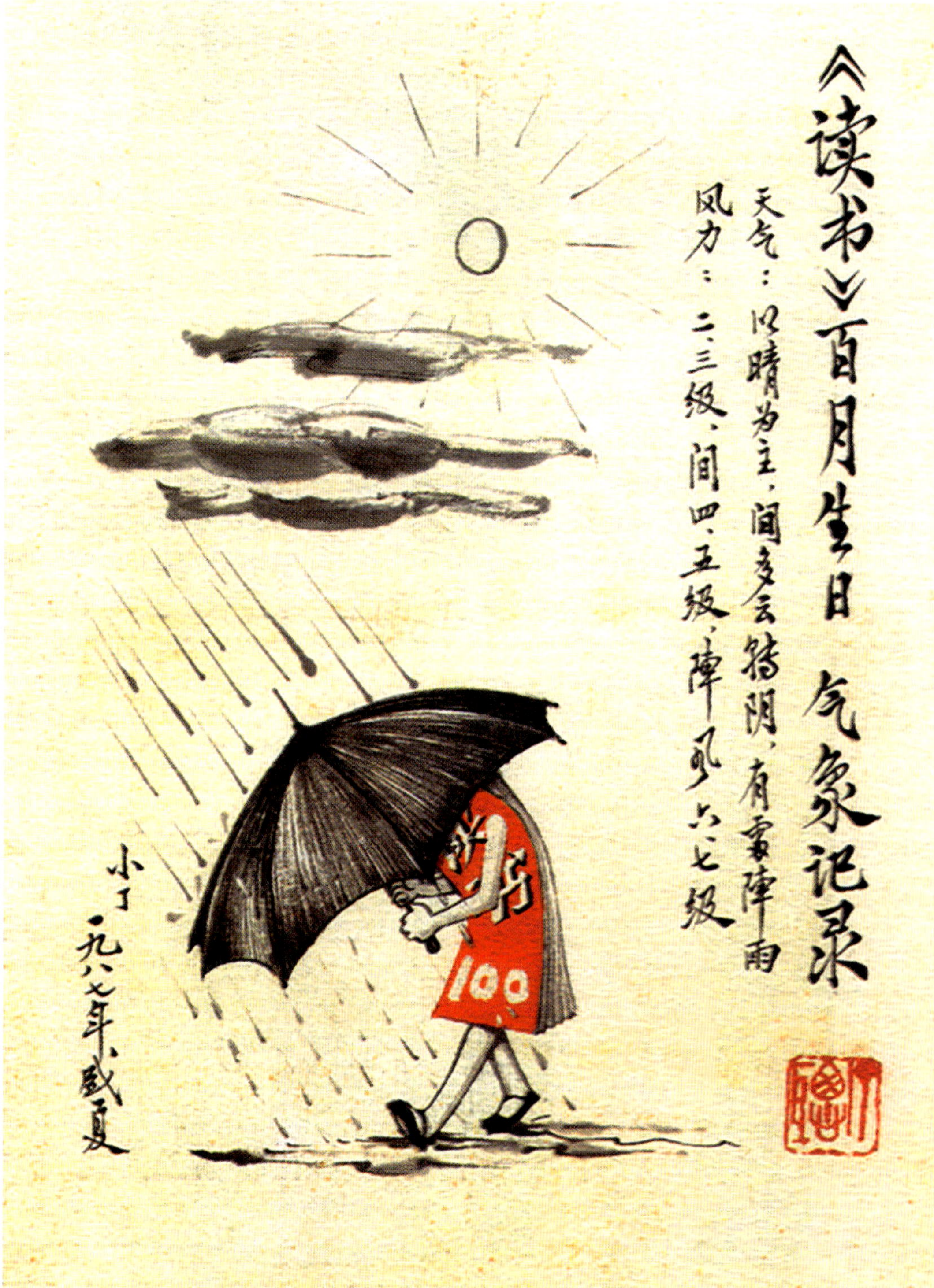

100. Even to commemorate its 100th issue, Du Shu *hesitates to publish anything riskier than a weather report*

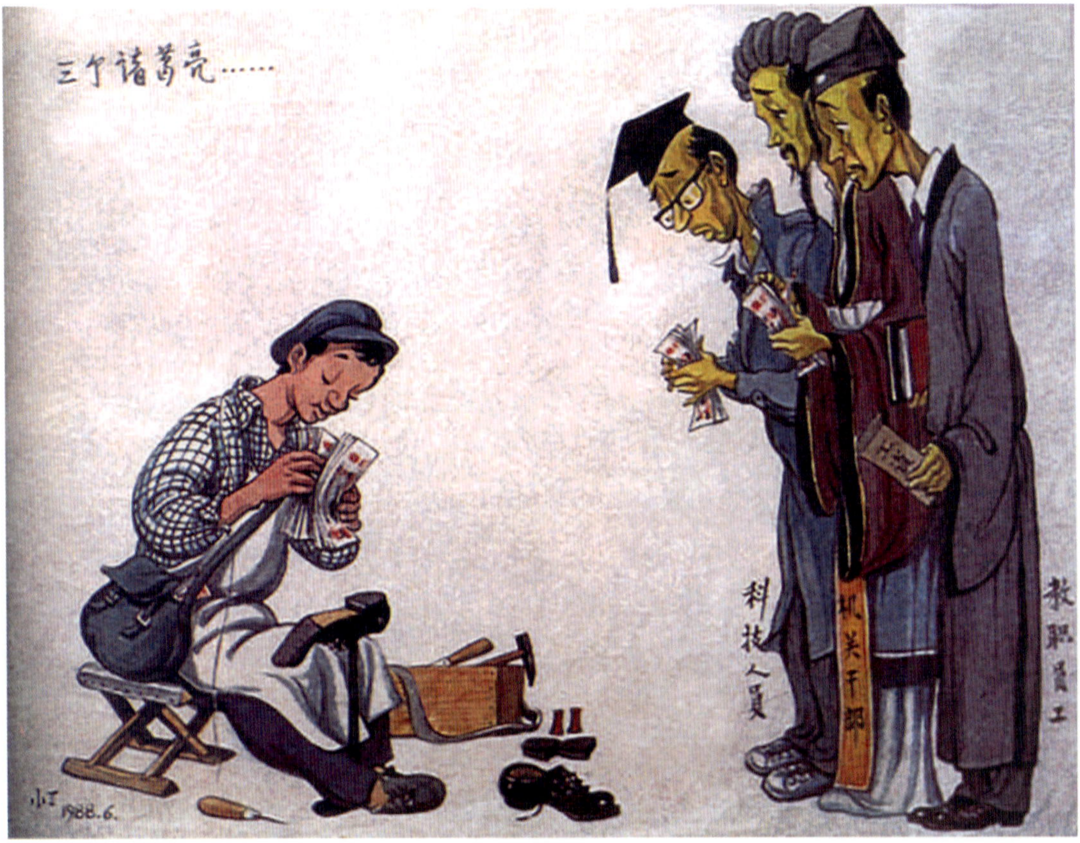

101. *Three Zhu Geliangs (intellectuals) are worth less than one cobbler (1988)*

publication, Xiao Ding satirized the editor's reluctance to publish anything other than benign subject matter during such still uncertain times. His cartoon was a mock cover for the journal, showing the issue's main content as nothing more than a long and detailed weather forecast (fig. 100). The sad plight of intellectuals, in this case university professors, is satirized in a drawing (fig. 101) showing "Three Zhu Geliangs" (after a revered wise man in Chinese history) as earning less, and by implication having less value to society, than an ordinary street cobbler. The diminished status of intellectuals continued to limit their influence, and to reduce their quality of life (fig. 102).

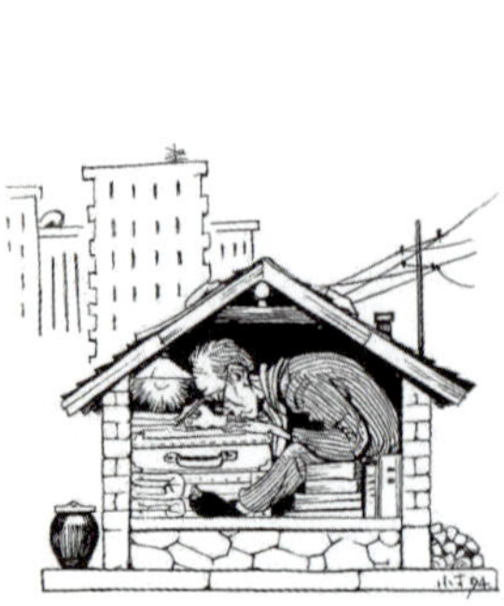

102. *The plight of intellectuals: "no golden room inside the book"*

During the unusual winter of 1978–79, citizens in Beijing participated in the celebrated Democracy Wall gatherings, plastering the brick structure with banners and posters calling for freedom and political reform. In March of 1979, one of the leading participants of the movement, Wei Jingsheng, was arrested for his advocacy of a fifth modernization, to coincide with the official Four Modernizations Campaign. He had in mind political democracy, popular advocacy of which was a "forbidden zone" (*jinqu*) that the Party could not tolerate. Wei received a sentence of fifteen years of hard labor. His recommendation had been clearly for a political alternative to Party rule, and as such was especially risky.

Discretion in one's writing and painting still remained the prudent course. A few pioneering artists, in particular a group dubbed "The Stars," did manage to hold some well attended exhibits in the fall of 1979 of their relatively edgy paintings, graphics, and sculpture. Although clearly a call for artistic freedom in an atmosphere of creative suppression, edgy meant the inclusion of more sexual content, a kind of artistic rebellion that was more viable than one clearly political. Still, many artists, sensing a possible hardening of the Party's positions, grew restless and finally decided to sever their connections to China to build their artistic careers in Tokyo, Paris, London, and New York.

Throughout the 1980s, Beijing sent conflicting signals about how to handle what it called "undirected art." There were turnabouts on the part of some formerly tolerant leaders, including Deng Xiaoping, who now wanted to curb free artistic expression, and others promoting a new campaign against "spiritual pollution." This new chill cast over the cultural world was soon followed by a popular reaction, one that released the energy of massive, countrywide student demonstrations. They boldly attacked censorship, blasted a corrupt dictatorship, and called for more freedom and the hope of a better future. In Beijing, demonstrations in remembrance of Party Secretary Hu Yaobang accelerated into huge and surging student protests, a massive outpouring of defiance and desperation, complete with

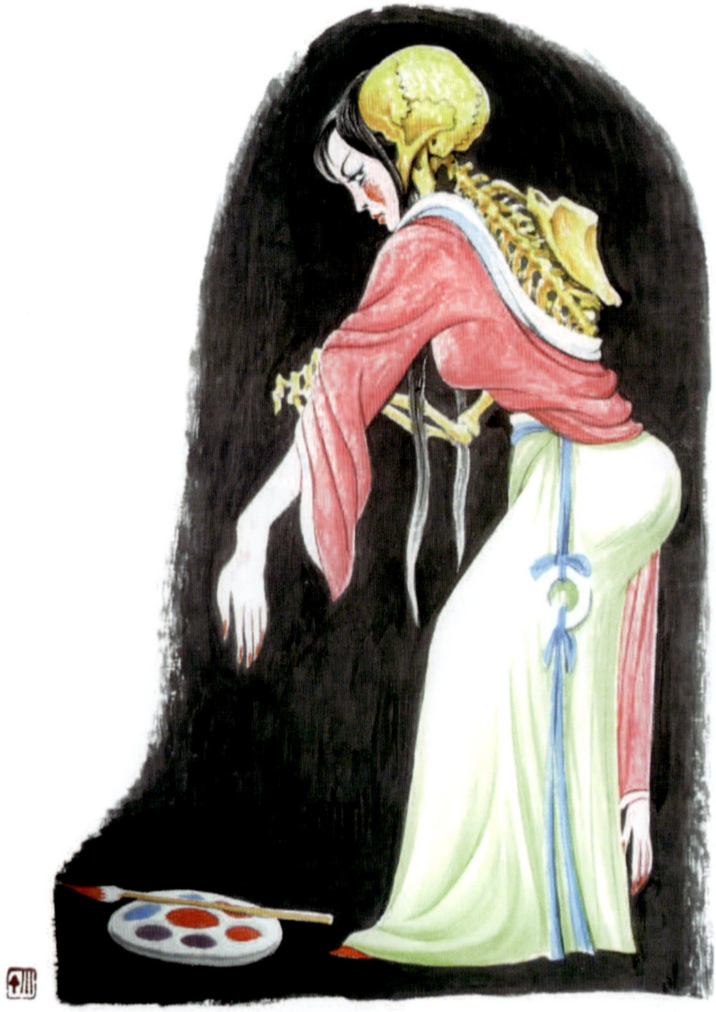

103. Done in Dadaist spirit, Hua Pi (Painted Skin) *reflects on beauty and mortality. Courtesy of Michael Sullivan*

a statue of the Goddess of Democracy made by students of Beijing's Central Art Academy. The government's response, mild at first, culminated in the brutal June 4, 1989, Tiananmen Incident, in which many hundreds were killed as army troops ended the student occupation of the great square. In aftermath of this disaster, an embarrassment for China with the world watching, the Secretary General of the Party, Zhao Ziyang, was removed from his position for being too easy-going in his handling of the crisis.

In the wake of this cataclysmic event, artists again heeded caution and returned to safe subjects such as patriotism and the

Party's one-child-per-family policy. But the genie seemed to be out of the bottle, as new artists' groups appeared that continued to energetically pursue all "modern" trends from the West, including Cubism, Dadaism, Impressionism, Expressionism, and Surrealism. Xiao Ding had been a pioneer in incorporating some important elements of Dadaism in the 1930s and 40s, and there were obvious signs of the influence of Cubism in his early paintings. As has been shown in his cartoon art, he had often favored the use of shocking, distorted, or elongated figures to awaken his viewers to his message (fig. 103).

In 1988, the film *River Elegy* (*He shang*) appeared, making the claim that Chinese culture should be quickly modernized, mostly by looking to the West, like the river flowing westward and reaching the ocean. Throughout the decade, many salons emerged and numerous exhibits were presented, varying thematically and in the intensity of their rebelliousness according to the changing political climate and fine-tuned to each fluctuation. However, most young artists had lost interest in heroism, having been convinced that their ability to bring about change, or even to try, was impossible and there-

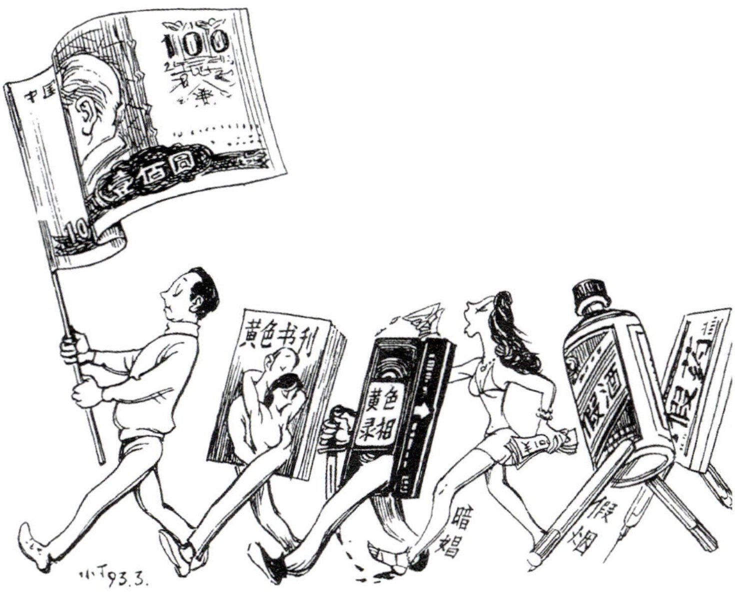

104. Follow the money: pornography, prostitution, fake cigarettes, liquor, and medicine (1993)

fore pointless. These were heady and often enriching years of "culture fever," but also risky times, especially in the capital.

New Themes for New Times

In the 1990s, a variety of new projects occupied Xiao Ding's attention. His close friend and fellow artist, Zhang Guangyu, began work as the designer of the cartoon movie *Uproar in Heaven*, based on the classic Ming dynasty novel *Journey to the West (Xiyouji)*. In 1944, Zhang had produced a much esteemed series of sixty cartoon paintings called *Xiyoumanji*, which at that time had been too provocative in its allusions to see publication, although his work became quite famous. In the new version of the story of the Monkey King and his exploits, the search for Buddhist scriptures includes the quest for democracy, and the modern government's failure to provide it were exposed. Instead of democracy, the Monkey King encounters fascism and oppression, in the guise of leaders like Japanese Admiral Tōjō. In meeting his challenges, the Monkey King shows great ingenuity, tenacity, and courage against powerful foes.

In his own work during the 1990s, Xiao Ding began to express trends that he observed in contemporary Chinese society. Following the Tiananmen disaster the enthusiasm for Western culture and cosmopolitanism of the previous decade gave way to greater concern for indigenous Chinese values, including Confucianism and other elements of a great tradition, accompanied by a growing spirit of nationalism. The return to China of Hong Kong in 1997, the U.S. bombing of the Chinese Embassy in Belgrade two years later, followed by China's accession within six months to the World Trade Organization, all promoted a new focus on China's national interests and accomplishments. The Chinese perspective on its place in the world, and its sometimes precarious position, was broadening and reaching deeper into the population.

One prevalent trend, which became the subject of several of Xiao Ding's cartoons, was the popular fixation on seeking and making money (fig. 104). The new theme followed the southern tour made by Deng Xiaoping in February, 1992, when he is said to have declared to the nation that "getting rich is glorious." Stymied by members of the entrenched and conservative bureaucracy in Beijing in his efforts to reform the Chinese economy and to open it up to the world, Deng knew he would have greater impact by making his declaration away from the capital. Opposition forces in Beijing had seen the outcome of radical reform measures in the Soviet Union, and worried that Deng's expansive economic program would lead to a similar result. Deng is also quoted as saying: "it matters not whether the cat is black or white, as long as it catches the mouse." A pragmatic approach leading to making China strong and prosperous was his mantra; how "revolutionary" the Party programs needed to be to effect this change were secondary. This viewpoint, which would have been an anathema to Mao, was not palatable to any of his conservative cohorts of the old guard. Fortunately for Deng, his

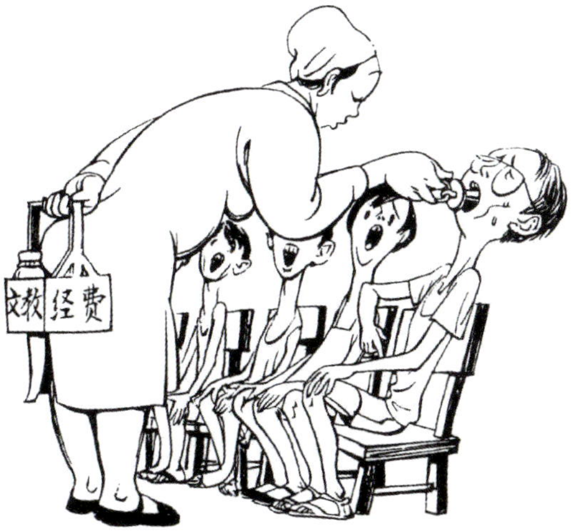

105. The meager education and arts budget has little left to feed the many hungry student mouths

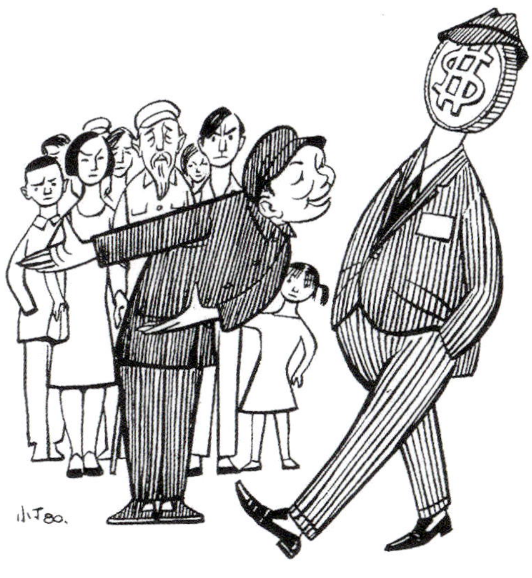

106. "Please, money always goes first"

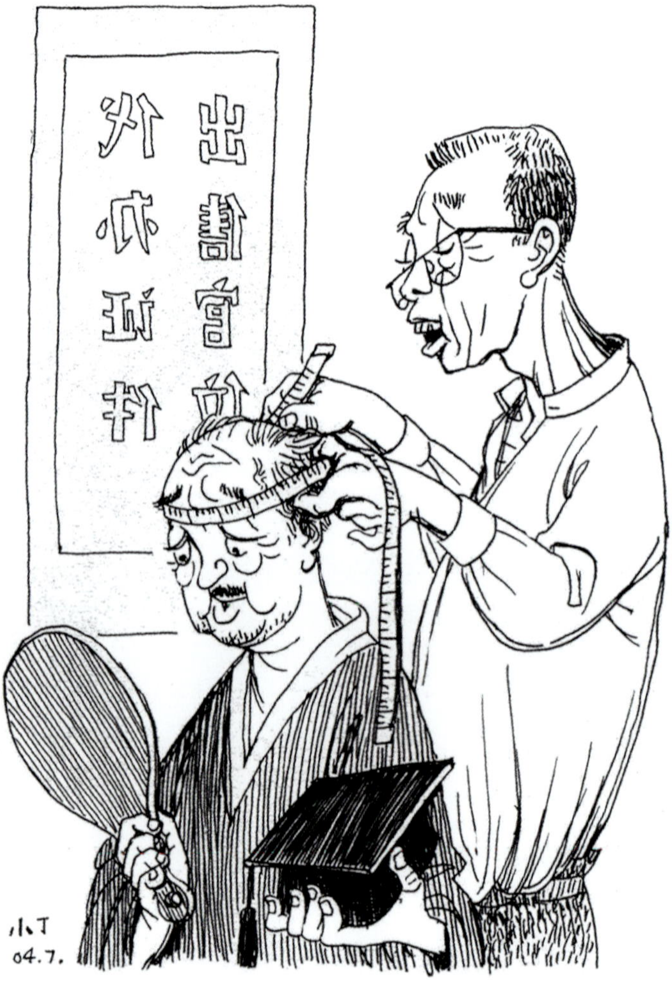

107. A seller of positions and degrees measures a client's head for his regalia (2004)

strongest opponents were one by one dying off; he himself succumbed in February 1997.

Into the Twenty-first Century

The People's Republic of China has prospered under a succession of more forward-looking and internationally minded leaders, including Jiang Zemin and Hu Jintao, who implemented and fine-tuned a broad program called "Socialism with Chinese Characteristics" aimed at creating a "harmonious society." Achieving a balance between tight central control and a more relaxed response toward public expression and discussion have remained a challenge, while the disparity in incomes among urban areas, especially between coastal cities and those in the hinterland, has been recognized as a potential threat to stability. Government corruption and the setting of economic priorities (figs. 105, 106) were issues that continued to be of popular concern and to inspire Xiao Ding's art.

Meanwhile, against a backdrop of urban prosperity, Xiao Ding began to develop new themes related to the social tenor of the times. One was the decline of ethical thinking and behavior in a period imbued with a materialist, even decadent spirit. Catering to the rush to attain a position or advance oneself, businesses emerged dedicated to selling professional certificates and positions (fig. 107). Xiao Ding depicted the frenzied race to gain higher position as transparent and artificial as playing musical chairs (fig. 108), with competitors rushing to claim the best position at the sound

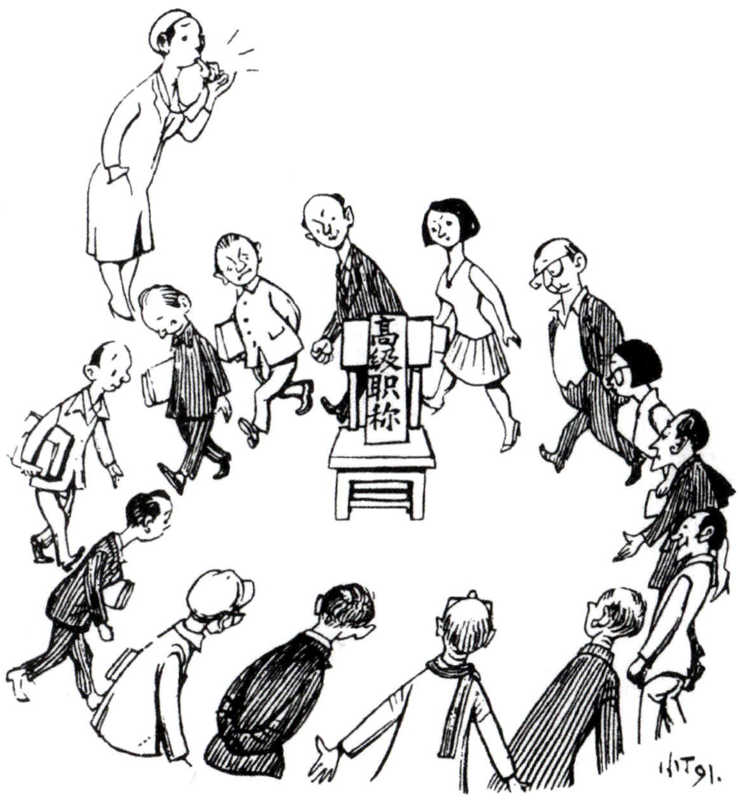

108. Grabbing a senior position, "Let's see who gets lucky" (1991)

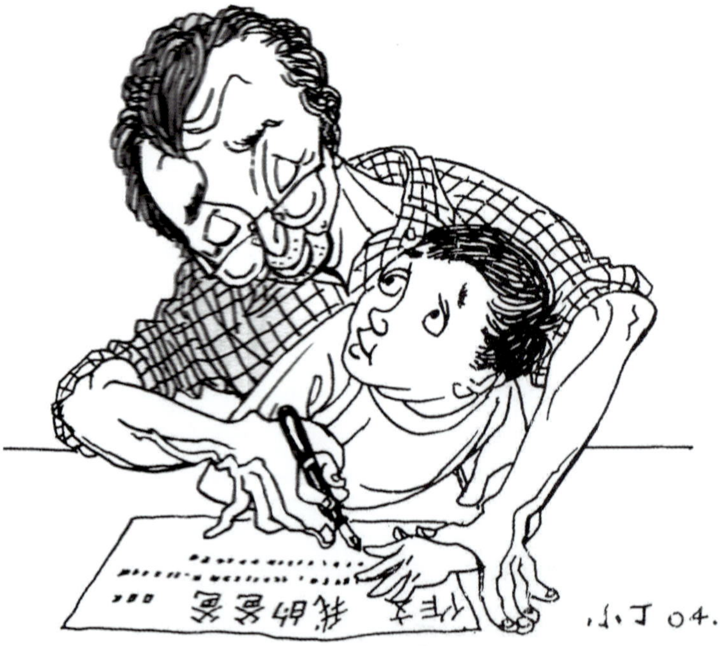

109. The young author's work is too mature; it was done by his father (2004)

of the whistle. Parents anxious about the success of their children assumed doing their homework for them would help them compete (fig. 109). Coddling of children, especially boys, or tolerating their rude and self-centered behavior

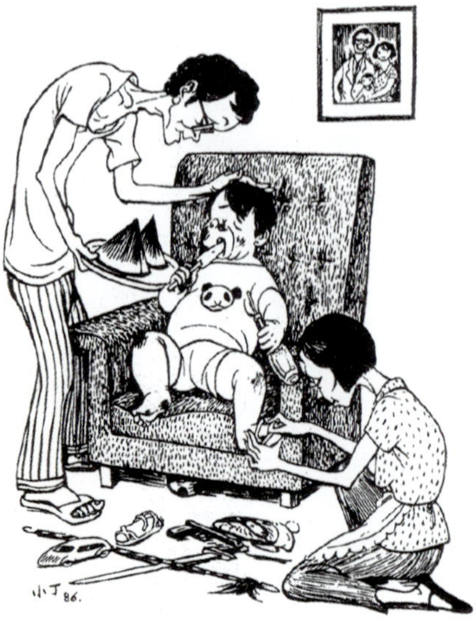

110. The only son cannot be indulged too much (1986)

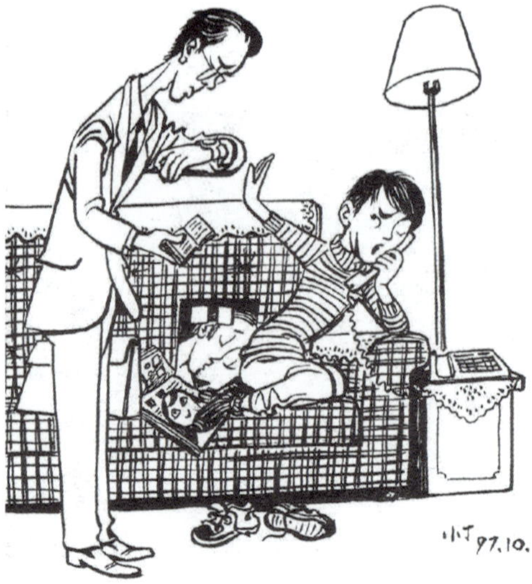

111. A father must wait until it is convenient for his young son to end his phone call (1997)

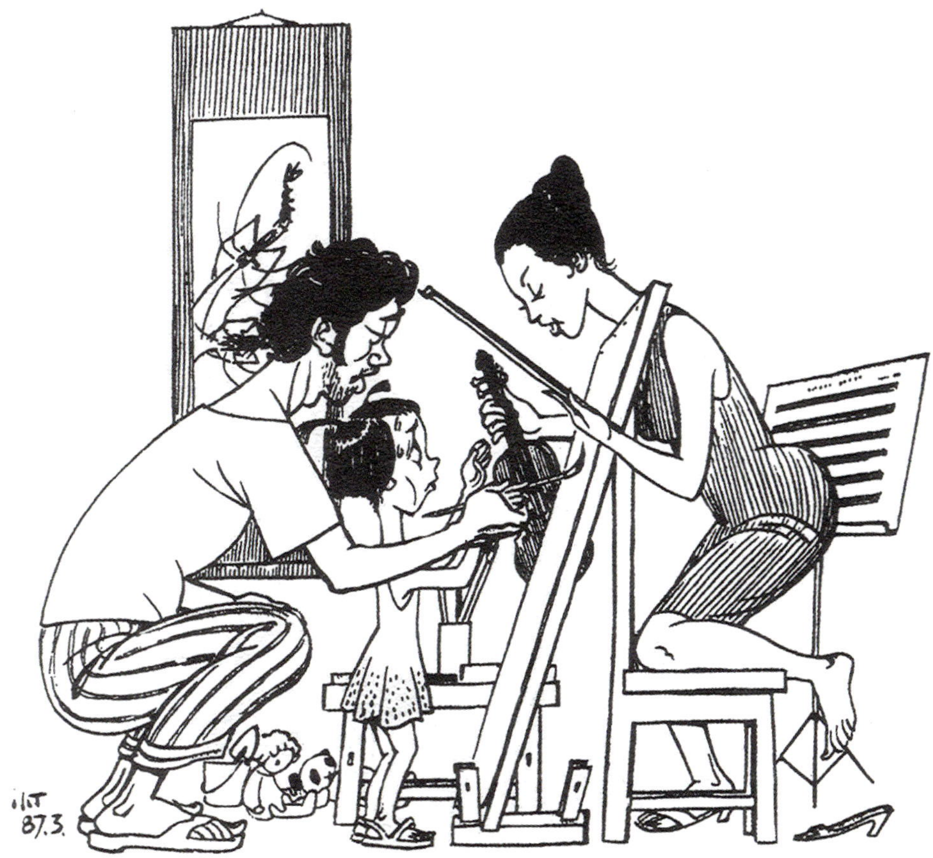

112. *Pushing the child too hard is like "pulling up seedlings" to see if they have grown (1987)*

became increasingly common parental behavior (figs. 110, 111). All were the focus of Xiao Ding's ready brush.

Increasing competition for social status, the desire for the latest and best consumer goods, *nouveaux riches* parents pressuring their children to achieve in multiple fields, from academics, to music, to art, personal appearance, and so on, preoccupied especially young and would-be professionals. The spirit of modern Chinese parenting was captured in the expression "pulling up seedlings," in order to measure their progress before replanting them, a counterproductive effort (fig. 112). While parents continually prodded children to achieve, television remained preoccupied with showing events like ribbon cutting ceremonies and upbeat news or light entertainment, rather than providing programs with real substance.

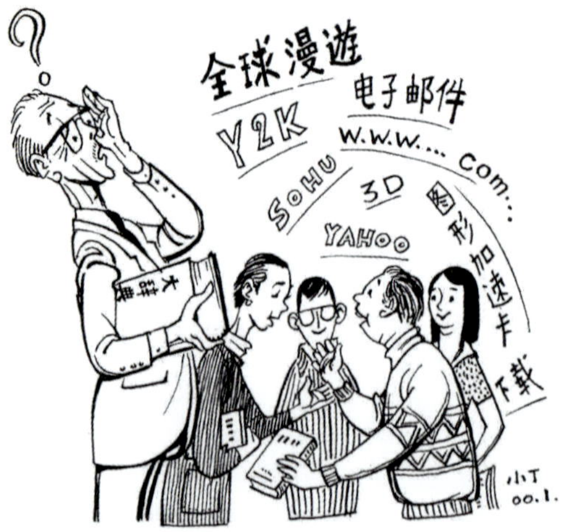

113. *The modern world challenges parents to keep up with the new terminology (2000)*

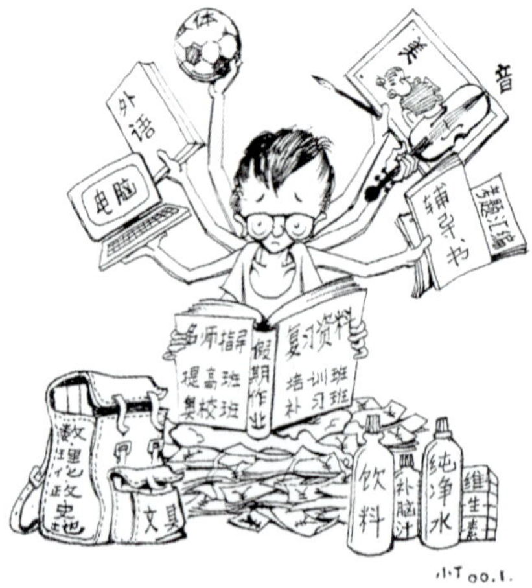

114. *Children are overwhelmed with learning (2000)*

The difficult task of keeping up with what was new and relevant fell to parents, for whom the responsibility could be daunting, even overwhelming (figs. 113, 114). These problems became fodder for Xiao Ding's art, and remind us of similar parenting problems in modern Western society. Finally, a playful humor had always had a place in Xiao Ding's cartoon art, often highlighting common human foibles that never seemed to escape his notice and interest (figs. 115, 116).

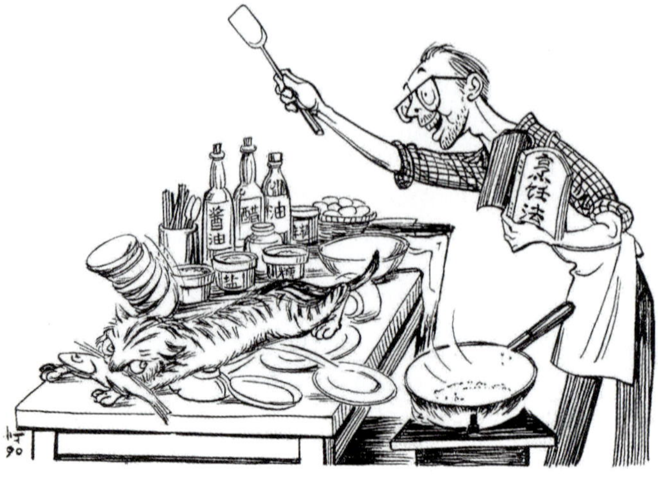

115. *"You stole the fish but I have the recipe" (1990)*

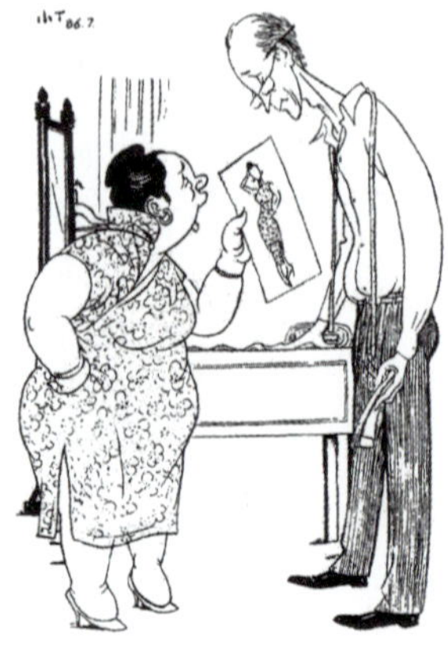

116. *A woman scolds her tailor, who failed to make her look like the model in the picture (1986)*

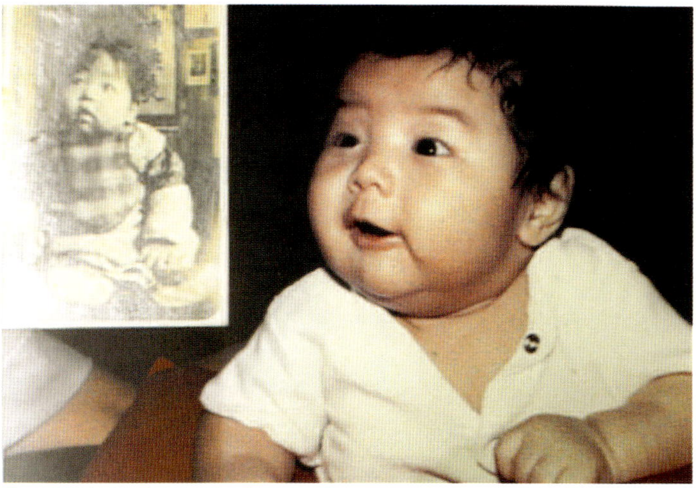

117. A photograph of Xiao Ding as a baby and his look-alike grandson.

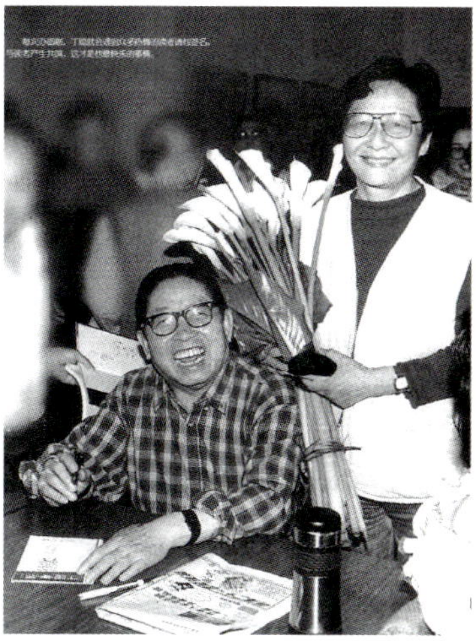

118. Xiao Ding and his wife, Shen Jun, celebrating his success

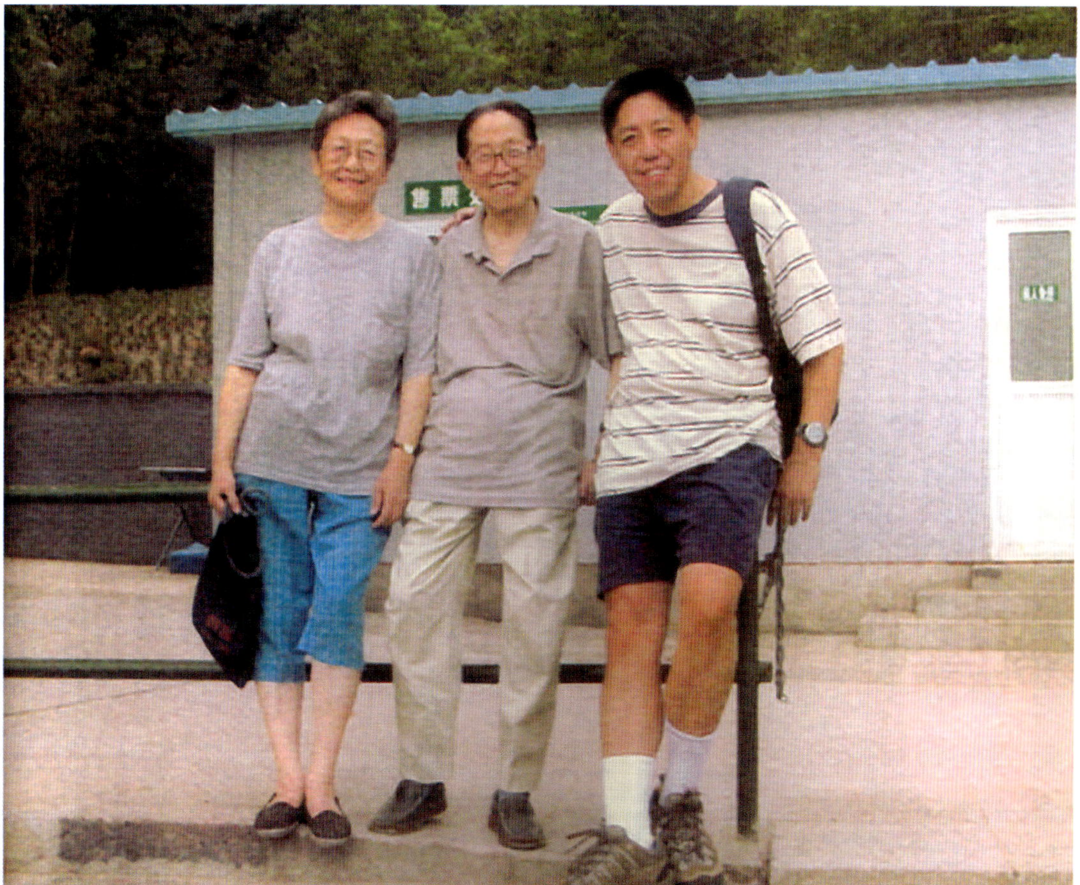

119. The family together for only the second time, in 2004

Xiao Ding began his remarkable career as a clerk, gradually mastering drawing through his own efforts and persisting in the face of many obstacles to become a renown painter and cartoonist. During the 1980s and 90s, he was especially prolific, trying to make up for the many years of creative output he had lost. He continued to paint and draw until he reached the age of ninety, rare for artists who had suffered as he had. He published more than a dozen books and liked to say that the happiest thing for him in later years was to draw pictures without Jiang Qing's interference. Life for him in recent years has been stable and peaceful, with no worries about food or clothing, or even politics (figs. 117–120). Until his death in 2009, he was finally able to enjoy with his wife the simple pleasures of coffee and fruit or dessert on any pleasant afternoon.

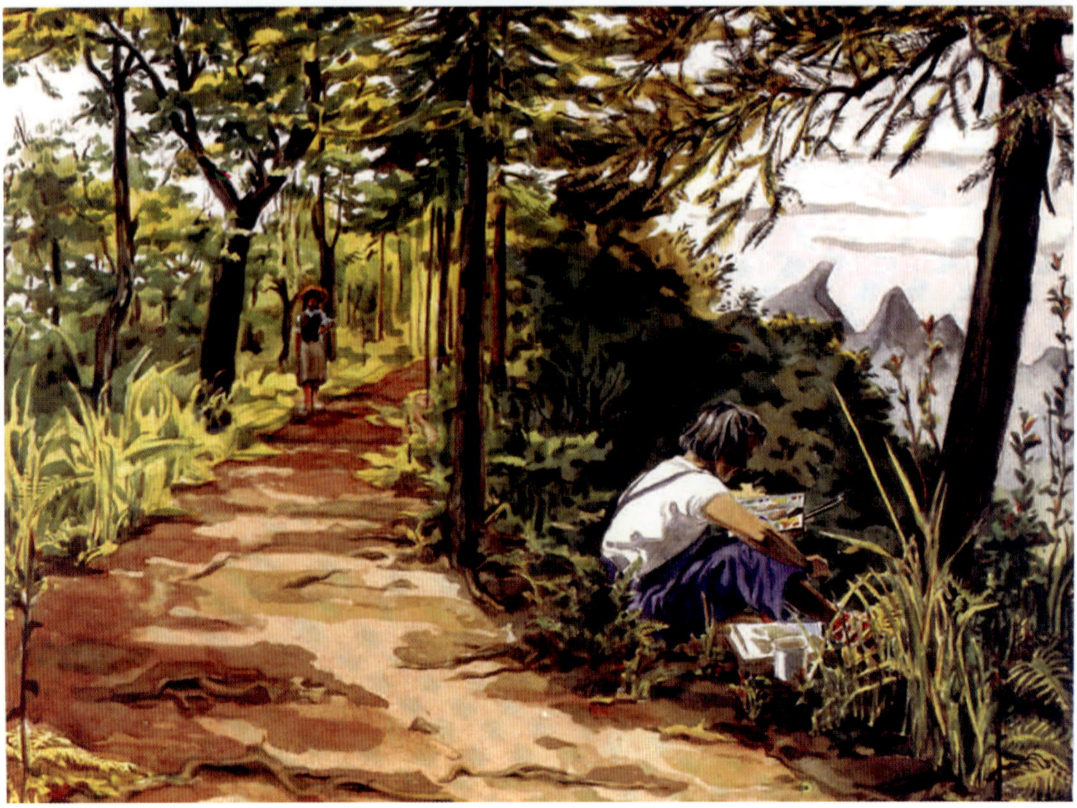

120. Simple pleasures

Afterword

Xiao Ding has been called "Old Hard Bones" as a title of respect and affection by those who have known him well. This, indeed, is a label that seems truly to fit. His fierce independence, passionate commitment to his art, strong sense of humanity toward his subjects, and deep love of his country have all combined to feed a determination to follow his own conscience and never to fold even under harsh beatings and cruel humiliation. Like so many Chinese of his generation, he lived through a war of resistance against Japan, a world war, a civil war, and then, under the dictatorship of Mao Zedong, a series of wrenching social movements culminating in the Cultural Revolution. During the course of these chaotic events, he was twice exiled, tortured, and rehabilitated, to ultimately emerge a citizen of a nominally Communist, yet semi-capitalist and up-and-coming world power, which recently paraded its accomplishments at the 2008 Beijing Olympics.

Xiao Ding played a revealing role in the titanic Chinese conflict between tradition and modernity, an abiding struggle to somehow re-state valuable parts of the ancient tradition and culture into a modern political and economic structure, in ways that would allow for a strong sense of root-

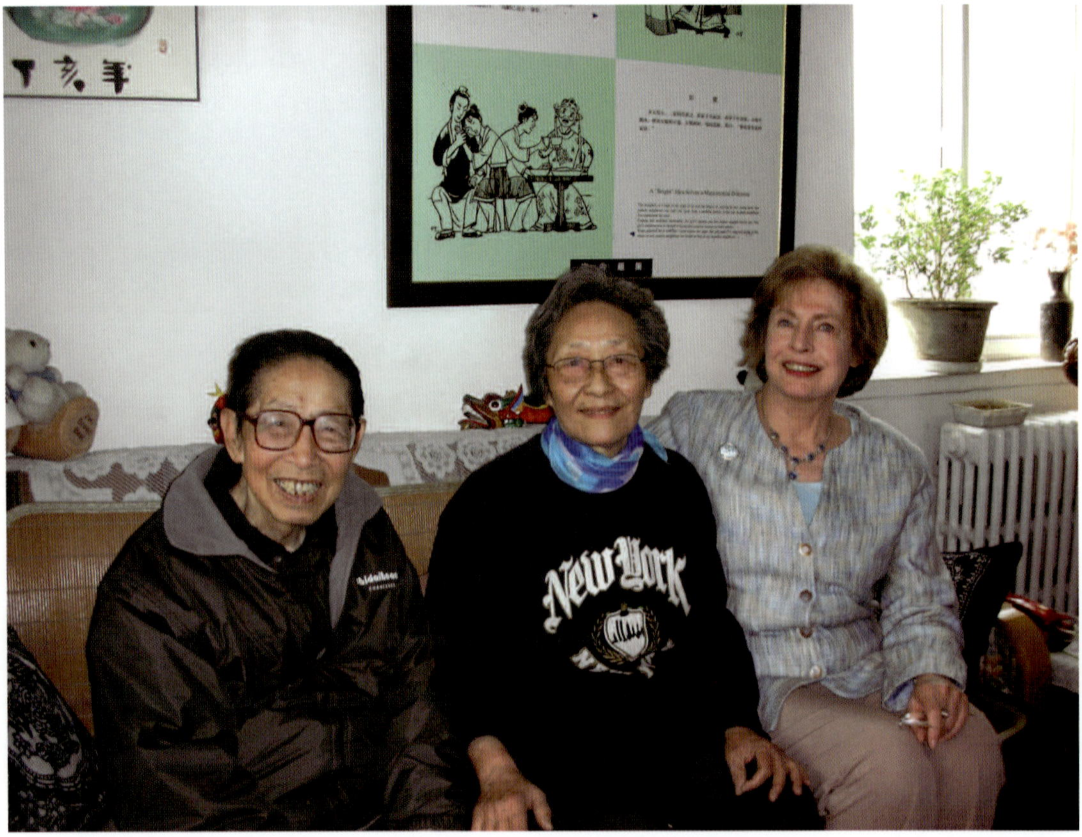

121. Author and Dings (2008)

edness and Chinese authenticity to permeate and shape the new. One can only hope that future Chinese leaders and cultural historians will not misunderstand or misrepresent this canny observer and interpreter of Chinese society, and will not, as has happened so frequently during his lifetime, find him beyond the pale of Chinese acceptance. One hopes rather that they will embrace Xiao Ding, and so learn from the life and work of perhaps the country's most intrepid critic and most ardent supporter.

Notes

1 C.T. Hsia, *History of Modern Chinese Fiction,* p. ix.

2 Sullivan, Michael, *Art and Artists of Twentieth Century China,* p. 30.

3 Leo Ou-fan Lee, *Shanghai Modern,* pp. 82–85; Yingjin Zhang, ed. *Cinema and Urban Culture in Shanghai, 1922–1943,* pp 76–77.

4 *Ibid.*, p. 16.

5 Lynn Pan, *Shanghai Style,* p. 135.

6 *Ibid.,* pp. 138–39.

7 Ding Cong, *Wode manhua shengwo* (My Cartoon Life), p. 38–9.

8 Lao She, *Rickshaw Boy,* p. 289.

9 Chang-tai Hung, *War and Popular Culture,* pp. 129–130.

10 John Lent and Xu Ying, "Cartooning and Wartime China," p. 92.

11 *Ibid,* "Cartooning and Wartime China," p. 130.

12 Chang-tai Hung, *War and Popular Culture,* p. 94.

13 John Lent, *op. cit.*, p. 109.

14 Michael Sullivan, *Art and Artists,* p. 96.

15 Ma was the only major cultural figure to escape China during the Cultural Revolution. See *Life Magazine*, June 2 & July 14, 1967.

16 Sullivan, *Art and Artists, p. 96.*

17 *Ibid, p. 122.*

18 Fang Chen, "Long Live Brother Bing," p. 645.

19 Elizabeth Lee, "A Letter to My Aunt," p. 192.

20 *Ibid*, p. 502.

21 *Ibid*, p. 487.

22 Chang-Tai Hung, "*The Fuming Image*," p. 128.

23 *Ibid.*, pp. 141, Plate 15.

24 Sullivan, *Art and Artists*, p. 129.

25 Information provided by Dr. Zhu Hongzhen, a close friend of the Dings.

26 *People's Daily*, Aug. 18, 1957.

27 Roderick MacFarquar and Michael Schoenhals, *Mao's Last Revolution*, p. 124.

28 *People's Daily*, Aug. 18, 1957.

29 *People's Daily*, Dec. 13, 1967.

30 MacFarquar and Shoenhals, *Mao's Last Revolution*, p. 262.

31 *Ibid.*, p. 306–307.

32 *Ibid.*, p. 358.

33 *Ibid.*, p, 422.

34 John Lent, interview with Ding Cong, 2002. In "Cartooning and Wartime Shanghai," p. 131.

Selected Bibliography

Barmé, Geremie, and John Minford. *Seeds of Fire: Chinese Voices of Conscience.* Newcastle-upon-Tyne, 1989.

Buck, Pearl. *China in Black and White.* New York, 1944.

Crozier, Ralph. "Art and Society in Modern Society—A Review Article." *Journal of Asian Studies* 49, no. 3 (August 1990) p. 587–602.

Ding Cong. *Manhua Xiao Ding.* Beijing, 2008.

Ding Cong and Shen June, Video (45 min.) by Marcia R. Ristaino and Nick Liu, Beijing, June 2008.

Ding Cong. Interview with Marcia R. Ristaino, Beijing, 2008.

—. *Ding Cong: Manhua jilie* (Compilations of Cartoons) 4 vols., Beijing, 1999–2007.

—. Interview with Marcia R. Ristaino, Beijing, 2007.

—. *Wode manhua shengwo (My Cartoon Life). Beijing, 2004.*

—. *Wenhuaren xiaoxiang (Portraits of Intellectuals), vol. 2. Beijing, 2002.*

—. *Ding Cong: Manhua, chatu, suxie, xiaowiang, sheji ji (Ding Cong:* Collection of Cartoons, Illustrations, Drawings, Portraits, and Designs). Hebei, 1996.

—. *Guji: Wit & Humour from Ancient China—100 Cartoons by Ding Cong,* trans., Ma Mingtong. Beijing, 1986.

—. *Ding Cong: Manhua, chatu, suxie* (Ding Cong: cartoons, illustrations, sketches). Hong Kong, 1983.

—. *Ding Cong chatu ji* (Collection of Ding Cong's illustrations). Shanghai, 2000.

Gigliesi, Primerose. "Ding Cong's Drawings." In *Eastern Horizon*, vol. 18, no. 4. April, 1979.

Goldman, Merle. *Literary Dissent in Communist China.* Cambridge, Mass., 1967

Gunn, Edward. *Unwelcome Muse: Chinese Literature in Shanghai and Peking, 1937–45.* New York, 1980.

Harbsmeier, Christoph. *The Cartoonist Feng Zikai: Social Realism with a Buddhist Face.* Oslo, 1984.

Hsia, Chih-tsing. *A History of Modern Chinese Fiction.* New Haven, CT., 1971.

Hung Chang-tai. *War and Popular culture: Resistance in Modern China, 1937–1945.* Berkeley, 1994.

Lao She. *The Two Mas.* trans. Kenny K. Huang and David Finkelstein, illus. by Ding Cong. Hong Kong, 1984.

Laing, Ellen. *The Winking Owl: Art in the People's Republic of China.* Berkeley, 1988.

Lee, Leo Ou-fan. *Shanghai Modern: the Flowering of a New Urban Culture in China, 1930–1945.* Cambridge, Mass., 1999.

Lent, John A. *Asian Popular Culture.* Boulder: Westview Press, 1995.

—. *Comic Art in Africa, Asia, Australia, and Latin America through 2000: an International Bibliography.* Westport, Conn.: Praeger, 2004.

Lent, John A. and Xu Ying. "Cartooning and Wartime China." In *International Journal of Comic Art,* Spring 2008, pp. 76–139.

MacFarquhar, Roderick. *The Hundred Flowers Campaign and the Chinese Intellectuals.* New York, 1960.

—. *The Origins of the Cultural Revolution.* 2 vols. New York, 1987.

—. *Mao's Last Revolution.* Cambridge, Mass., 2006.

Mao Zedong. *On Literature and Art.* Beijing, 1967.

Pan Ling. *In Search of Old Shanghai.* Hong Kong, 1982.

Schram, Stuart. *Ideology and Policy in China since the Third Plenum, 1978–84.* London, 1984.

Schwartz, Vera. *The Chinese Enlightenment.* Berkeley, CA, 1986.

Spence, Jonathan D. *The Gate of Heavenly Peace.* New York, 1981.

Sullivan, Michael. *The Arts of China.* 4th ed., Berkeley, CA, 1999.

—. *The Art and Artists of Twentieth-century China.* Berkeley, CA, 1996.

—. *Modern Chinese Artists: A Biographical Dictionary.* Berkeley, CA, 2006.

Warner, John. *Chinese Papercuts.* Hong Kong, 1978.

Wu Ching-tzu. *The Scholars.* Beijing, 1973.

Xin, Shuwei. *Ding Cong zhuan* (Ding Cong Classics). Beijing, 1993

Zhang Yingjin, ed. *Cinema and Urban Culture in Shanghai, 1922–1943.* Stanford, CA, 1999.

Zhang Zhen. *An Amorous History of the Silver Screen: Shanghai Cinema, 1896–1937.* Chicago, 2006.

Index

Academy of Arts and Literature 28
All Men are Brothers 22
Art 26
Aurora University 8
Ba Jin 18
Baowe zhongguo datongmeng (Defend China Alliance) 37
Beacon 26
Beidahuang 80
Beijing Technical College vi
Big Dipper 26
Block, Herbert 5
Boxer Rebellion (1898–1901) 2
Buck, Pearl 22
Central Academy of Fine Arts 73
Central Reserve Bank 61
Chiang Kai-shek 14, 28, 29, 53, 59, 67–68
China Film Studio 40
Chinese Academy of Sciences 87
Chinese Communist Party 14, 32, 41, 68, 86
  11th congress 101
  1st congress 7
  admits to errors during the Great Leap Forward 83
  dissention within ranks of 25
  establishes bases in rural areas 27
  invites artists to return to China 68
Chinese Communist Youth League 71
Cold Nights 44
Comintern 14, 27
Confucianism 112
Confucius 98
Covarrubias, Miguel vii, 22
Cubism 110
Cultural Revolution 85–88, 93–96, 101–102
Culture (Wenhua) 64
Da Gongbao 17
Dadaism 110
Darwin, Charles 20
Daumier, Honoré 4
Dawn 26
Democracy (Minzhu) 64
Democracy Wall gatherings 108
Deng Xiaoping 96, 99–100, 109–112
Dewey, John 20
Diary of a Madman 17–18
Dickens, Charles 20
Ding Cong 1, 6, 92
  and Chinese influences 17–20
  and Mexican influences 22–23

and the *Erliutang* 40–42, 76
and Western influences vii, 71, 110
anti-Japanese work 25, 31–39, 47, 57
anti-war work 63
becomes part-time editor of movie magazine 11
becomes part-time student at the Shanghai Painting and Art Institute 10
criticism of corruption 51–52, 62–64, 113
development as an artist 4–5, 9–11
early work 11–12
enters work at first national exhibit of cartoon art 11
in Beidahuang 77, 81
in Beijing 69, 71–72, 74, 81–85
in Chengdu 44–45, 47–49
in Chongqing 40–42, 54
in Hong Kong 31–39, 44, 68–69
marries Shen Jun 71
meets family in Zhejiang 84
officially pardoned 102
participation in exhibition at Sino-Soviet Cultural Association 54
participation in Woodcut Movement 26
pen name of "Xiao Ding" 9
personality 12
rehabilitated 102
relations with Zhou Enlai 98
teaches painting at a local school for girls 11, 12
trip to Burma 40, 42–44
work for the Americans 57–59, 72, 93
Ding Song 3–4, 9, 13
Dushu 106–108
Erliutang 42, 88, 99
and Zhou Enlai 96
founding of 40–42
Expressionism 110
Feng Zikai 3
Fenn, Dr. William F. 57
Fine Arts Institute of Shanghai 3
Four Modernizations Campaign 109
French Concession 8, 23
Gang of Four 96, 98–100, 103–104
Gogol, Nikolai 20
Goya, Francisco 22–23
Great Leap Forward 83, 86
Grosz, George 5
Guo Morou 32, 41, 87
Guomindang 14, 50, 54, 68, 90
and commercial Shanghai 62
and the National Salvation Propaganda Corps 32
censors 26, 31, 63, 85
Hitler, Adolf 5
Hong Kong Central Theater 35
Hong Kong Theater Association 44
Hu Jintao 113
Hu Yaobang 109
Hua Guofeng 101
Hua Lu (Flower Street) 55
Huashang bao 42
Hundred Flowers Campaign (1956–57) 74, 75
Ibsen, Henrik 20
Impressionism 110
International Bookstore 85
International Youth Festival 69
Jiang Qing 96, 103–104, 120
Jiang Zemin 113
Journey to the West 111

Kangzhan manhua (Resistance Cartoons) 34–35
Khruschev, Nikita 87, 101
Lao She 20–21, 94
League for the Resistance Against Japanese Aggression 36
League of Left-Wing Writers 18
Liao Bingxiong 54
Life 39
Lin Biao 96, 98
Liu Haisu 8
Liu Shaoqi 87, 101
London Daily News 9
Long March 28
Lu Xun 16–18, 28, 54, 103
Ma Sicong 45
Mao Dun (Shen Yanbing) 18, 44, 47
Mao Zedong 72–75, 87–88, 90, 95–96, 99
  and the Red Terror 86
  announces founding of PRC 69
  death of 101
  speech at the Yan'an Literature Conference 42
Marx, Karl 20
Masses (*Qingzhong*) 64
May Fourth movement 7, 17, 20
Mexican Mural Renaissance 22
Mexican Revolution (1919–20) 22
Midnight 18
Ministry of Culture 73
Modern Art Society 51
Nagy, Imre 100
Nast, Thomas 5
National Art Institute 102
National Salvation Cartoon Association 26
National Salvation Cartoon Propaganda Corps 30–31, 35
National Salvation Movement 26
New Art Movement 30
New Culture Movement 6
New Fourth Army incident 40
New Yorker vii, 9, 22
New Youth 18
Nixon, Richard 93, 96
Northern Expedition 14
Opium War (1839–42) 2, 7
Orozco, José 22
Orwell, George 1
Outcry 26
Peking Spring 104
Petöfi Club 90, 99
Picasso, Pablo 37
Red Guards 87–89
People's Daily (*Renmin ribao*) 88, 102
People's Liberation Army 75, 87, 95
People's Pictorial (*Renmin huabao*) 71
Republican Revolution (1911–12) 7, 23
Rickshaw Boy 20
River Elegy 110
Rivera, Diego 22
Rockwell, Norman 71
Shanghai International Settlement 8, 26
Shanghai Painting and Art Institute 8
Shen Bao 17
Shen Jun 71, 93
Shen Yanbing. *See* Mao Dun
Shenzhen Art Gallery 42
Sichuan Provincial Art Academy 44
Sino-Western Drawing and Painting School 8
Siquieros, David Alfaro 22
Siren 26

Snow, Edgar 35
Spencer Museum of Art 53
Spring (Qingming) 65
Stars 109
Struggle 26
Sun Yat-sen, Madame (Song Qingling) 35–36
Surrealism 110
Tang Yu 40
Taowang (Fugitives) 36
The Family 18
Tiananmen Square 69
  democracy movement 108, 110
  homages to Zhou Enlai (Qingming festival) 99–100
Tōjō Hideki 112
Tolstoy, Andrey 19, 22
Torrent 26
Trotsy, Leo 22
True Records of the Japanese Agressor's Atrocities 35
True Story of Ah Q 54
Turgenev, Ivan 19
Uproar in Heaven 111
Vanity Fair vii, 9, 22
Weekend Magazine (Zhoubao) 63
Wei Jingsheng 109
Western China University 57
Wu Zuguang 40, 54, 88
Xianshitu (Picture of Reality) 53
Xianxiangtu (Looking at Images) 50, 68
Xiao Ding. *See* Ding Cong
Xihua wanbao (West China Evening Newspaper) 54
Xiyoumanji (Journey to the West) 111
Yan'an group 71, 74
Yan'an Literature Conference (1943) 42
Ye Jianying 69
Ye Qianyu 35, 44
Young Companion Pictorial 31, 39
Yu Dafu 43
Yu Qiangyu 54, 85
Yuan Shi-kai 7
Zhang Guangyu 9–10, 54, 111–112
Zhang Leping 12
Zhao Ziyang 110
Zhou Enlai 32, 69, 75, 96, 98–100
Zhoubao (Weekly) 63G–64H
Zhu De 28

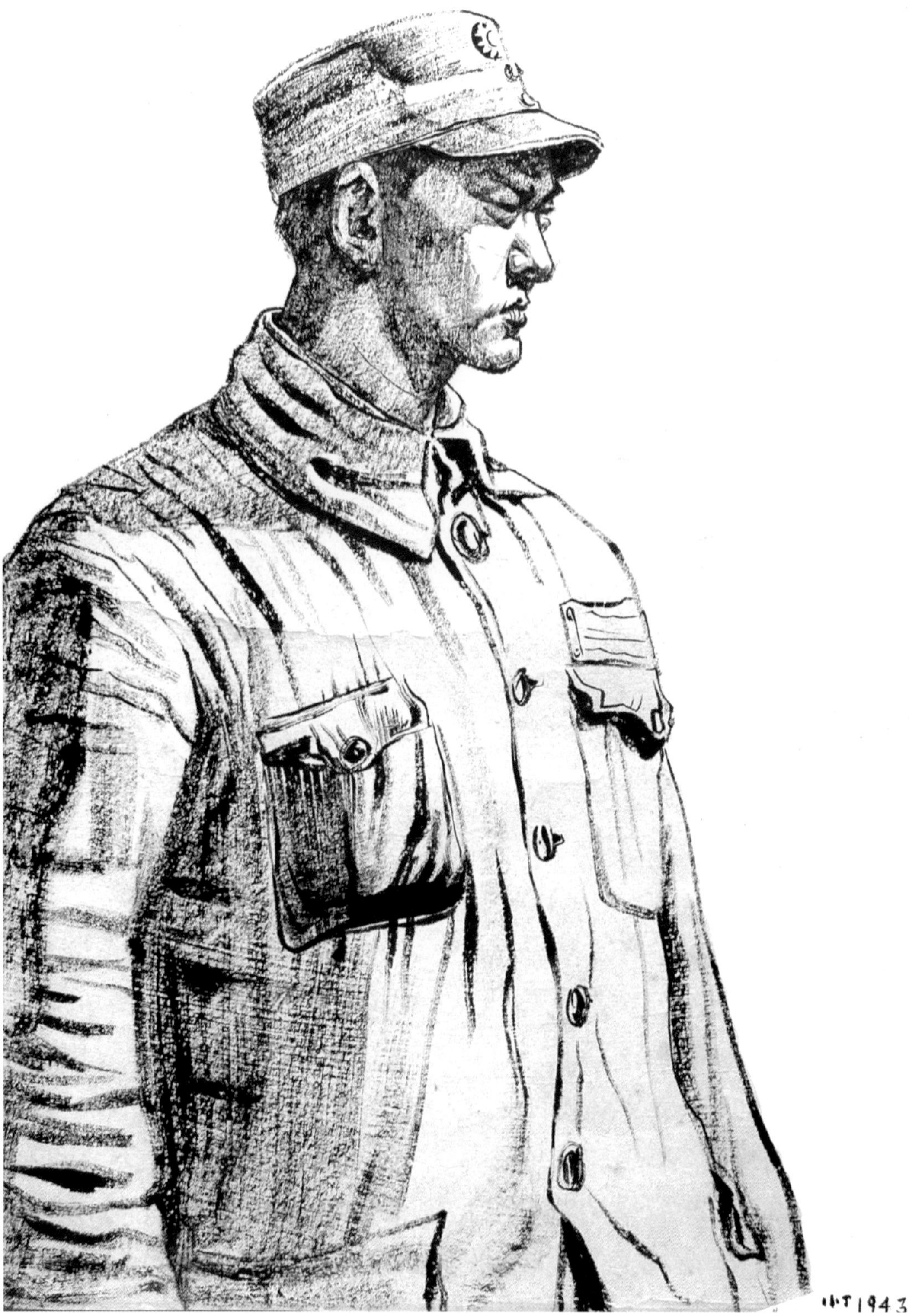

Guomindang soldier (1943). Courtesy of Michael Sullivan

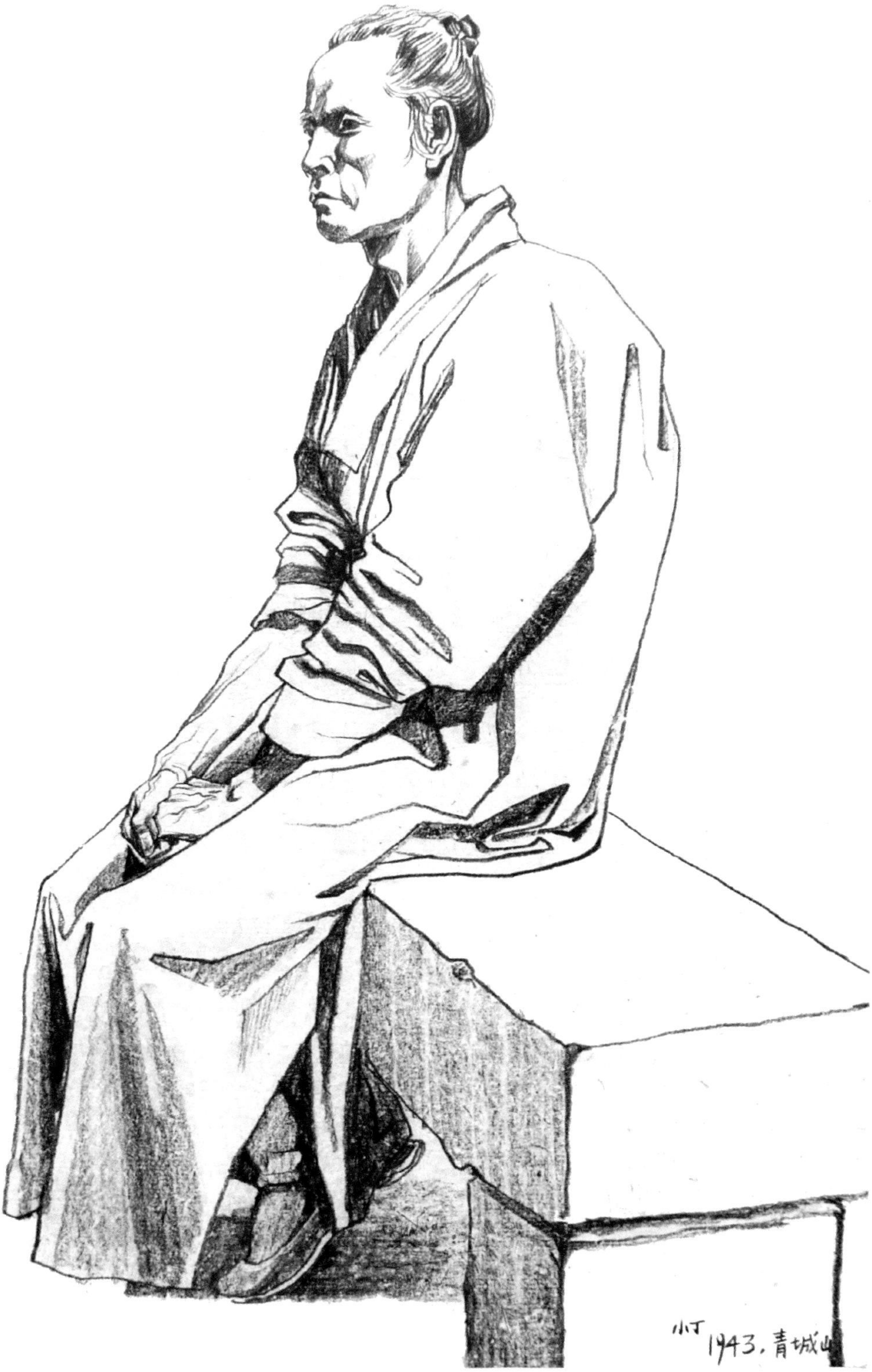

Daoist priest on Qingchengshan (1943). Courtesy of Michael Sullivan

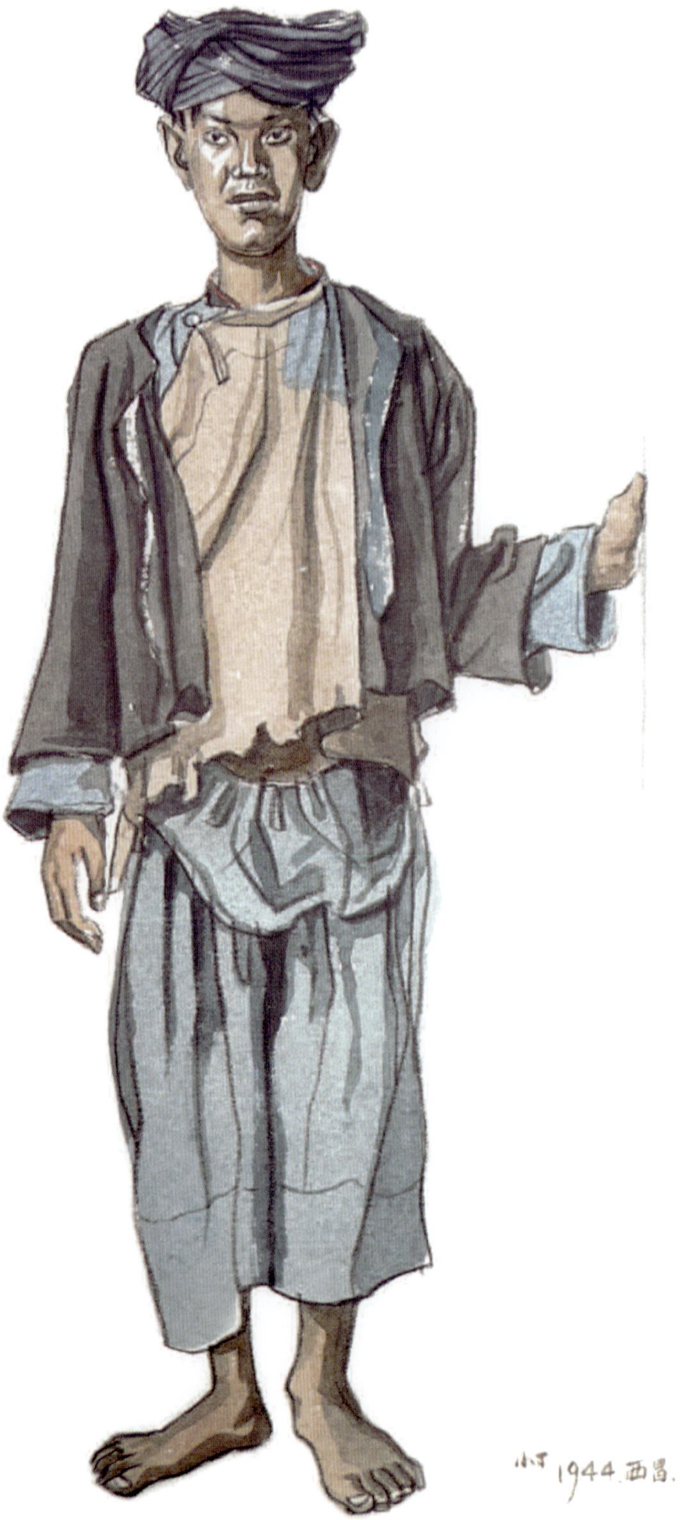

Borderland tribesman, Xichang (1944). Courtesy of Michael Sullivan

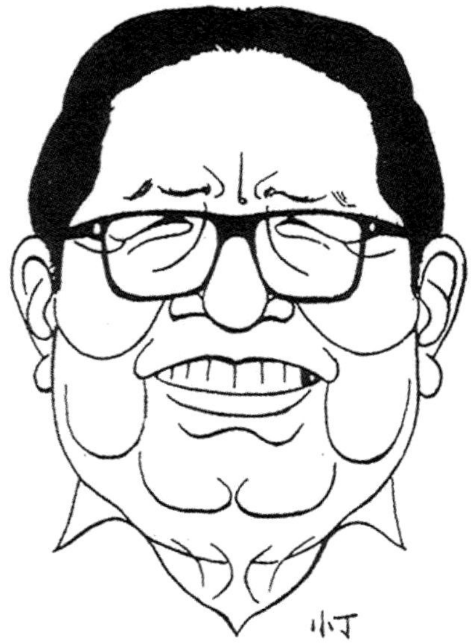

Self-portrait of an older Xiao Ding

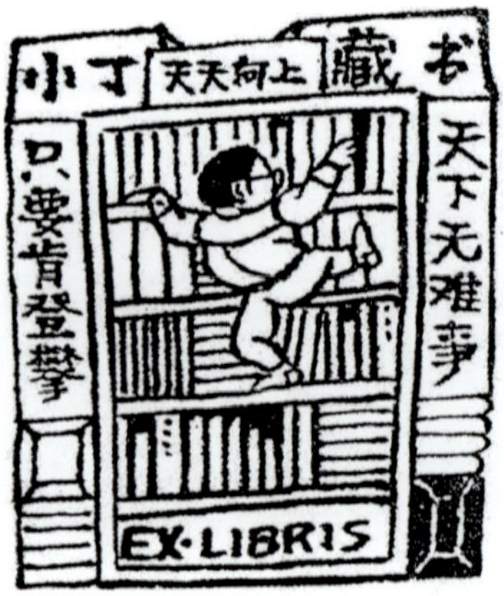

Floating World Editions publishes books that contribute to a deeper understanding of Asian cultures. Editorial supervision: Ray Furse. Book design: William de Lange. Cover design and page composition: Digital Dragon Designery. Production supervision: Bill Rose. Printing and binding: SNP Leefung Printers Limited. The typeface used is Purloin.